Traditions of Natural Law
in Medieval Philosophy

Studies in Philosophy and the History of Philosophy

General Editor: John C. McCarthy

Volume 65

Traditions of Natural Law
in Medieval Philosophy

Edited by Dominic Farrell

The Catholic University of America Press
Washington, D.C.

We would also like to thank the University of Gdańsk Press for the
permission to publish revised and translated material from "Wola
a rozumność" [The Will and Rationality], chapter 3 of *Natura woli.
Wolność a konieczność. Stanowisko Jana Dunsa Szkota na tle koncepcji
św. Augustyna, św. Anzelma z Canterbury i św. Tomasza z Akwinu*
[The Nature of Will. Freedom and Necessity: The Analysis of John
Duns Scotus's Theory in Comparison to St. Augustine, St. Anselm of
Canterbury, and St. Thomas Aquinas] (Gdańsk, Poland: University of
Gdańsk Press, 2019), 308–35. The original was published in Polish and
has been translated by the author, Martyna Koszkało, and appears in
her chapter of this book, "John Duns Scotus and Natural Law."

Cataloging-in-Publication Data available from the
Library of Congress

ISBN 978-0-8132-3538-7

Contents

Abbreviations

a.	articulus
a. un.	articulus unicus
ad dub.	ad dubium
arg.	argumentum
c.	capitulum
co.	corpus
d.	distinctio
facsim.	facsimile
f. / fols.	folium / folia
lect.	lectio
lin.	lines
n.	numerus
obj.	objectio
praenot.	praenotata
prol.	prologus
prooem.	prooemium
q.	quaestio
q.^{la}	quaestiuncula
q. un.	quaestio unica
ra	recto, column a
rb	recto, column b
resp.	respondeo
s.c.	sed contra
tit.	titulus
v	verso
va	verso, column a
vb	verso, column b

Traditions of Natural Law in Medieval Philosophy

Introduction

The natural law tradition has a distinguished history, counting figures such as Cicero, Suárez, Grotius, and Locke among its exponents. Arguably, it reaches its highpoint during the Middle Ages. While the notion of natural law has its roots in the Stoics and Roman law and is taken up by early Christian theologians, it is only during the medieval period that systematic theories are worked out. This is done explicitly by scholastics, such as Jean de la Rochelle, Thomas Aquinas, and John Duns Scotus. They may influence modern moral and political thought less directly than post-Reformation Iberian scholastics or the seventeenth- and eighteenth-century Protestant theorists of natural law. Still, the natural law tradition reaches its highpoint with their work because they articulate the framework for all subsequent reflection on natural law.

This is not the only reason for situating the highpoint of the natural law tradition in the Middle Ages. During this period, Eastern Christianity works out its own account of natural law. The Jewish and Islamic traditions also develop their own canonical statements on how much authority reason, working independently of divine law, has on moral matters. In this way, each of these traditions addresses the central issue of the natural law tradition, even if neither thereby endorses a theory of "natural law."

The contribution of the Latin tradition of medieval thought has been studied extensively though not exhaustively.[1] Furthermore, with a grow-

---

1. Odon Lottin, *Le droit naturel chez saint Thomas d'Aquin et ses predecesseurs*, 2nd ed. (Bruges: Charles Beyaert, 1931); Michael Bertram Crowe, *The Changing Profile of the Natural Law* (The Hague: M. Nijhoff, 1977), 72–110; Rudolf Weigand, *Die Naturrechtslehre der Legisten und Dekretisten von Irnerius bis Accursius und von Gratian bis Johannes Teutonicus* (Munich: Max Hueber, 1967).

ing number of studies on the natural law theory of the Byzantine, Jewish, and Islamic traditions, a fuller picture of medieval reflection on the matter is emerging.[2]

There has been a comparative study of the Jewish, Christian, and Islamic understandings of natural law.[3] It does not focus on the medieval period, however. There is need, therefore, of work which looks at the various medieval traditions of natural law theory together and their relation to one another.[4] This volume of essays aims to fill this gap in part.

Is this a worthwhile enterprise, though? Maybe not, judging by the current mainstream in moral and political philosophy. For much of the history of Western thought, belief in the existence of a natural law has been prevalent. And yet, at present most professional philosophers deem natural law doctrines to be no longer tenable. Despite the skepticism and naysaying, there are various reasons to believe that medieval discussions of natural law are still relevant to current debates in moral, political, and legal philosophy.

First, there is a greater awareness than there was during much of the last century that the study of philosophical thought from the remote past is likely to enrich and advance contemporary reflection in moral, political, and legal theory. There are certainly indications to the contrary. Much contemporary work in these fields is conducted according to the methods of analytical philosophy. As a result, not only does it privilege the rigorous clarification and assessment of concepts and arguments but also it tends to attribute less importance, if any, to another mode of in-

2. On the Byzantine tradition, see Paul Babie, "Natural Law in the Orthodox Tradition," in *Christianity and Natural Law: An Introduction*, ed. Norman Doe (Cambridge: Cambridge University Press, 2017), 36–57.

On the Jewish tradition, see Jonathan A. Jacobs, "The Reasons of the Commandments: Rational Tradtion without Natural Law," in *Reason, Religion, and Natural Law: From Plato to Spinoza*, ed. Jonathan A. Jacobs (New York: Oxford University Press, 2012), 106–29; David Novak, *Natural Law in Judaism* (New York: Cambridge University Press, 1998); Tamar Rudavsky, "Natural Law in Judaism," in *Reason, Religion, and Natural Law*, 83–105.

On the Islamic tradition, see Anver M. Emon, *Islamic Natural Law Theories* (New York: Oxford University Press, 2010).

3. Anver M. Emon, Matthew Levering, and David Novak, *Natural Law: A Jewish, Christian, and Islamic Trialogue* (Oxford: Oxford University Press, 2014).

4. This has been done to some extent by Élisabeth Dufourcq, *L'invention de la loi naturelle. Des itinéraires grecs, latins, juifs, chrétiens et musulmans* (Montrouge: Bayard, 2012). The book has been republished as Dufourcq, *Intuitions et pièges de la loi naturelle* (Paris: Éditions du Cerf, 2019).

quiry: the study of important philosophical works from the past. Furthermore, philosophers are currently under pressure to back up their claims with the results of empirical work in the natural and social sciences. Dusting off and studying works from the supposedly prescientific Middle Ages might strike the empirically minded as an unproductive investment of one's time and energy, especially when much of that literature is theological. There are several signs, however, that many professional philosophers do not take such a dim and narrow view of the history of philosophy. Not only do a growing number of analytical philosophers appreciate the importance of the history of philosophy[5] but there is also more research on the history of ethics coming from analytically trained scholars.[6] Most significant perhaps is the way in which several contemporary classics of ethical and political theory either adopt a historical approach or engage with major thinkers of the past.[7] There are various indicators, therefore, that moral and political philosophy, as currently practiced, not only benefits from bringing earlier figures and debates into the conversation but can no longer pretend to be an ahistorical and purely analytical enterprise. There is every reason, then, to study medieval theories of natural law. They constitute an important chapter in the history of moral, political, and legal philosophy. As such, they may contain valuable conceptual distinctions and arguments for contemporary debates in these fields.

One reason to suppose so is that medieval thinkers approach ethics as part of a more comprehensive account of human nature, action, and metaphysics. As a result, their statements on natural law are nested within sophisticated discussions of law, God, human nature, and action, not to mention moral epistemology, motivation, and anthropology. They

---

5. Tom Sorell and G. A. J. Rogers, *Analytic Philosophy and History of Philosophy* (Oxford: Clarendon Press, 2005); Erich H. Reck, *The Historical Turn in Analytic Philosophy* (Basingstoke, UK: Palgrave Macmillan, 2013).

6. Two examples are Roger Crisp, *The Oxford Handbook of the History of Ethics* (Oxford: Oxford University Press, 2013); Terence Irwin, *The Development of Ethics: A Historical and Critical Study*, 3 vols. (Oxford: Oxford University Press, 2007–09).

7. Gertrude Elizabeth Mary Anscombe, "Modern Moral Philosophy," *Philosophy* 33, no. 124 (1958): 1–13; Christine M. Korsgaard, *The Sources of Normativity* (Cambridge: Cambridge University Press, 1996); Alasdair MacIntyre, *After Virtue: A Study in Moral Theory* (London: Duckworth, 1981); Charles Taylor, *Sources of the Self: The Making of the Modern Identity* (Cambridge, Mass.: Harvard University Press, 1989); Bernard Williams, *Ethics and the Limits of Philosophy* (London: Fontana, 1985).

thereby alert us to how inquiry in moral, political, and legal philosophy is not a self-contained enterprise. To ground its principles, such inquiry needs to move beyond the conventional confines of these disciplines and address the broader underlying questions.

One such question with which medieval theories of natural law grapple, and that surfaces in this volume, is the modal metaphysics of morality. Ash'arite theologians and Scotus argue that there can be a possible world in which human beings, identical to us in all respects, are under different moral demands. In their view, moral demands are contingent. Hence, some are binding in our world only because God has freely decided that this should be the case. Mu'tazilite jurists and Aquinas, on the other hand, reject this view. They too believe that all possible worlds are contingent. They also believe that God, in choosing to create human beings, is always constrained to create them under the same moral demands.

Both sides are engaged in a sophisticated debate over divine voluntarism, a central issue within the philosophy of religion. However, these opposing views also evince how medieval reflection on "natural law" overlaps with contemporary metaethics, action theory, moral epistemology, and philosophy of religion. This medieval debate raises the question of the supervenience of moral properties upon natural ones, and so that of moral naturalism and cognitivism. It thereby opens the way to different conceptions of virtue's relation to human nature. It also yields different moral epistemologies: a divine command ethics, on the one hand, and a variety of ethical naturalism on the other. By inquiring into what reasons God has for creating something in the way that he does, it goes into the questions of moral motivation and whether there are external reasons for action or only internal ones. This in turn entails different conceptions of practical reason. Furthermore, the broader religious background of all medieval theories of natural law means that they develop nuanced accounts of the role of tradition in moral epistemology and the significance of theistic commitments.

This debate over the modal metaphysics of morality illustrates certain respects in which medieval reflection on "natural law" is still relevant to moral philosophy, particularly to metaethics. But what about normative ethics, political theory, and the philosophy of law?

As already noted, medieval natural law theories are often continuing and committed to the ethical naturalism of ancient philosophy. In this regard, they pursue a project that overlaps to some extent with that of contemporary virtue ethics. Much of the latter is also inspired by ancient Greek ethics, endorses its underlying ethical naturalism, and attempts to rearticulate it.[8] Furthermore, virtue ethics is one of the main currents within contemporary normative ethics. By developing arguments much like those of Neo-Aristotelian virtue ethics, the medieval discussions of natural law can be relevant to current work in normative ethics.

Like modern proponents of ethical naturalism, the medieval natural law theorists are opposed to both consequentialism and to the kind of constructivism that is often attributed to Kant. They maintain that, given the constitution of human beings, there are certain moral demands, accessible to reason, that hold for everyone, regardless of place, culture, and consequences. Unlike Kantian constructivism, however, they generally ground human good in the real existence and normativity of natural teleology. They also differ in a significant regard from Neo-Aristotelian accounts of ethical naturalism. They set the ethical naturalism that they inherit from ancient philosophy within the framework of their mono-theistic faith (Judaism, Christianity, or Islam). As a result, they develop a theistic and religious ethical naturalism. They consider what it means to hold that reason has authority on moral matters if we are in fact created, subject to divine retribution, and called to follow the path that God has revealed. In this regard, they constitute a distinctive paradigm within the current conceptual map of normative ethics. The medievals formulate very sophisticated conceptions of the role of reason and its authority—but also its limits—given that they believe there is a source of the intelligibility and authority of morality that transcends reason. These questions about the role and authority of reason in moral life continue to be relevant in our very different context.

This commitment to ethical naturalism and Revelation affects the way in which medieval thinkers view the law. Traditionally, one of the main purposes of natural law discourse has been the critique of legal positivism. According to natural law theory, a society's laws, though largely con-

---

8. Philippa Foot, *Natural Goodness* (Oxford: Clarendon, 2001); Rosalind Hursthouse, *On Virtue Ethics* (Oxford: Oxford University Press, 1999); Michael Thompson, *Life and Action: Elementary Structures of Practice and Practical Thought* (Cambridge, Mass.: Harvard University Press, 2008).

ventional, are subject to preexisting moral constraints that are not of our making. Natural law theory often goes on to propose an analysis of those constraints. Indeed, this antipositivism is not only present in much medieval reflection on natural law but also systematized there for the first time. However, it would be wrong to assume that said reflection simply brings its theological and philosophical assumptions to bear on jurisprudence. Jurisprudence is often its source. The centrality of the Torah in Judaism and of Shari'a in Islam means that "medieval natural law discourse" within these traditions falls generally, if not primarily, under the purview of legal experts. Unlike Christian natural law discourse, which is primarily theological and doctrinal in character, the Jewish and Islamic varieties are juridical at every turn. Nevertheless, Christian natural law discourse also draws heavily on Roman and canon law. To some extent, it is even an outgrowth of jurisprudence. It is heavily influenced by the *Corpus iuris civilis*, compiled at Constantinople at the behest of Justinian I. The subsequent revival of interest in Roman law in eleventh-century Italy not only leads to the systematization of canon law in the West but, through it, also provides Catholic theologians of the period with many of the categories they use to articulate a more systematic account of natural law.

The Christian jurists and theologians who discuss natural law or kindred categories are concerned with the making, interpretation, and administration of civil and canon law. That said, they are almost always dedicated to academic work rather than the actual practice of the law. There is evidence, though, that natural law theory is not a mere conceit of academics but exerts real influence in courts and chancelleries across Christendom during the Middle Ages and beyond.[9]

Scholars have noted how, during the Middle Ages, theological reflection on natural law influences the canonists in developing certain principles that then pass into civil law by way of the *ius commune*, the amalgam of civil and canon law that is central to European law until the nineteenth century and also influences English common law. One example is the principle of hearing both sides of a case (*audi alteram partem*). This principle is first treated as a matter of divine and natural justice by the Church Fathers. The most notable argument is that of Lucifer of Cagliari (†370).

---

9. On the reemergence of the legal profession in the Christian regions of medieval Europe, see James A. Brundage, *The Medieval Origins of the Legal Profession: Canonists, Civilians, and Courts* (Chicago: University of Chicago Press, 2008).

After Adam eats of the forbidden fruit, God, despite being omniscient, calls him to present himself and give an account of his actions. Lucifer thereby attributes to Adam the right to defend himself before being sentenced. This line of argument resurfaces in an eighteenth-century judicial decision of common law.[10] John of Legnano (c. 1320–1383) invokes the same line of reasoning to explain why citation is essential to due process under canon law.[11] Natural law reasoning also informs the positions that the canonists reach on substantive issues such as: freedom and slavery; property; marriage and family.[12]

In this regard, a study on the role of natural law reasoning in a later period of legal practice is illustrative. The study in question regards European and English courts between 1500 and 1800 and those of the early American republic (1776–1861).[13] Nevertheless, the story it tells can be assumed to be largely representative of legal practice in medieval Europe too.

As it turns out, lawyers of this period do not take any one theorist, not even Aquinas, as their authority on natural law. They look instead to the commonly held opinion (*opinio communis*), generated over time by a wide range of jurists and theologians. They appeal to natural law in dealing with concrete cases and do not attempt to work out an analytical, systematic statement of its precepts or exact content. Rather, their understanding of natural law is drawn from Roman and canon law. As a result, they, unlike the philosophers and theologians, remain in substantial agreement about the nature and normative implications of natural law. Their appeals to natural law often fail to win the case and have limited applicability. They are nonetheless of critical importance. They win the case just as often as they do not. Furthermore, lawyers of the period believe deeply that natural law is essential to legislation and jurisprudence.[14] This is in keeping with their legal education. There they are taught about the basic features of natural law, its normative priority vis-à-vis man-made law. Over the course of their training, they also gain some famil-

---

10. John M Kelly, "*Audi Alteram Partem*," *Natural Law Forum* 9 (1964): 103–10.

11. Richard H Helmholz, "Citations and the Construction of Procedural Law in the Ius Commune," in *The Creation of the Ius Commune: From Casus to Regula*, ed. John W. Cairns and Paul J. du Plessis (Edinburgh: Edinburgh University Press, 2010), 247–75 at 256–57.

12. Weigand, *Die Naturrechtslehre der Legisten und Dekretisten*, 259–361.

13. Richard H. Helmholz, *Natural Law in Court: A History of Legal Theory in Practice* (Cambridge, Mass.: Harvard University Press, 2015).

14. Helmholz, *Natural Law in Court*, 5–12.

iarity with the extensive literature on it. Consequently, they believe that natural law is the source of positive law rather than incongruous with it. However, they only invoke it in a minority of the recorded cases, especially when moral principles are at stake. Indeed, natural law discourse is the medium through which they establish fundamental principles of justice in legal practice, even if they do not always use it consistently. In fact, they fail to show conclusively that slavery and judicial torture go against natural law.[15]

Medieval thought on natural law, therefore, plays an important role in legal history. Indeed, it is one possible doorway into the legal theory of Judaism, Christianity, or Islam, three religions, each of which has shaped the legal systems of certain countries significantly and continues to do so. Unpacking their respective conceptions of the law is important if we are to understand the sources of the principles and conflicts debated in current legal and political disputes.

By bearing on jurisprudence, medieval natural law discourse must also touch upon central questions of political theory. It must clarify how a society makes and enforces laws legitimately. To answer this question, it must account for the origin, nature, scope, and workings of political authority. Current debates on these central problems of political philosophy tend to adopt, in the West at least, a secular standpoint. Medieval natural law discourse, however, is explicitly religious in character and bound up with reflection on the theologico-political problem. It needs to work out whether the state should be theocratic or constitutionalist: whether its institutions should be rooted in divine law or only in natural law. Natural law, therefore, is a central element of medieval political thought or at least a central issue. It constitutes the framework through which theorists grapple with these questions.

Furthermore, given the religious character of their natural law discourse, the medievals believe not only that there is a higher, divine law but also that we rely on it to know natural law. The latter is accessible to reason in principle but not necessarily in practice. While the religious traditions of medieval philosophy largely agree on this, the divine law of each is different in character and content. This is one of the main reasons why Jewish, Christian, and Muslim thinkers hold different conceptions of "natural law," the law, and the state. Their varying conceptions of the

---

15. Helmholz, *Natural Law in Court*, 173–78.

divine law are obviously a point of contention, but, as the essays in this volume demonstrate, they also open the way to interesting theoretical alternatives.

By working against this theological backdrop, in which the relation between the authority of Revelation and that of reason becomes a central problem, the natural law theories of medieval thinkers are also framed to address the ever-pressing issue of religious pluralism. In this regard, they are dealing with an issue prominent in much contemporary political philosophy: the challenge of legislating in a pluralist society. It is worth examining, therefore, whether medieval philosophers, committed as they are to belief in a divinely revealed morality, but also aware of how some societies of their time are marked by a limited degree of religious and ethical pluralism, provide rational standards for settling moral disagreements between parties holding different comprehensive doctrines.

In addition to ethical and religious pluralism, there is pluralism within medieval natural law theories themselves. Even thinkers belonging to the same religious tradition disagree over important features of natural law. Ostensibly, the existence of rival views within the tradition undermines its claims about the purported universality of natural law itself. For this reason, there is need of work on the convergences and divergences that exist between the various medieval theories of natural law, especially those of Abrahamic religions. This is where this book comes in.

It has two sections. Each looks at a different kind of pluralism that characterizes medieval theories of natural law.

The first section provides a survey of the "natural law theory" of each of the religious traditions of medieval philosophy; Judaism, Islam, and then Christianity (both Eastern and Latin). To some extent, it also considers how each is related to the others. This is only an initial foray into the issue rather than a definitive treatment. A fully satisfactory comparison of each religious tradition's reflection on "natural law" during the Middle Ages would require an extensive reconstruction, analysis, and comparison of each one's conception(s) of the matter. The essays in this volume provide, nonetheless, a good working picture of the subject and the issues at stake.

The second section looks at the rival accounts of natural law that existed within the Latin tradition. It contains essays on several representative Scholastic theories of natural law.

Each chapter of the first section presents the "natural law theory" of one of the religious traditions of medieval philosophy: Judaism, Islam, Eastern Christianity, and Latin Christianity. Each one thereby points to the tradition's distinctive views on the authority and place of reason in ethical discussions.

In this regard, a first issue that needs to be addressed is whether each of the religious traditions of medieval philosophy espouses natural law. Natural law discourse figures explicitly in the Christian tradition, but there are more complex interpretative issues concerning its presence in medieval Judaic and Islamic thought. Some contemporary scholars maintain that medieval Jewish and Muslim thinkers develop natural law theories, if only implicitly. Others argue that they do not develop a theory of natural law but, at most, hold a series of positions that resemble natural law theories in important regards. They warn against reading these thinkers through the lens of concepts that are extraneous to their religious tradition.

In Chapter 1, Jonathan Jacobs considers to what extent medieval Jewish philosophers develop a natural law theory. To do so, he looks at the writings of Saadia Gaon, Bahya ibn Pakuda, Judah Halevi, and Moses Maimonides. He argues that, while medieval Jewish thought seldom adopts the idiom of natural law, its reflection on "the reasons of the commandments" should not be construed as an implicit theory of natural law or practical wisdom. Although medieval Jewish thinkers have access to the works of ancient philosophy that are read by their peers in the other religious traditions, they conceive "the reasons of the commandments" in the light of Judaism's specific sources and authorities. As a result, they conceive them as part of an authoritative rational tradition. A tradition can be understood in a relativistic manner or as a truth-directed process of accessing rationally justified moral judgments. It is the latter sort of tradition that is operative here. Medieval Jewish thinkers argue that the faithful observance of the Torah enables one to understand which moral requirements are universal and why they are rational. This understanding of Judaism as an authoritative rational tradition overlaps in various ways with theories of natural law and practical wisdom. Nevertheless, medieval Jewish moral thought cannot be equated with an Aristotelian account of practical reason and wisdom. Due to its religious sources, it is non-Aristotelian in important regards, just as Aquinas and Scotus are equally non-Aristotelian on account of their theological commitments. Nor can it be equated with natural law theories, such as those of Aquinas and Scotus, even though it coincides with them in various regards. Medieval Jewish moral thought does not become a natural law theory for several reasons. It focusses on the significance that morality acquires in connection with the covenant. Second, it is concerned mainly with the practice of leading a righteous life and imitating God's holiness rather than with grounding morality in its principles. Third, it is difficult for it to make a clear demarcation between moral precepts and specifically religious ones. In all this, Jewish moral thought is not opposed to natural law, but is working with a different concept of "law."

Anver Emon, on the other hand, charts the disciplinary terrain in which medieval Islamic thought discusses the questions underlying natural law, even when it does not use the term. In his view, medieval Sunnite scholars do not broach those questions by doing theology (*kalam*) but within an area of Islamic legal theory, *usul al-fiqh*. The Islamic world does not draw the Gelasian distinction between the sacred and the secular. Its literature on legal doctrine (*fiqh*) often treats ritual and religious issues together with, say, an ordinary contract. Medieval Islamic scholars also write in a genre of literature, usul al-fiqh, that mediates between theology and law. In it, they deploy their training in both theology and law to debate the ontological first principles of the former and to develop a framework for deriving laws from them. This framework enables them to think jurisprudentially and reach decisions on those matters for which the Shari'a does not contain explicit norms. It thereby grants a certain ethical authority to reason and yields a sort of natural law theory. Two broad kinds of natural law theory emerge, though, since there is disagreement over the theological principles. The disagreement is between Ash'arite theologians, who defend a strong version of divine voluntarism, and the Mu'tazilites, who favour a more rationalist conception of creation. Consequently, there is a hard conception of natural law, defended mostly by Mu'tazilite jurists (e.g., al-Qadi 'Abd al-Jabbar, Abu al-Husayn al-Basri), and the soft conception of the Ash'arites (e.g., Abu Hamid al-Ghazali, al-Tufi, al-Shatibi, al-Ghazali). Notwithstanding their theological disagreements, jurists of each current reach substantially the same conclusions, due to their reliance upon legal reasoning. This confirms, in Emon's view, that law and not theology is where Islamic scholars of the Middle Ages work out a natural law theory. However, as he points out, the purported universality of natural law is in tension with the tradition-boundedness of any theory thereof. This suggests that natural law cannot be worked out through a mere process of discovery but only through an ongoing dialectical engagement between rival traditions.

Unlike the Jewish and Islamic traditions, medieval Christian thought, both Byzantine and Latin, makes explicit appeals to natural law, though not to the same extent. The Latin tradition produces extensive theoretical work on natural law, the Byzantine tradition comparatively little. The former produces extended treatises on natural law; the latter does not.

Even so, as Christiaan Kappes argues, medieval Byzantine authors do develop a common, systematic theory of natural law. Rather than write extended treatments of natural law, they are content to restate certain maxims of Roman law. Through this convention, they express their deeply held belief that natural law constitutes the foundation of ethics and civil law and is summed up in the Decalogue. Similarly, under the influence of Roman law, they believe that the law of nations (*ius gentium*) reflects natural law. The Church Fathers of the East and medieval Byzantine theologians also draw on Stoicism to articulate their natural law theory. This is not fortuitous. Kappes argues that both Roman law and the New Testament passage that prompts the Church Fathers to use the concept of natural law—Paul's teaching on how the gentiles do by nature what the Torah requires (Rom 2:14–15)—draw on Stoic thought. Consequently, Byzantine thinkers draw on Stoic virtue theory. They adopt, for example, the theory of the four general (cardinal) virtues and repurpose Epictetus for monastic spirituality. Stoicism also leads them to think of natural law as a commandment of practical reason that enjoins one to acknowledge God's existence.

As to the Latin tradition, Dominic Farrell considers how the natural law theory of Thomas Aquinas, the most celebrated figure within medieval Latin thought, is related to that of the other religious traditions. To this end, he examines the way in which representatives from those traditions figure in Aquinas's discussion of natural law and even influence it. Not only does Aquinas draw on the other traditions but he does so whenever they provide him with resources the better to articulate his Aristotelian account of practical reason. This suggests that virtue ethics rather than natural law discourse may constitute the proper framework by which members from these traditions can debate ethical issues in common. Natural law discourse is less suitable because it is related to divine law, a subject on which the religious traditions disagree. Each tradition's doctrine of "natural law" is concerned with the same central questions. Can reason establish, authoritatively yet independently of divine law, what we must do to attain our ultimate end? If so, can we attain that end merely by living in accord with reason? Nevertheless, Aquinas's own answer to these questions is intriguing and puzzling. He gives a qualified yes to the first question but answers no to the second. By insisting that we need grace to attain our ultimate end, he appears to render natural law otiose. A closer examination of his account of divine law reveals that natural law is still necessary and plays two important functions. On the one hand, it directs us toward the happiness attainable within political society, which consists in the practice of the acquired virtues. In this regard, it constitutes a universal ethico-political standard. On the other hand, it plays a religious function. It is the framework by which we understand divinely revealed morality. It directs us toward acquired moral virtue and our natural end, whereas divine law directs us toward infused virtue and our supernatural end. Still, though directed toward a higher end, an infused moral virtue bears on the same material object as its acquired counterpart. The moral precepts of divine law, therefore, regard the same matters as those of natural law. Indeed, for Aquinas, any revealed moral teaching belongs to natural law in this regard and supposes reason's understanding of the acquired moral virtues.

While Aquinas's natural law theory is perhaps the best known, it is just one of the various medieval scholastic accounts. The essays of the second part survey a sample, give a taste of the pluralism that exists within the medieval natural theories of the Latins, and indicate the main positions that they adopt on a common set of problems.

A good place to start is Aquinas's Franciscan contemporary, Bonaventure. To this end, Andrea Di Maio conducts a lexicographical analysis of the syntagma "natural law" in his writings and of the related terms, "nature," "law of nature," "right," and "natural right."

This allows us to appreciate Bonaventure's complex thought—theological, philosophical, and even jurisprudential—on how different kinds of law evolve and are related to one another. Of particular interest, though, is his account of the reciprocal dependency that exists between natural right and positive right; natural law and civil law. While Bonaventure insists that the law of the city grows out of natural law, positive right is also necessary at times to make explicit certain moral demands that are only implicit in natural law. Nevertheless, Bonaventure believes that the preceding tradition of political philosophy, both pagan and Christian, has failed to provide an adequate theory of social life. In his view, there are four functions of politics and jurisdiction, each being more fundamental than its successor. These are: conscience and its values, centered on the worship of the one God; the laws (the golden rule, natural law), which govern life in society; the structure and exercise of government; the judiciary. Whereas modern political thought stresses the separation of powers, Bonaventure insists that there is a subordination of lower functions to higher ones. In this regard, his political thought is a natural law variety of constitutionalism. The exercise of government and judiciary powers is constrained by natural law. Indeed, positive laws are valid only if they grow out or issue from natural law and can be traced back to it: if they stand in continuity and are consistent with it. He is particularly alert to the historical evolution of law and the need of practical wisdom to mediate between eternal truths or principles and concrete contingencies.

To highlight the development and pluralism of scholastic reflection on natural law, Riccardo Saccenti examines how two major theologians of the second half of the thirteenth century develop their understanding of natural law against the backdrop of Aquinas's thought. He focuses on one of Aquinas's confreres and colleagues and then on one of Bonaventure's disciples. On the one hand, there is the Dominican Peter Tarentaise (c. 1225–1276). He is a colleague of Aquinas during Thomas's second period of teaching at Paris and goes on to become Pope Innocent V. On the other hand, there is the Franciscan Matthew of Acquasparta (1240–1302). Both Peter and Matthew work with the same sources as Thomas. Each, however, develops a very different moral epistemology from his. Whereas Aquinas argues that we can work out the content of natural law through reasoning, they believe that the supreme rules that shape the moral life are impressed upon reason from without, by divine grace. Peter, nonetheless, approaches natural law from the same standpoint as Aquinas. He addresses it within an analysis of how our natural human powers work and interact with one another in producing human action. Matthew, on the other hand, focuses on law as a general metaphysical category.

The major Scholastic theologian of the early fourteenth century is the Franciscan John Duns Scotus. It is commonly believed that he initiates within the Latin tradition a more voluntarist and nonteleological conception of natural law. In his view, if creation is an expression of God's freedom, the second tablet of the Ten Commandments, which regards our treatment of our neighbors, is not natural law in the strict sense. It is merely consonant with natural law, which is stated in the first tablet. Furthermore, God can dispense us from the commandments of the second table since these are as contingent as creation itself.

Martyna Koszkało, however, argues that dispensation, in this case, refers not to the suspension of these moral demands but to the introduction of a new law. Furthermore, she addresses the scholarly debate over what Scotus means when he claims that the second tablet of the Decalogue is consonant with the natural law expressed in the first tablet. Scholars disagree over whether Scotus is thereby claiming that God establishes the second tablet of the law for aesthetic reasons, in view of ethical naturalism, or simply as one of many equally valid ways by which he can make humans express their obedience to him. For Koszkało, all three readings prove inconsistent with Scotus's moderate divine voluntarism. The first two are incompatible with voluntarism, whereas the third entails an extreme rather than moderate divine voluntarism. Indeed, it is difficult to explain why his divine voluntarism is internally coherent rather than inconsistent. Scotus does not spell out what, in his view, renders the second tablet of the Decalogue consonant with the first. Rather, his thought on this matter needs to be teased out or reconstructed to some extent. A more consistent reading emerges, Koszkało argues, if we attend to a claim made by Scotus: that the second table of the law is not merely consonant, but very consonant with the first. This means that, in his view, one set of contingent moral commandments is more consonant with the first table than others. This would be the case if one set enables the rational creature to love God better, by imitating his love for creation more perfectly and by loving him in one's neighbor more deeply. Scotus's account of natural law, therefore, is not centered on obeying God nor, in the manner of ethical naturalism, on achieving the full potential of human nature. Rather, it is centered on becoming like God by imitating his love.

The preceding medieval Latin thinkers are primarily systematic theologians. However, natural law is equally important to jurisprudence and politics. In this regard, a particularly significant figure is Marsilius of Padua (c. 1275–c. 1342), whose *Defensor Pacis* (1324) is one of the most important works of medieval political thought.

Alessandro Mulieri discusses the relevance of Marsilius of Padua's conception of natural law for his overall theory of human law. Marsilius is often considered to have rejected natural law by identifying it with human convention. This is the view of Alan Gewirth and Leo Strauss. Mulieri, on the other hand, argues that Marsilius does not reject natural law nor reduce it to human conventions but deems it politically irrelevant, nonetheless. This can be gleaned from his only detailed discussion of natural law in the *Defensor Pacis*. There he proposes two definitions of natural law. The first is grounded in Averroes's interpretation of Aristotle's remarks on the variability of things that are naturally just. Under this first definition, natural law is equated with convention. The second definition, however, equates natural law with dictates of right reason and thereby makes it a subspecies of divine law. Marsilius believes that divine law, which comprehends natural law, defines what is licit and illicit. In his view, however, it is an extrapolitical standard that does not have any legal force. He argues instead that, to make good laws, a polity needs to draw on the collective experience and practical wisdom of the people rather than natural law. This amounts to a dismissal of the traditional medieval belief that natural law should constitute an extra-legal standard for assessing the quality and function of human laws in the political community. In this regard, Marsilius may have been influenced, through his contact with Peter of Abano and John of Jandun, by Jewish-Arabic elaborations on natural law.

The preceding survey illustrates how each essay in this volume aims to clear up some misreading that surrounds the writings of one or several medieval thinkers and their reflection on natural law. In this regard, they resemble, both singly and collectively, the work done by the restorer of a painting, who removes, say, a film of grime and thereby lets us see the artwork in its pristine condition. Moreover, much in the manner of an art restoration project, where the specialist will often work on one aspect or sector, each contribution has focused on one area of a broader canvas. So, while each essay deserves to be read by itself, we also need to step back and, viewing it relation to the others, look carefully at the overall picture that this volume frames.

Taken together, the essays sketch medieval reflection on natural law in a way that either renders some of its features more accurately than the existing literature or captures them more vividly.

The essays in the first part highlight how "natural law theory" can only be predicated univocally of medieval Christian thought. Even there its scope, nature, and efficacy are disputed. Whenever it designates a feature common to each of the religious traditions of medieval philosophy, the term can only function as an analogical or an equivocal name. Taken together, these traditions do not share a common concept or theory of natural law. Only the Byzantines and Latins do. Nevertheless, in one way or another, the three monotheistic traditions do address the questions that underlie natural law discourse. On these grounds, Emon characterizes a certain kind of reasoning within Islamic jurisprudence, usul al-fiqh, as natural law. In this case, the term functions as an analogical name. However, if as Jacobs argues, Jewish law and moral thought should really be characterized as an authoritative rational tradition, then "natural law" can only be predicated of it in the manner of a strictly equivocal name. This does not mean that attributing theories of natural law to medieval Islamic and Jewish thought involves a category mistake. Rather, the essays in the first part indicate that the concept of natural law, central to Christian thought, provides an apt framework for singling out and labelling a series of questions and concerns that are common to the moral and legal thought of the various traditions of medieval philosophy. In this regard, it plays a hermeneutical function rather than designate a common doctrine. It also has a dialectical function. It constitutes a point around which proponents of the various traditions can initiate debate and inquiry with one another on their rival conceptions of morality.

A second feature highlighted in the essays is the inseparability of natural law discourse from juridical texts and categories. The chapters on Judaism and Islam confirm how these two religions are centered primarily on the observance of a divine law rather than the acceptance of a doctrine. Nonetheless, as several other chapters underline, Christian reflection on natural law is also rooted in law. Byzantine natural law discourse is largely articulated through the citation of maxims taken from Roman law. There are also recurring indications of how medieval Latin theologians draw on the work of Romanists and canonists. One example is Bonaventure's detailed examination of the reciprocal relation between civil and natural law. Another is the way in which Scotus accounts for the contingency of the commandments of the second table of the Decalogue by analyzing the juridical practice of granting a dispensation. As discourse about a law, natural law theories are grounded in jurisprudence and draw on it. They also shape the law when accepted within the broader culture. They give it an antipositivist thrust and provide reasons for adopting certain norms and procedures. Indeed, there are also some indications of how natural law discourse informs legal practice. Jacobs notes how, in the Middle Ages, Jewish courts and legal commentators work out the practical implications of the Torah for concrete cases. By situating natural law reasoning within usul al-fiqh, Emon underlines how it is part and parcel of Sunnite legal reasoning. However, Marsilius of Padua argues that it is not operative in the framing of laws. This, however, is not the standard view of Byzantines and Latins. Virtually all medieval Christian thinkers are convinced that natural law is a decisive criterion of the laws that we make. They thereby reinforce this conviction in the culture of their time. We can also assume that legislators and lawyers share this conviction, even if they do not always put it into practice.

Third, just as the various traditions of medieval philosophy do not work with the same concept of natural law, they do not have a common understanding of its status as a standard for regulating ethical or religious pluralism within society. This is largely due to their different conceptions of divine law. The Gospels distinguish Caesar's prerogatives from those of God. Islam, on the other hand, does not make such a sharp distinction between the sacred and the secular. Its natural law discourse regards that which is only implicit in the Shari'a. It is not conceptually distinct from divine law. Similarly, the ethical reasoning of Judaism cannot be distinguished conceptually in its entirety from divine law. It is grounded in God's Covenant with Israel. Still, by comparing the natural law discourse of the various traditions of medieval philosophy and highlighting its heterogeneity, the contributors also point toward the challenges of ethical and religious pluralism and to some ways of tackling them.

According to the standard understanding of natural law, all humans, regardless of their culture, are under the same moral order and can access it through reason, by considering the structure of either human nature or thought. However, several contributions not only consider a particular tradition but also stress how any tradition has its own inherent particularity (chapters 1 and 2). In other words, whoever articulates or draws on a theory of natural law to address moral, legal, or political questions necessarily does so within a specific conceptual framework or tradition. That conceptual framework will be incommensurable with others, both those classifiable as theories of natural law and those that are not. Defending a natural law theory, therefore, requires that one consider how to engage with both kinds of rival tradition. Once the imposition of one's conceptual framework is ruled out, what constitutes the proper procedure for engaging them will depend largely on whether one's own tradition allows for the possibility of establishing first principles through rational inquiry. One might believe that such a process of dialectical engagement between incommensurable traditions can lead to the discovery of a universally valid set of moral truths. This may be the view of medieval Jewish philosophers and some Islamic jurists. It is also the view of virtually all medieval Christian philosophies. However, there is a difference between an engagement between members of different traditions at an individual level and at a societal or political one. In the latter case, maybe all that can be expected is that society maximize the space for the various traditions to practice their beliefs and make their case. This is what Emon proposes, after surveying the natural law theories of medieval Islamic thought. Alternatively, one might conclude, as Marsilius does, that a conception of natural law, no matter how correct, plays no role whatsoever in the process of framing and revising a society's laws. Rather, the law is developed by drawing on the collective wisdom and experience of the people. This strategy has the advantage of making people focus on what they have in common rather than what separates them. It leaves unsettled, though, how a society and its members determine which of the insights and arguments that they draw from their collective experience count as wise and correct. Inevitably, a society will base its law on some conceptual framework. The challenge of engaging with other traditions, far from being settled, merely resurfaces. Marsilius notwithstanding, the general view of medieval Christian theories of natural law in this regard is that the fundamental norms of law and political morality should be based on a sound conception of human nature and good: on natural law. At the same time, medieval Christian thought acknowledges that normally it is difficult to discover the fundamental norms of law and political morality with sufficient reliability, whether on an individual or social level. It insists that, in practice, we rely on divine revelation. This implies that a society whose members do not share this commitment to divine revelation is not only unlikely to agree on the proper moral principles but will also find it difficult to reach such a consensus. At any rate, not only do medieval theories of natural law point to the central problems of ethical and political pluralism but also to several ways of addressing them. In one way or another, though, each medieval theory of natural law points to the continual need for engagement between rival traditions rather than a straightforward formula for resolving pluralism once and for all.

Moreover, the various medieval theories of natural law not only postulate such engagement but often practice it to some extent. In articulating their account of natural law, authors of one of the religious traditions draw on the thought of those belonging to another. This is a fourth characteristic underscored in this volume. Aquinas draws on Avicenna to develop his Aristotelian account of practical reason, whereas Marsilius may be influenced by medieval Jewish thinkers in formulating his views on natural law. Similarly, Joseph Albo probably adopts the concept of natural law from Aquinas. They also share common ground to the degree in which they all engage critically and speculatively with Greek philosophy.

These, then, are some of the findings of this collection of essays. Earlier versions of the papers, with the exception of chapters 3 and 8, were presented at the Pontifical Athenaeum *Regina Apostolorum*, on April 10–11, 2018, as part of the conference, "Natural Law in Medieval Philosophy: Traditions, Convergences and Divergences." The conference was organized by the Cattedra Arosio di Alti Studi Medioevali. A special word of thanks goes to its sponsors, Franco Arosio and the late Olimpia Arosio, and to the faculty and staff who helped organize it: Fr. Rafael Pascual, LC, Fr. Alex Yeung, LC, Fr. Eamonn O'Higgins, LC, Fr. Alain Contat, Carmelo Pandolfi, Guido Traversa, Marco Martorana, Renato Zeuli, and Roberto Vercellone.

The authors of this volume are also grateful to the collaborators and staff of The Catholic University of America Press. Much of the merit goes to John Martino, who has guided the book through the submission, review, and editorial process, and to John C. McCarthy, the editor of the Studies in Philosophy and the History of Philosophy series. The two anonymous reviewers who read the initial draft with great care also helped to improve it with many useful comments and suggestions.

Hopefully, this collection of essays illustrates how medieval theories of natural law, drawing on Judaism, Islam, or Christianity, offer valuable insights not only on ethics, law, and politics but also on how to engage with rival traditions on these issues. If so, it may help advance the ongoing conversation on these important matters.

Part I ∞ Natural Law in the Religious Traditions
of Medieval Philosophy

Jonathan Jacobs

1 ⁂ Natural Law in Medieval Jewish Philosophy

INTRODUCTION AND SOME BACKGROUND

It is a striking fact about medieval Jewish philosophical thought—and Jewish philosophical thought overall, for that matter—that there is so little discussion of natural law in it. Joseph Albo (1380–1444) regarded natural law as one of the three major types of law, along with divine law and conventional law, but his discussion of natural law is very brief and has had almost no influence. Enlightenment-period and more recent Jewish thought reflects some interest in natural law, but its impact has been modest. However, the absence of natural law in Jewish thought is not a defect, not a lack indicative of a significant failure to ground moral judgment in a sound manner. There are rich and extensive resources for moral thought in the Jewish tradition. The present discussion will focus on those and how they are like and unlike conceptions of natural law.

There are some significant respects in which certain currents of Jewish thought overlap with natural law theorizing. In addition, some contemporary scholars argue that Jewish moral thought should be interpreted as reflecting natural law.[1] They maintain that absence of the idiom is

I would like to express my gratitude to the Fulbright Scholar Program and the Faculty of Law at the University of York in England. A grant from the former made possible a half-year visit, graciously hosted by the latter. Much of this paper was written during that period in 2017–18.

1. David Novak, Lenn Goodman, and Tamar Rudavsky have each argued that there are important respects in which Jewish thought—especially medieval Jewish thought—either can and should be interpreted as including natural law elements or, as Tamar Rudavsky has argued, it includes "natural law sentiments" if not clear examples of natural law elements. See, for example, Lenn Evan Goodman, *Judaism, Human Rights, and Human Values* (New York: Oxford

not to be taken as absence of the relevant conceptions; their presence is implicit. Acknowledging the presence and role of natural law, it is contended, will help show that Jewish moral thought is committed to a number of universal values and principles. There is probably more discussion of how to understand the relations between Jewish moral thought and conceptions of natural law at this time than at any earlier time.

One of the main claims in the present discussion is that while there are important likenesses between medieval Jewish thought and natural law theorizing, there are good reasons to recognize Jewish moral thought as distinct from it. It is illuminating to highlight the points of overlap, but it is important, also, to recognize the distinctive features of each of the views, noting some differences between them. Also, we should keep in mind that there are numerous conceptions of natural law. For present purposes we can employ a general characterization of it. However, even within Catholic natural law theorizing there are significant differences between, for example, Thomistic natural law and Scotist natural law, and, later on, Protestant thinkers elaborated conceptions of natural law with still other distinctive features. In addition, there are different interpretations of Thomistic natural law, and in recent philosophical literature there are important examples of those different views.[2] With a topic such as this one the level of description at which one addresses the issues can be quite important. At high levels of abstraction and generalization we can find important affinities among all of the views mentioned. At lower levels of abstraction, the differences become more apparent. I will make some remarks about each level.

Medieval Jewish thinkers had access to many of the same ancient and classical sources as their Christian contemporaries. And by the late thirteenth century numerous works of Aristotle had been retrieved and made accessible as well as numerous Arabic commentaries and commentaries on Aristotle and others. The Abrahamic monotheisms shared an

---

University Press, 1998); David Novak, *Natural Law in Judaism* (New York: Cambridge University Press, 1998); Tamar Rudavsky, "Natural Law in Judaism," in *Reason, Religion, and Natural Law: From Plato to Spinoza*, ed. Jonathan A. Jacobs, 83–105 (New York: Oxford University Press, 2012).

2. For example, consider the differences between the interpretation of Thomistic natural law in the work of Henry Veatch and that in the work of John Finnis. See, for example, Veatch, *Human Rights: Fact or Fancy?* (Baton Rouge: Louisiana State University Press, 1985), 49–112; Finnis, *Natural Law and Natural Rights* (New York: Oxford University Press, 2011).

interest in the philosophical inheritance from antiquity, and in numerous respects medieval philosophy exhibits impressive intercultural intellectual respect and exchange. Solomon ibn Gabirol and Isaac Israeli, for example, are two Jewish thinkers whose philosophical views were known to numerous Christian philosophers. Still, each tradition had its own key sources. Thus, Augustine, John of Salisbury, and Anselm were not likely to have been among the thinkers studied by Maimonides and Levi ben Gerson. Likewise, Saadia Gaon and Judah Halevi were almost certainly not studied by Albert the Great and Duns Scotus. While in each tradition we find versions of the sentiment, "Hear the truth from whoever says it," and there is discernible philosophical interaction, each tradition had its own crucial sources and authorities as well as commitments and perspectives.

The main point I wish to make here is that given the sources, the authorities, and the perspectives of medieval Jewish moral thought we can see that it involved a conception of *authoritative rational tradition* that merits being distinguished from conceptions of practical wisdom and conceptions of natural law. The way that Jewish philosophers addressed the issue of "the reasons for the commandments" is central to this claim. The notion of authoritative rational tradition overlaps with practical wisdom and natural law in important respects but there is still a point in distinguishing them.

We need to be careful here because all three approaches to moral/practical epistemology can be consistent with each other; in some very influential bodies of thought—Aquinas's, for example—they are interconnected. Still, we will see that each can also be the core conception of a moral/practical epistemology largely in its own terms, and there are explanatory gains in seeing medieval Jewish thought, or at least one important current of it, as centrally shaped by the notion of authoritative rational tradition.

NATURAL LAW AND RATIONAL TRADITION

For purposes of clarity, I suggest the following (nondogmatic) characterizations of practical wisdom and natural law. A conception of practical wisdom maintains that through the exercise of reason, supported and oriented by well-formed dispositions of appetite and the passions, a person can arrive at correct judgments of how to understand the ethical features of situations and how to act in them, and has a reliable (if imperfect) disposition to enact those judgments. That might or might not be connected with a conception of natural law. A conception of natural law maintains that: (i) there are rationally ascertainable general principles of practical reason (or right action) reflecting objective goods for human beings; these may or may not involve teleological considerations; (ii) as universal, those principles and/or objective goods are accessible to all human beings; (iii) there is a relation between general principles of practical reason (or right action) and the specific requirements in particular cases though that relation might not be one of logical derivation. Other forms of determination are sometimes indicated: (iv) whether or not a theory of natural law includes explicit commitment to the God of Abrahamic monotheism natural laws are taken to be authoritative norms integral to the world-order. They are not conventional, and they are not discretionary.

To distinguish the relevant current of Jewish moral thought from those two approaches I will refer to that current as "authoritative rational tradition." In recent years there has been increased interest in the role of tradition, especially with regard to morality. One might think that tradition would be especially important in conceptions of morality that are noncognitivist or relativist. The thought would be that perhaps traditions are important as sources of guiding norms, principles, perspectives, and judgments in the absence of objective or rational considerations underwriting those judgments. To persons who have internalized norms and values they seem objective but, in fact, they are not. However, the notion of tradition relevant here is not relativist or noncognitivist. It is a notion that regards tradition as a mode of access to rationally justified moral judgments, and does so in an epistemologically reflective manner, which is not merely a matter of convention, even if some of its elements are not fully evident. For instance, neither mere antiquity nor mere endurance is adequate as a basis for a tradition's authority. The authority includes epistemic authority.

Notions of "tradition" and of what is "traditional" can apply in a diversity of ways. For example, we could say that there is a tradition of criticism and innovation in Western science. Yet, this is just the sort of intellectual disposition that might seem to be at odds with an institution or practice being traditional or traditionalist. In philosophy we speak of "the rationalist tradition" and the "empiricist tradition," each of which exhibits a good deal of internal criticism and development. We sometimes (appropriately) distinguish between modern societies and highly traditional societies. Yet, in a modern society there may be significant elements of tradition. A tradition of respecting individual liberties, for example, can be strongly conservative in some ways but it may also develop and be responsive to changing conditions, while in a strongly traditional society social and cultural change is very slow, and customary ways are preserved with considerable tenacity.

The notion of tradition has a pronounced presence in medieval Jewish philosophy. Judah Halevi wrote:

> The approach to God is only possible through the medium of God's command, and there is no road to the knowledge of the commands of God except by way of prophesy, but not by means of speculation and reasoning. There is, however, no other connexion between us and these commands except truthful tradition.[3]
>
> Tradition in itself is a good thing if it satisfies the soul, but a perturbed soul prefers research, especially if examination leads to the verification of traditions. Then knowledge and tradition become united.[4]

The quotation indicates the importance of the epistemological aspect. Bahya ibn Pakuda wrote: "Wisdom is the life of their [human beings'] soul, the light of their mind, their way to the favor of God (glory and praise be unto Him), and their guardian from His anger in this world and the next."[5] Sustaining tradition and the study of tradition are parts of our finite, imperfect way of imitating God and a way for us to come closer to God. Only in that way can the people Israel become a "kingdom of priests and a holy nation."

Thus, the notion of tradition does not in itself imply a relativistic or noncognitive character, and the epistemology of a tradition may be strongly connected with rational justification, truth-seeking, and the growth of understanding. Influential medieval Jewish philosophers understood their tradition and the project of seeking "the reasons for the

---

3. Judah Halevi, *The Kuzari* (*Kitab Al Khazari*): *An Argument for the Faith of Israel*, trans. Hartwig Hirschfield (New York: Schocken Books, 1964), 183 [Part Three].

4. Halevi, *The Kuzari*, 248 [Part Five].

5. Bah.ya ben Joseph ibn Pak.uda, *The Book of Direction to the Duties of the Heart*, trans. Menahem Mansoor (Oxford: The Littman Library of Jewish Civilization, 2004), 85.

commandments" in just that way. That project concerns the question of whether the commandments—all six hundred and thirteen of them, not only the Ten Commandments—have rational justifications and whether we can ascertain them. It has been a central concern of Jewish thought throughout its history. Much of Jewish thought concerns the reasons for the commandments because the commandments constitute a way of striving for holiness, and that we are to be holy, to walk in God's ways, is the guiding imperative of life.

Are the commandments to be interpreted in terms of divine voluntarism or in terms of divine wisdom? If Torah and its interpretation supply adequate guidance to leading a life of holiness are we able to appreciate this through ascertaining and understanding the reasons for the commandments, or are we to regard the commandments as shaping a discipline of perfection but without human beings attaining a deepened understanding of that discipline? With respect to the motivation to fulfill the commandments, is that exclusively a matter of having been commanded by God or is there a role for understanding in our motivation? Is deepened, enlarged understanding integral to fulfilling the commandments? Or is faithful, rigorous observance sufficient?

Two important points of clarification need to be mentioned here. One is that Torah is understood by Jewish tradition to include Mishnah and Talmud as well as the Five Books of Moses. It is part of Jewish understanding that interpretation, explanation, argument, judgment, and consideration of new cases and applications are part of what is included in fulfilling the commandments. That is what Rabbinic Judaism maintains. It is not a form of brittle legalism employing a fully fixed code, with no questions to be asked or understanding to be attained. At the core is a living tradition making demands on intellect, imagination, and interpretation. The second point is that medieval Jewish thinkers regarded Torah as a fully adequate source regarding how one is to live in all departments of life, though study, reflection, dialogue, argument, and elaboration are needed to find what is in it. It requires thoughtful engagement, not simple compliance. Fulfilling the commandments is both an intellectual and a practical project and the way in which practice and understanding are mutually informing is centrally important to the tradition. In its aspiration to holiness, each generation must do its own thinking as well as studying what has been bequeathed as an intellectual inheritance. Study is not merely committing to memory. It is an inexhaustible project of understanding divine wisdom and benevolence through appreciation—in multiple senses—of what the commandments require. That is how the human condition and the proper perfections of a human being's end are best understood. It is part of the life of any Jewish community that striving to live in accord with the commandments requires reasoning. The elaboration, articulation, and application of commandments are not mechanical; these involve active, engaged thinking and consideration of different views.

An important source of evidence for this is that even though Jews did not have political sovereignty they were often permitted by Christian or Muslim rulers to operate their own courts, and the total body of commandments and the commentaries upon them were the laws governing Jewish life. The commandments and the interpretations of them had direct practical significance in all departments of life. Ascertaining just what the commandments require in novel circumstances and situations that were not anticipated by earlier commentators required insight and imagination while also needing to be oriented by values and norms with familiar resonances. The practical dimension of the commandments was fully present in the daily life of the community.

At the same time, that the Law itself is to be studied, is among the commandments. At Deuteronomy 4:6–8 we find the Lord telling Moses to speak to the people, saying to them that the Lord has said of the commandments: "Observe them faithfully, for that will be proof of your wisdom and discernment to other peoples, who on hearing of all these laws will say, 'Surely, that great nation is a wise and discerning people!' For what great nation is there that has a god so close at hand as is the Lord our God whenever we call upon Him? Or what great nation has laws, and rules as perfect as all this Teaching that I set before you this day." Reasoning about the law and reasoning from the law are regarded as inseparable from following the law.

Jewish thinkers held a variety of views about the reasons for the commandments but rationalistically inclined thinkers such as Saadia Gaon, Bahya ibn Pakuda, and Maimonides argued that there are reasons for the commandments and that it is possible for us to ascertain the reasons for many of them, even if the reasons are not fully evident. Those who held a more voluntarist view often did so as a way of acknowledging God's sovereignty. (Jewish philosophers tended not to be voluntarists though, among the works of others besides philosophers, voluntarist views are sometimes found. The voluntarist tradition has been very prominent in Islam for several centuries. While there are currents of mystical thought in Judaism voluntarism has not been widely defended by Jewish philosophers.) However, Maimonides, for example, argued that it is an affront to divine wisdom and benevolence to suppose that any commandments are without rational justification. The rational justifications for many of the commandments might not be fully evident, but *a great deal of* knowledge generally is not fully evident, and the lack of self-evidence or demonstrative necessity does not signal lack of justification. The notion that divine will is connected with divine reasons is a widely held view among Jewish thinkers.

Saadia Gaon, two centuries before Maimonides, was very clear in taking tradition to be a vitally important source of knowledge, one that is in a relation of mutual reinforcement with the senses and reason (in the intuitive sense of reason). In the "Introductory Treatise" to *The Book of Beliefs and Opinions* he presents a number of epistemological considerations. Among them are these:

> 1. "That is [to say, we believe in] the validity of authentic tradition, by reason of the fact that it is based upon the knowledge of the senses as well as that of reason."[6]

> 2. "We remark that this type of knowledge (I mean that which is furnished by authentic tradition and the books of prophetic revelation), corroborates for us the validity of the first three sources of knowledge."[7] [Those are direct observation, intuition of the intellect, knowledge inferred by logical necessity.]

> 3. "Furthermore [authentic tradition] verifies for us the validity of the intuition of reason. It enjoins us, namely, to speak the truth and not to lie."[8]

> 4. "Besides that it confirms for us the validity of knowledge inferred by logical necessity, [that is to say] that whatever leads to the rejection of the perception of the senses or rational intuition is false."[9]

---

6. Saadia Gaon, *The Book of Beliefs and Opinions*, trans. Samuel Rosenblatt (New Haven: Yale University Press, 1976), 18.

7. Saadia Gaon, *Book of Beliefs*, 18.

8. Saadia Gaon, 18–19.

9. Saadia Gaon, 19.

5." Next [tradition] informs us that all sciences are [ultimately] based on what we grasp with our aforementioned senses, from which they are deduced and derived."[10]

6. "Were it not for the fact that man felt satisfied in their hearts that there is such a thing in the world as authentic tradition, no person would be able to cherish legitimate expectations on the basis of the reports he receives about the success of a certain commercial transaction, or the usefulness of a speci-fied art—and, after all, the realization of man's potentialities and the satisfac-tion of his needs depend upon enterprise."[11]

7. "Again, were it not for the assumption that there exists in the world [such a thing as] authentic tradition, men would accept neither the command nor the interdict of their ruler, except when they saw him with their own eyes and heard his words with their own ears.... But if things were like that, it would mean the end of law and order, and the death of many human beings."[12]

8. "Also, were it not for the existence in the world of such a thing as authentic tradition, no man would be able to identify the property of his father or his inheritance from his grandfather. Nay, he would not even be certain of being the son of his mother, let alone of his being the son of his father. The result would then be that the affairs of men would always be subject to doubt, to the point where human beings would believe only what they perceive with their senses at the time of perception."[13]

9. "Now the Scriptures, too, assert that authentic tradition is as trustworthy as things perceived with our own eyes."[14]

10." The Bible is not the sole basis of our religion, for in addition to it we have two other bases. One of these is anterior to it; namely, the fountain of reason. The second is posterior to it; namely, the source of tradition."[15]

These claims might seem basically congenial to Maimonides's own view later on, though Maimonides was critical of Saadia for employing *ka-lam*, the method of the dialectical theologians, and thereby—Maimonides claimed—being insufficiently philosophical and rigorous in his method. Maimonides had a conception of philosophical explanation and justifica-

10. Saadia Gaon, 19.
11. Saadia Gaon, 156.
12. Saadia Gaon, 156.
13. Saadia Gaon, 157.
14. Saadia Gaon, 174.
15. Saadia Gaon, 174.

tion somewhat more rigorous and systematic than Saadia's, and it was important to Maimonides to distance philosophy from dialectical theology. Nonetheless, Maimonides clearly agreed with Saadia that tradition has an important epistemological role and that there is epistemic interaction between tradition and reason.

Indeed, Maimonides was emphatic that there are reasons for all of the commandments, even if some elude our grasp. He wrote:

> Every commandment from among these six hundred and thirteen commandments exists either with a view to communicating a correct opinion, or to putting an end to an unhealthy opinion, or to communicating a rule of justice, or to warding off an injustice, or to endowing men with a noble moral quality, or to warning them against an evil moral quality. Thus all [the commandments] are bound up with three things: opinions, moral qualities, and political civic actions.[16]

There is always a point in striving to understand the reasons for commandments, even if we find that the reasons are obscure. It helps that we know what the overall aim of the Law is—namely to abolish idolatry—and that is achieved through the Law's *telos* regarding beliefs, moral character, and civic life.

Bahya ibn Pakuda's (eleventh century) focus in his main work was somewhat different from Saadia and Maimonides's, but he, too, highlighted the significance of tradition. Bahya was committed to revivifying the spiritual aspect of Judaism. He thought that, too often, it had become preoccupied with details of scholarship rather than gratitude, joy, and delight in the Lord along with seeking deeper understanding. He wrote: "If you are a man of sound mind and understanding, which qualify you to verify the traditions passed down to you from the prophets concerning the roots of religion and the origins of the acts of worship—then you are obliged to use your faculties in order to verify things both logically and by tradition."[17] He sought to reanimate devotion and religious feeling but that was to accompany intellectual depth and enlarged understanding, not replace it.

Seeking the reasons for the commandments is integral to the activity by which one is perfected. That activity shapes moral virtues, virtues

16. Moses Maimonides, *The Guide of the Perplexed*, trans. Shlomo Pines, 2 vols. (Chicago: University of Chicago Press, 1963), 524 [III, 31].

17. Bahya ben Joseph ibn Pakuda, *Book of Direction*, 94 [introduction].

of the intellect, and shapes our striving to lead lives of holiness. Suppose there is a practice, a ritual, a form of worship, the reason for which remains unclear. It is not for us to judge that such a commandment is discretionary or is so anachronistic that it now lacks relevance. For one thing, divine wisdom and benevolence assure us that fulfilling that commandment does have a role in perfecting us even if we do not fully recognize it. Moreover, as our understanding deepens, we may come to see the reason for the commandment and thereby be strengthened in our disposition to fulfill it. In Bahya's view as well, practice and understanding can form a braid, a spiral of mutual reinforcement.

Understanding the reasons for a commandment can strengthen the disposition to fulfill it, and the practice of fulfilling it can lead to a fuller understanding of the good realized by it. In some respects much of the reasoning required in order to apply commandments to the particularities of life is not so different from the sort of reasoning Aquinas referred to when an agent is arriving at "determinations" of natural law—judgments based upon, but not strictly derivable from, principles. The commandments, like principles of natural law, often need to be specified in ways that address the particular features of situations. There is not just one set way to welcome the stranger, to rebuke a wrongdoer, love one's neighbor, or to act generously. What is to be done in acting in those ways often depends on judging how to best meet needs and realize goods in particular situations.

At the same time, we should observe that while the material in Talmud, the key text for the interpretation of a great deal of Jewish law, is organized into six Orders divided into sixty-three Tractates, it does not constitute a fully systematic codification. There are several different types of arguments and interpretive claims in Talmud, along with commentary and suggestions and points that are neither narrowly jurisprudential nor in strict accord with formal rules of inference. Also, the rationale for the organization of the material in it is often not clear. This is not to say that Talmud is just a complicated jumble of things. It is much more coherently organized than that. But it is also a very rich source of illustrations of how Jewish thinkers often seek rationales and justifications by intellectual methods other than logical derivation from principles. Many other forms of explication of claims are also included.

Still, in many cases the exercise of capacities involved in fulfilling the commandments might seem very much like the exercise of capacities in practical wisdom and following the requirements of natural law. In addition, recent defenders of the view that Judaism includes natural law elements point to the fact that moral judgment, thought, and argument are present in the Hebrew Bible from the very beginning, prior to the giving of the Law. There are numerous examples of moral knowledge independent of Torah. Part of the view's appeal is that it is a way of showing the universal validity of many of the moral elements of the commandments and the overall view of human nature and morality presented in Scripture.

Consider, for instance, Abraham's argument with God over the fate of Sodom and Gomorrah (Gn 18:17–33) and Avimelekh's moral blamelessness regarding Sarah and Abraham (Gn 20:2–7). There are several others, including Cain's apparent awareness of the wrongfulness of murder and Jacob's understanding of the wrongfulness of his deceit of Isaac. These are all instances in which the persons involved showed clear awareness of moral considerations, and they all precede the giving of the commandments to the People Israel. Thus, it is argued, when the people entered into covenant with God they did so on the basis of antecedent moral understanding, and this is to be interpreted as a role for natural law.

The argument might also note that Jewish tradition holds that all of mankind is subject to the Noahide covenant with God, and most of its elements are concerned with important moral matters. That is yet another basis for finding natural law elements in Jewish thought. The Noahide commandments are as follows:

1. It is forbidden to deny God.
2. It is forbidden to blaspheme God.
3. Murder is prohibited.
4. Incest, adultery, and homosexual relationships are prohibited.
5. Stealing is prohibited.
6. It is not permitted to eat a part of a live animal.
7. Courts/legal system must be established.

It is fairly clear that most of these concern recognizably significant moral matters, whether or not one agrees entirely with them. Jewish tradition regards these as accessible to all people; they are not found only in a revelation to the Jewish people. They are for all of mankind in making a new start after the floodwaters have receded.[18]

LIKENESSES AND CONTRASTS WITH NATURAL LAW

Why, then, hesitate to regard Jewish moral thought as involving natural law elements? I will suggest three reasons. One is that the notion of covenant with a particular people and the reciprocal relation with God is integrally important. That does not mean that the values are not universal or that the ethical importance of the Law is domesticated to the Jewish people. The commandment to welcome the stranger and the moral lesson of recalling being enslaved in a strange land teach—powerfully and universally—the value of compassion and of justice. That lesson is repeated again and again in Torah. However, that is not inconsistent with interpreting the value as inseparably bound up with all of the commandments and their special significance for a particular people leading a life of holiness. Thus, one might highlight the distinctive religious, moral, and political character of the covenant with the Hebrews. That does not diminish the universality of the moral values but it does place them in a way that has unique significance for a particular people.

A second reason is that Judaism has a fundamental orientation to practice, to how one lives, rather than being primarily a set doctrine or counterpart to a catechism. The commandments inform and orient a way of living, of striving to be holy. Numerous Jewish thinkers have articulated philosophical understandings of Judaism and some have produced fundamental principles of Judaism (in fact, Maimonides did) but the focus has almost always been on how deepened understanding illuminates the way of life of a righteous person. The formulation of principles has generally been a response to critiques or challenges on the part of Christians and Muslims requiring Judaism to specify just what its basic claims are. It has not been a mainly internally motivated project.[19] During the medieval period Jews were called upon to defend their religion, to make

18. The rabbinic (Talmudic) tradition regards the Noahide commandments as applying universally and not only to the Jewish people. They are moral/life-guiding requirements to be fulfilled by all people, and though not identified explicitly in Torah as "Noahide commandments" they are interpreted as elaborations of commandments given to Adam and Noah.

19. See the discussion of this issue in Menachem Marc Kellner, *Dogma in Medieval Jewish Thought: From Maimonides to Abravanel* (Oxford: Littman Library of Jewish Civilization, 1986).

a case for showing that it was not theologically and morally superseded and anachronistic. Often, to clarify what Judaism involved it was helpful to articulate basic principles even though that was not the approach taken by Jews to educate persons within their own community.

The emphasis on practice and how a life is led does not imply any incompatibility with natural law. Rather, it is a point about the focus of normative concern. At the conclusion of the *Guide of the Perplexed*, where Maimonides highlights what is most crucially involved in *imitatio Dei*, he writes: "My attributes, i.e., God's actions—as we have shown when commenting on the verse: show me now thy ways (Exodus 33, 13). In this verse we are informed that the actions one must know and imitate are 'mercy, justice and righteousness.'"[20] And, "It is My purpose that you should exercise mercy, justice, and righteousness in the earth, similarly as we have explained before, when speaking of the Thirteen Dispositions, that the intention was that we should imitate them and that they should form our model of conduct."[21] Part of what is striking about this is that it comes *after* Maimonides has developed at considerable length, a conception of intellectualist perfection as the end proper to a human being.

The apparent shift from intellectualist perfectionism to virtues of practice need not indicate an inconsistency in Maimonides's view. We can see the latter virtues—informed by the former—as needed for a human being to best and most fully walk in God's ways, imitate divine activity. This does not undo the braiding of intellectual perfection and ethical perfection; it characterizes it, each type of virtue reinforcing the other and both being reflected in the person's life-activity. In addition, the commandments are concerned with more than political order and more even than moral life. They are guidance to the holiness of individuals and a people.

A third reason has to do with the fact that there is no clear, bright line distinguishing moral commandments from nonmoral ones. There are numerous commandments that concern ritual, others that concern diet, others concern compensation for injury, punishment for offenses, and several concern various forms of worship and tithing at specific times in the calendar. Nonetheless, because they are all commandments concerning what makes for a life of holiness it is not as though some can

20. Maimonides, *Guide*, 201 [Part I].
21. Maimonides, 202.

be regarded as discretionary or as lacking moral significance. Maimonides argued that all of the commandments are integral to the Law and that even those that are suspended because the relevant conditions do not obtain while Israel is in exile and without the Temple as the center of priestly ritual remain parts of the Law.

The primary purpose of the Law is to eliminate all traces of idolatry in the world and to orient us to true good through understanding—to the extent we can attain it—of "the existence and oneness of the deity."[22] Our knowledge of God through our knowledge of the created order, which includes the Law, is to be deepened and enlarged; that is an aspect of the abolition of idolatry. "For Maimonides this cultivation of the intellect is unthinkable apart from the study of Torah, or to be more specific, it is only possible when one reflects on the reasons for divine commandments as well as obeying them."[23] It might seem problematic that the Law contains many elements concerning sacrifice and other practices that seem emblematic of idolatry or at least needless for a people of deep understanding. However, Maimonides refers to God's "wily graciousness" in giving commandments that do not require an abrupt, radical change in people's lives in ways they could not manage.

In his view, the highest worship is a loving cognition that informs action. To attain that loving cognition, significant accommodation of human nature is necessary. Maimonides writes:

> If you consider the divine actions—I mean to say the natural actions—the deity's wily graciousness and wisdom, as shown in the creation of living beings, in the gradation of the motions of the limbs, and the proximity of some of the latter to others, will through them become clear to you. Similarly His wisdom and wily graciousness, as shown in the gradual succession of the various states of the whole individual, will become clear to you.[24]

There is wily graciousness in the organization and processes of nature, and also with regard to how the commandments promote the multiaspect good of a human being. Wily graciousness is evident in the Law, inasmuch as what it requires of people is doable, given what human pro-

---

22. Maimonides, 527 [III, 32].

23. Michael P. Levine, "The Role of Reason in the Ethics of Maimonides: Or, Why Maimonides Could Have Had a Doctrine of Natural Law Even If He Did Not," *The Journal of Religious Ethics* 14, no. 2 (1986): 282.

24. Maimonides, *Guide*, 525 [III, 32].

pensities, susceptibilities, and tendencies in fact are. Accustomed practices are sometimes maintained just because of how entrenched they are in people's second nature, but their meaning is altered, their *telos* is changed so that they are no longer connected with beliefs that are unsuited to monotheism. Expecting people to undertake an abrupt, radical change in practice—accompanying a radical change in belief as part of a process of reorienting people to a fundamentally different way of understanding the world—may be expecting too much, something that is not feasible, given human nature. There is divine wisdom in the way God allows for the endurance of habits of certain kinds while redirecting them to the service of genuine good.

In discussing Maimonides and the question of whether the *Guide* and the Mishneh Torah present not only different but divergent views (one concerned with thought, the other concerned with practice), Isadore Twersky wrote, "However, law, as we shall see, is also propaedeutic and a prophylactic for true belief, i.e., laws protect and promulgate true opinions, solidify and concretize abstract notions. You know from what I have said that opinions do not last unless they are accompanied by actions that strengthen them, make them generally known, and perpetuate them among the multitude."[25]

Belief and practice are not compartmentalized. The dispositions informing each have an impact on the other. One reason ritual and practice are so important is that they can be in the service of sustaining correct understanding.

Monotheism marked a radical change in belief and perspective but the achievement of such a revolution is *work,* involving disciplined, sustained attention and efforts of thought and practical activity. Familiar practices can be maintained though they come to have new and very different meanings. The fact that some familiar forms of practice might be required is important evidence of how thought and action are related in human beings.[26]

The susceptibility to idolatry does not suddenly disappear, and there is the risk of people falling back into prior beliefs—indeed, there is a bib-

---

25. Isadore Twersky, *Introduction to the Code of Maimonides* (*Mishneh Torah*) (New Haven: Yale University Press, 1980), 363.

26. Maimonides discusses this issue in the *Guide,* III, 29. The reasons of the commandments need to be understood in relation to the many surviving practices associated with idolatry.

lical record of that. Thus, the commandments by which we guard against such a lapse remain relevant even if they seem to be no longer needed. The concern about lapsed commitment and moral discipline is one Saadia also addressed. He wrote, "The repetition by the prophets of the injunction already dictated by reason served to put man on his guard, and make him beware, and take the necessary precautions in the fulfillment of these precepts."[27]

There is some likeness here to Aristotle's view of the relation between habits, on the one hand, and ethical virtue and practical wisdom on the other. The more perfect our understanding, the less susceptible we are to specious authority and false values. The more righteous our way of life, the better positioned we are to understand and appreciate the true and the good. To support and preserve practical wisdom many persons might need certain habits mainly as supports, directing attention rightly, and preserving good judgment. In a highly general sense, temperance preserves practical wisdom, Aristotle says, and some of the medievals took note of this feature of human nature, that regular practice, repetition, and encouragement in certain respects can have a vital role in shaping focus and understanding.

Also, no one's practical wisdom (or holiness) is altogether complete, in need of no additional enlargement, coherence, integration, and depth of understanding. It is likely that even persons with a notable degree of virtue of character will rely on habit and the guidance of others in many respects and they might lack full understanding of just why some of their right actions are right. Still, the regular practice of fulfilling the commandments develops virtuous dispositions, which in turn enable people to act well and to enjoy doing so, which reinforces gratitude to God, strengthening the motive to fulfill the commandments, aiding the understanding of the goods thereby realized, further motivating faithful commitment ... and so forth in a reinforcing interaction of thought and practice.[28]

Having highlighted some of the chief features of one important way of regarding "the reasons for the commandments" and Jewish tradition

27. Saadia Gaon, *Book of Beliefs and Opinions*, 192 [Treatise IV].

28. I discuss this view of Maimonides's conception of tradition in Jonathan Jacobs, "The Epistemology of Moral Tradition: A Defense of a Maimonidean Thesis," *Review of Metaphysics* 64, no. 1 (2010): 55–74.

we can look again at similarities and differences regarding natural law. We will use the theories of Aquinas and Scotus as examples of two significant, different approaches to natural law by medieval Christian thinkers. Aquinas's theory takes natural law to reflect objective, substantive considerations of good for human beings, ascertainable by reason. Scotus's view represents the voluntarist approach to natural law, taking the sovereignty of divine volition as the ground of natural law.

There is some resemblance between Scotus's view and Saadia's in that both held that the first two statements in the Decalogue are evident to reason. They are truths of reason concerning the love, gratitude, and obedience owed to God. Saadia held that the existence and uniqueness of God and our debt of gratitude to God are approved by reason immediately; that is, they are rationally self-evident. Scotus said much the same, maintaining that those principles have the status of natural law, and the rest of the Decalogue and moral requirements in general are "exceedingly in harmony" with those truths though not strictly derivable from them.[29]

In addition, there are some likenesses between the tradition of Jewish moral thought and Thomistic natural law, and we can see this by looking at Maimonides and Aquinas's views. Aquinas held that sound reasoning from natural law is not always (or even generally) a matter of derivation in the sense of deduction. Rather, reasoning well from principles of natural law requires exercising practical wisdom, through which the agent arrives at a determination of what is required. Consider a nonethical counterpart. Suppose an architect is asked to design a home for a family. While there are some general principles of physics and engineering governing the project, the actual design is not arrived at by deduction from those principles. It is arrived at by a determination responsive to how large a home the buyer wants and can afford, what are the most appropriate materials, whether it will be a shelter for a great deal of property too or just the family members, what the climate is, and so forth. This is a matter of reasoning, to be sure, but it is not demonstrative reasoning. It is more a matter of arriving at an appropriate specification of the home-

---

29. Scotus's account of natural law in *Ordinatio* III, d. 37, q.un., can be found in Allan B. Wolter, *Duns Scotus on the Will and Morality* (Washington, D.C.: The Catholic University of America Press, 1997), 198–207; John Duns Scotus, *Selected Writings on Ethics*, edited and translated by Thomas Williams (Oxford: Oxford University Press, 2017), 248–58.

owner's end—in this case, a house—taking into account relevant conditions.[30]

In Maimonides's view, Adam's disobedience is what led to human beings' need to make moral judgments. Human beings were no longer completely occupied with intellectual comprehension and judgment, and now needed to be responsive to the imagination as well. That is what led to Adam making judgments of the seemly and the ugly, the becoming and the unbecoming, and what motivated his concern with sensual gratification. Morality concerns a class of judgments that are rationally supportable but not fully evident. The account of how morality and moral judgment came into the human world is supplied in Genesis.

Maimonides held that many moral judgments are in the category of the "generally accepted." Such judgments are not evident to reason but neither are they merely matters of convention or stipulation. Much can be generally accepted in the sense that reasonable persons, considering the matter in question, would agree in arriving at a particular view. The view is rationally supportable but neither a priori nor demonstrated. Maimonides employed the notion of the "generally accepted" in numerous places in the *Guide*, when he discussed moral matters, and also in *Eight Chapters*, the closest thing to a text devoted on (philosophically considered) ethics among his works.[31]

Maimonides speaks there of ethical requirements that rational agents would have been able to recognize as requirements even had they not been revealed. These are: "The things generally accepted by all the people as bad, such as murder, theft, robbery, fraud, harming an innocent man, repaying a benefactor with evil, degrading parents, and things like

30. The example of designing a house is an elaboration of an example Aquinas presents at *Summa Theologiae* (hereafter, *ST*), 5 vols. (Ottawa: Harpell's Press, 1941–45), I-II, q. 95, a. 2, co. For the translation, see *Summa Theologica* (henceforth, Benziger Edition), trans. Fathers of the English Dominican Province, 3 vols. (New York: Benziger Brothers, 1948), 1:1014. He writes: "But it must be noted that something may be derived from the natural law in two ways: first, as a conclusion from premises, secondly, by way of determination of certain generalities. The first way is like to that by which, in sciences, demonstrated conclusions are drawn from the principles: while the second mode is likened to that whereby, in the arts, general forms are particularized as to details: thus the craftsman needs to determine the general form of a house to some particular shape."

31. Examples of its use can be found at *Guide*, 517 [III, 29], 523 [III, 30], and 526 [III, 32]; Maimonides, *Eight Chapters*, in *Ethical Writings of Maimonides* (New York: New York University Press, 1975), 79 [Ch. 6]; Maimonides, *Treatise on the Art of Logic*, in *Ethical Writings of Maimonides*, 158 [Ch. 8]. Also, Alfarabi uses the expression.

these. They are the laws about which the sages, peace be upon them, said: 'If they were not written down, they would deserve to be written down' [BT *Yoma* 67b]."[32]

Nonetheless, he did not mean that they are self-evident or that they can be demonstrated. In Aquinas's view, many moral judgments and decisions are rationally supportable but not demonstrable. They can be rationally determined but are not demonstrably derived from principles of natural law. Maimonides and Aquinas were not making exactly the same point, but they were both drawing attention to the fact that reason's role in ethical thought is not strictly a matter of disclosing evident truths or demonstrating conclusions.

Both the Maimonidean and the Thomistic conceptions of human nature and virtue were influenced by Aristotle's moral anthropology but were also anchored in Scripture, and Aristotle's anthropology and the anthropology of Scripture differ in important respects. Sometimes Maimonides uses Aristotelian concepts while making un-Aristotelian claims. For example, Maimonides acknowledged the significance of habit in shaping states of character but his view of the possibility of repentance involved an important departure from Aristotle concerning the power of the will and the possibility of changes in states of character. In Maimonides's view repentance and moral reorientation are possible. Maimonides endorsed the doctrine of the mean but was explicit in arguing that, with regard to anger and humility, we are to go the extreme of minimization. We are to discipline ourselves not to feel the passion of anger even if angry behavior is appropriate, and we are to strive to be humble, in fact, very humble.[33]

Moses is mentioned as the example of humility. Moses represents a muscular version of humility, but this is also a way of pointing to the fact that humility is not inconsistent with dignity, courage, leadership, judgment, resolve, and other virtues. Aristotle, too, held that we are not the noblest beings in the world, but he did not regard humility as a virtue, and he held that anger, like other emotions, can be felt and can influence action in ways that are appropriate. Maimonides repeated the remark rooted in tradition that a person who is angry is like an idolater. Anger can so easily distract a person from what should be the focus of concern

32. Maimonides, *Eight Chapters*, 79–80 [Ch. 4].
33. See Maimonides, *Laws Concerning Character Traits*, in *Ethical Writings of Maimonides*, esp. 30–33 [Ch. 2].

and it can result in needlessly harmful conduct through succumbing the passions it involves.

Aquinas's conception of the virtues was powerfully influenced by Christian doctrine, and that led to significant non-Aristotelian views concerning pride and forgiveness, to mention just two examples. Moreover, Aquinas held that the fundamental principles of natural law are accessible to all (normal) human beings, and the first principle (that good is to be pursued, and evil is to be avoided) cannot be blotted out from men's hearts. *Synderesis*, nonacquired habitual knowledge of that principle, is not part of Aristotle's view.[34] He did maintain that in all rational activities human beings aim at what they take to be good, but that is not quite the same as the Thomistic notion that human beings are naturally inclined to the goods proper to them (though they need to engage in reasoning in the deliberate pursuit of them). Thus, "to the natural law belongs those things to which a man is inclined naturally: and among these it is proper to man to be inclined to act according to reason."[35]

In addition, it is not part of Aquinas's view that only those who acknowledge the God of Abrahamic monotheism have a grasp of natural law. Recognition of God as the creator of the world, providentially governing it, and making redemption of human beings possible is not a condition for the grasp of natural law. Referring to Romans 2: 14–15 Aquinas says that just men, whoever they are, "'show the work of the law written in their hearts,' as the Apostle says (Rom 2:14–15)."[36] Earlier, Maimonides had argued that there are some fundamental moral matters persons can understand despite not being a party to the covenant between God and Israel. That is the point of the Noahide requirements.

Thus, there are numerous important differences between Aristotle, on the one hand, and Maimonides and Aquinas on the other. Here we have considered only a few examples. Aspects of the moral epistemology of a Jewish or Christian thinker, and the conception of the scope and power of the will according to a Jewish or Christian thinker will differ from their counterparts in Aristotle's philosophy. The theist will argue that there is guidance offered to human beings no matter how corrupt they are; guidance that is accessible. And it is guidance that is effectively

---

34. Aquinas discusses *synderesis* in *ST* I, q. 79, a. 12, and *ST* I-II, q. 94.

35. *ST* I-II, q. 94, a. 4, co.; Benziger Edition, 1:1011.

36. *ST* I-II, q. 96, a. 5, ad 1; Benziger Edition, 1:1021.

followable; one's moral corruption need not be irredeemable. It is possible for even the very worst of people to orient themselves to the good. It is possible for even the very bad man to turn his will to the good and to pursue it. That does not seem to be part of Aristotle's view.

While Judaism does not involve the notion of fallenness in the same sense as Christianity they both share the understanding of human nature needing guidance on account of its original lapse. They also share the view that guidance was offered, and that guidance is accessible to all who will look to it. That is an important difference between the monotheistic view and Aristotle's. In Aristotle's view, persons who lack practical wisdom and who are without the guidance of persons with practical wisdom are likely to be epistemically cut off from it. There is no assurance that they will or could somehow attain it on their own, and they might become settled in ethically corrupt second natures, effectively unable to judge and to be motivated in ethically sound ways. Thus, with regard to various aspects of human history, anthropology, and moral epistemology there are some important similarities between a broadly Maimonidean view of moral judgment and a broadly Thomistic view. In addition, Thomas accepts that God and Israel shared a distinctive covenant, though Aquinas also held that it was superseded by a later divine dispensation.

CONCLUSION: WHY NOT NATURAL LAW?

In highly influential currents of Jewish thought human beings are regarded as capable of rational comprehension of what is ethically required even if that grasp is incomplete and uncertain in some respects. Much of it is not in the category of the rationally evident. God's unrevealed will and the human capability to seek understanding of the created order make such knowledge possible. Also, given the Noahide commandments the covenant with Israel does not mean that moral judgment is only possible for persons participating in that latter covenant. Many moral judgments clearly are universal; in fact, that is a well-attested element of Jewish tradition, not something in tension with it. Those facts might seem especially apt for explanation in terms of natural law.

However, even when reason operates on its own the authority of its results with respect to moral requirements and prohibitions still has an important connection with divine sanction. The role of divine sanction here does not imply a defect of reason. Rather, the point is that human action in whatever context is to be understood in terms of the aspiration to holiness, and in that sense, the authority of reason is not autonomous.

Maimonides insisted that recognition of the divine source of commandments is crucial to proper fulfillment of them. And we can plausibly suggest that it is part of the Jewish understanding of the commandments that their prescriptive force is rooted in being divine commands. They are *rational* commands; God does not prescribe anything contrary to reason or utterly without reason. But the normative authority of reasons depends on the notion of God's will being known through the rationally intelligible created order, and through God making demands on human beings through His revealed will.

The notion of covenant and some of what it implies is especially important here. Even those moral requirements—such as the Noahide laws—that apply to all of humanity are to be fulfilled because they are divine commandments, violation of which will meet with divine sanction. The covenant at Sinai expresses a unique relation between God and a particular people to whom He has offered distinctive responsibilities and possibilities. It is important to remember that, for the medieval—but also for observant Jews in the modern world—all of the commandments are integral to the striving for holiness. While Saadia, Bahya ibn Pakuda, Maimonides, and others recognized a distinction between the laws of reason and laws of revelation, it was also important to them that the integrity of a life of holiness should be responsive to the commandments as fully as possible. They are many and they are diverse in their requirements, but the medievals saw them as constituents of one covenant and in ways that are mutually reinforcing. That, I suspect, is one of the chief reasons why natural law has no presence in medieval Jewish philosophy.

It has not been my aim to "protect" Jewish Law and moral thought from being regarded as involving natural law, as though there is some significant respect in which natural law is antithetical to Jewish Law. The most influential conceptions of natural law have historical and conceptual roots in Hebraic thought even when it is regarded as theologically superseded. The concern for justice, for the dignity of the individual person, for the protection of the orphan, the destitute, the widow, and the stranger are all anchored in the Hebrew Bible. Moreover, the notion of a people or a state as being formed by law, by covenant, and the notion of wisdom-informed law governing a human community is part of the Judaic heritage. Nonetheless, regarding Jewish Law as involving natural law elements and interpreting Jewish thinkers as articulating views that can properly be categorized as natural law risks neglecting some especially important features of Jewish Law. They are important not mainly because they imply significant differences in moral content from natural law (natural law gets much of its moral content from Judaism) but because of how *law* is understood.

Anver M. Emon

2 ✑ Islamic Natural Law Theories
Between Theology and Law

Natural law has often been positioned as a promised intellectual site for dialogue amid difference. In 2009, the Catholic Church's International Theological Commission issued a report on natural law, implicitly suggesting that religious and value-based traditions the world over could locate functional equivalents in their own tradition.[1] In a volume dedicated to engaging that report, I issued my own critique of it, suggesting that in casting Islamic natural law in Islamic theological terms, the Commission did not fully appreciate the disciplinary logics in Islam that distinguished between theology, jurisprudence, and law.[2] Moreover, failure to do so allowed for a more suspicious, conspiratorial reading of the Commission's aim. In the report, the Commission distinguished the voluntarist theology of the Ashʿarites with the rationalist one of the Muʿtazilites, creating an intellectual binary in a way that reduced the "Islamic" in terms that were certainly familiar to the Commission, but not particularly enlightening about the complex Islamic tradition. But the conspiratorial reading comes from an appreciation of the material implications of each member of the binary. Where Ashʿarites dominated as

1. For the text, see International Theological Commission, "In Search of a Universal Ethic: A New Look at the Natural Law," in *Searching for a Universal Ethic: Multidisciplinary, Ecumenical, and Interfaith Responses to the Catholic Natural Law Tradition*, ed. William C. Mattison and John Berkman (Grand Rapids, Mich.: William B. Eerdmans Publishing Company, 2014), 25–92.

2. Anver M. Emon, "On Islam and Islamic Natural Law: A Response to the International Theological Commission's 'Look at Natural Law,'" in *Searching for a Universal Ethic*, 125–35.

orthodox, Mu'tazilites have been deemed heterodox, with the negative implications that arise from any association with heterodoxy.[3]

In this paper, I will map the relevant disciplinary terrain in which any discussion of Islamic natural law occurs. This intellectual map will require us to move from the field of theology to a distinctively Islamic genre of legal literature called *usul al-fiqh*. This genre has been variously translated as legal theory or jurisprudence; in short it is a genre of literature in which medieval scholars trained in both theology and law would debate ontological first principles and develop an epistemic framework that moves from those first principles to derivations of law. While some consider this genre committed to delineating a "legal method" of *deducing* the law, I suggest instead that this genre is designed to discipline the jurist to "think like a lawyer" while also providing sufficient space for "play" at the boundaries of orthodoxy. In a Foucauldian sense, it disciplines the subject-jurist into a compliant participant in the enterprise of governance through the deployment of a legal grammar and vocabulary that presumes to conclude what the law is, or at least, should be. But it also creates a wide enough space to contemplate ideas that might be too dangerous to consider in the genre of theology.[4] Indeed, to the extent that theology was a policed site of compliant belief, usul al-fiqh offered a space for intellectual play without the dangers that might come from such play in the field of theology. It is in this space of play that jurists articulated competing theories of natural law that, while starting from distinct theological/ontological first principles, ultimately reached the same conclusion on natural law, at least for the *epistemic* purpose of legal determination. This paper will conclude by examining one epistemic vehicle where jurisprudential play on natural law made possible an open-ended inquiry into the law in the absence of a voluntarist, expression of divine will. This epistemic vehicle, the *huquq Allah* and *huquq al-'ibad* ("claims of God" and "claims of individuals"), was a heuristic

---

3. On the material consequences of this binary, see the various literature recounting the apostasy-related trials of the Egyptian intellectual Nasr Abu Zayd: Declan O'Sullivan, "Hisba Law and Freedom of Expression in Islam: Two Case Studies of Prosecution in Contemporary Egypt," *Journal of Mediterranean Studies* 14, no. 1 (2004): 213–35; Baber Johansen, "Apostasy as Objective and Depersonalized Fact: Two Recent Egyptian Court Judgments," *Social Research: An International Quarterly* 70, no. 3 (2003): 687–710.

4. This indeed is the thesis of Rumee Ahmed, *Narratives of Islamic Legal Theory* (Oxford: Oxford University Press, 2012).

device by which jurists reached to what the law should be in circumstances where there was no expressed divine will in the form of source texts deemed to express that will.

THEOLOGICAL FIRST PRINCIPLES

Premodern debates on Islamic natural law began with a fundamental theological question about God and, in particular, God's justice (*'adl*). While all agreed that God is just, the theological debate centered on how best to characterize God's justice. Ash'arites, who were committed to theological voluntarism, argued that something is just when God says it is. In other words, if God commands us to do X, then X is necessarily just; if God prohibits us from doing Y, then Y is necessarily unjust. Whether we can appreciate why X is just and Y is unjust is irrelevant. In contrast, the Mu'tazilites were what some have called "ethical rationalists."[5] As rationalists, they argued that God only commands X because X is already understood as just; God prohibits Y because Y is already understood as unjust. The evaluation of justice and injustice, they argued, are things that humans can reason about and presume of God. Voluntarist Ash'arites, as one can expect, found the Mu'tazilite view outrageous; it violated the omnipotence of God by imposing upon His divinity standards of justice that are utterly human in their construction.

Depending on one's theology, it might be that one is more or less inclined to a natural law theory in which reason can articulate norms that can be attributed subjunctively to God, as if God has articulated them himself. If we frame a natural law account in these theological terms, we will immediately find ourselves in the throes of theological line drawing between orthodoxy and heterodoxy, where the material stakes of falling on one side of that line or another could be substantial, if not dire.

This understanding of theology and its consequences is perhaps not unsurprising to the readership of the International Theological Commission's document on natural law. Certainly, Church history has been replete with theological fights over right belief. From decrees of excommunication to the Spanish Inquisition, to the Reformation, and the Wars of

---

5. George Makdisi, "Ethics in Islamic Traditionalist Doctrine," in *Ethics in Islam*, ed. Richard G. Hovannisian (Malibu, Calif.: Undena Publications, 1985), 47–63; George F. Hourani, "Divine Justice and Human Reason in Mu'tazilite Ethical Theology," in *Ethics in Islam*, 73–84.

Religion, right belief is more than simply a matter of epistemic debate and deliberation. It was materially consequential, having potentially extreme implications for one's well-being, political, economic, and otherwise in relation to the Church and what it represented locally and globally. If it were not the case, then why should Henry have presented himself so penitently at Canossa? Whether he was sincere in his belief or not, he was certainly mindful of performing sincerity out of concern for a certain material well-being, however measured.

TO THE REALM OF JURISPRUDENCE

For medieval Muslim jurists, however, theology was not their only area of intellectual engagement. So too was law. Nevertheless, disputes about law did not occur under a similar shadow of boundary policing as in the case of theology. Whereas differences in theology could put someone outside the ambit of orthodoxy, differences of opinion in law were almost to be expected.

This is an important disciplinary distinction for the purposes of our inquiry into natural law in Islam. In the Latin West, we perhaps all too often take for granted what the Gelasian doctrine propounded as a compromise: a jurisdictional division of human experience into the world of the sacred and the profane. This jurisdictional division may have allowed two legal worlds to flourish, the ecclesiastical or canonical on the one hand, and what we might call the "secular" for purposes of governance on the other. But this division of jurisdiction—of legal subject matters into what moderns might call the religious and the secular—helped create the conditions for a secularism that both continues to animate how we understand the political project of the state and structures debates about the extent to which the state's legal arm can and should reach into what we might call our private or intimate lives.

Islamic law, however, does not operate in the shadow of such a Gelasian binary. The logic of Islamic legal reasoning traverses the boundaries that we often consider immune from the legal eyes of the state. For this reason, we can find distinctively legal debates about matters of ritual worship, formation of contract, and admissible evidence in trial all within a single title in Islamic law libraries across time and space. These doctrinal issues are addressed in a genre of literature called *fiqh*. Ranging from single volume handbook to multivolume encyclopedias, fiqh sources detail the doctrine of one legal school of thought (i.e., *madhhab*) or another, and in related genres, discuss the differences between the schools and why they exist (i.e., *khilaf*). To debate or disagree on matters of legal doctrine—whether concerning ritual worship or wrongful death liability rules—is not to engage in theological dispute despite the subject matter of the legal doctrine. Rather it is to engage in the art of legal reasoning.

Where theological disputes and fiqh disputes constitute different subject matters on a spectrum of intellectual history captured by both subject and genre, usul al-fiqh arguably served as a mediating device or bridge between the first principles of theology and the black letter rules that we know as fiqh. And within the genre of usul al-fiqh is an intellectual play space where debate about theological first principles, epistemes of legal analysis, and possibilities of legal futures came together. Neither in the battlefield of theology (*kalam*) nor in the waiting room of fiqh, but rather in the antechamber of usul al-fiqh do we find jurists thinking jurisprudentially about reason and its possible contribution to the possibility of law. It is here that we find a curious debate that bears the indicia of natural law thinking, allowing us to identify two versions of natural law among premodern Muslim jurists, which we will call hard natural law and soft natural law.

HARD NATURAL LAW

Hard Natural Law was mostly, though not exclusively, proffered by Mu'tazilite jurists such as al-Qadi 'Abd al-Jabbar (ca. 937–1025) and Abu al-Husayn al-Basri (d. 1044). It is important to emphasize that not all hard natural law jurists were necessarily Mu'tazilite. Indeed, sources are unclear or ambiguous about the theological affiliation of the Hanafi al-Jassas (d. 942). Whereas he offers a hard natural law account, it would be historically inaccurate to call him a Mu'tazilite, despite playing with Mu'tazilite first principles in his usul al-fiqh. Hard Natural Law advocates rooted their natural law jurisprudence in a particular understanding of God, or a theology of first principles. They began by asking whether humans can know the good and the bad (*husn, qubh*), and whether they can subjunctively attribute that knowledge of good and bad to God, thereby allowing them to articulate divine norms despite the silence of revealed scriptures on the matter. They argued that when God created the world, he did so for human benefit. If God had created the world to humanity's detriment, that would have been either futile or unjust of God, which for them was contrary to their understanding of God's justice (*'adl*). For them, God is not unjust, and consequently they concluded that he must have created the world to create a benefit.

As God was omnipotent, he had no need for such benefit. Consequently, he must have created the world as a bounty for humanity. These first principles about God were the bases by which they imagined the world itself and, in particular, what they could infer from their reasoned deliberation about the world. If the world is for the benefit of humanity, they argued, then one can reason about the world and human experience therein to reflect on norms for ordering human welfare. God's creative act both creates the *factual* reality of the world and gives positive *normative* content to that reality. In this manner, Hard Natural Law jurists fused fact and value in the natural order, enabling themselves to reason from an "is" to an "ought."

Modern philosophers will call this form of reasoning a "naturalistic fallacy," especially as the "is" certainly is not always something that is good or right. Sometimes what exists may be quite bad if not evil. Moreover, sometimes what we might think is good or right is contradicted by revelatory texts. For a Hard Natural Law jurist such as Abu al-Husayn al-Basri, though, Hard Natural Law offered a method of analysis that created a rebuttable presumption. That presumption could be rebutted by findings from revelation or elsewhere. The point for him, though, was that as a presumption it is sufficiently justified theoretically to inform the law unless countervailing evidence or considerations existed to rebut it.

SOFT NATURAL LAW

Soft Natural Law theory was proffered by Ash'arite theologians, such as Abu Hamid al-Ghazali (c. 1056–1111), al-Tufi (1276/7–1316), al-Shatibi (1320–1388), and others. They adopted different first principles in their usul al-fiqh debate about the good and the bad. They did not believe that God necessarily created the world for human benefit. Indeed, to assert such a position would be to limit God's omnipotence by reference to human presuppositions about justice (*'adl*). This is not to say, however, that they held the world was created to the detriment of human existence. Rather, they held theologically that God can create the world as he sees fit. This starting point allowed the Soft Natural Law jurists to ensure that nothing undermined God's omnipotence. However, they went further and argued that it just so happened that God created the world to benefit humanity, but only because of his grace (*rahma, tafaddul*). The argument from grace is important *theologically* because God can change his grace whenever he wants. However, and important for us, the argument from grace is significant *jurisprudentially* because it meant Soft Natural Law jurists could assert that, since God created the world for humanity's benefit, there is no evidence that he has changed his mind. Consequently, one can reason from the natural world to a normative conclusion, or, in other words, from an "is" to an "ought." In short, despite starting from different *theological* first principles, they ended up in the same *jurisprudential* position as the Hard Natural Law jurists, fusing fact and value, and arguing from an "is" to an "ought." This shared jurisprudential position is where we can locate a distinctively Islamic contribution to debates on natural law.

MAQASID AL-SHARIʿA AND THE IRONY OF THE MODERN ISLAMIC REFORMIST

The problem posed by this shared jurisprudential position was its theological implications. Though jurisprudence or usul al-fiqh is arguably positioned between theology and legal doctrine, its in-betweenness made the more theologically inclined Soft Natural Law jurists anxious that their approach might be mistakenly perceived as premised on heterodox theological views. Their Soft Natural Law theory was built on a very carefully constructed theological argument, the particulars of which might be lost on observers. They worried that merely distinguishing their position on the grounds of God's grace might be insufficiently distinct and run the risk of Soft Natural Law jurists being mistaken as Hard Natural Law jurists. This fear of mistaken perception, or perhaps simply an abundance of theological caution, led some Soft Natural Law jurists to articulate a method of legal reasoning (i.e., practical reasoning) that exhibited in legal guise the primacy of their voluntarist theological first principles.

Soft Natural Law jurists such as al-Ghazali articulated a circumscribed mode of legal reasoning that revolved around two terms of art, namely *maqasid* and *maslaha,* and which was designed (out of deference to voluntarist theological first principles) to limit the scope of reason's authority in matters of law and legal interpretation. *Maqasid* is the Arabic term for "aim, object or purpose"; *maslaha* is often defined as "welfare" or "public interest," and, in al-Ghazali's model, served as a particularized instance over which one might employ a *maqasid-based* analysis. In his account, al-Ghazali argued that there are five basic purposes of the law (maqasid), namely the preservation of life, lineage, mind, property, and religion. In the absence of scriptural authority, al-Ghazali argued that particularized public interests (maslaha) may very well uphold those aims when implemented as part of the law in a rule-like fashion. In some cases, a maslaha-based rule will uphold an aim that is deemed a necessity (*darura*), whereas in other cases the underlying interest is merely a "need" (*haja*) or purely edificatory (*tahsin*). For al-Ghazali, if a maslaha-based rule is rationally based, upholds the maqasid, and poses a necessary interest (*darura*), it has the authority of law. Framed subjunctively, this necessary maslaha-based rule is treated *as if* God had legislated it. Anything less than a necessary maslaha falls short of imputing legal authority in the same way. To expand the subjunctive scope of this maqasid-maslaha model beyond a necessary maslaha would so empower reason as to vitiate the primacy of voluntarist first principles about God's will. By focussing on those rationally based maslaha and hierarchizing them for legal purposes, al-Ghazali's model of legal reasoning both empowered a form of natural legal reasoning without undermining (to a great degree, at least) his voluntarist theological first principles.

TO THE REALM OF LEGAL DOCTRINE

The value of recasting the debate on reason and authority from theological terms of reference to jurisprudential ones lies in the intellectual and political possibilities it creates. It makes possible a new appreciation of modes of ordinary legal reasoning already deployed in premodern Islamic legal epistemology. One particular mode of legal reasoning that is illustrative is the premodern legal heuristic of the *huquq Allah* and *huquq al-ʿibad.* ("claims of God" and "the claims of individuals"). It is important to specify that by "claims of God" we are not suggesting some legal-theology in which God appears as claimant or litigant. Rather this phrase serves metaphorically to refer to the well-being of society, public policy interests, and the social weal. In the aggregate, the two terms of this heuristic highlight the fact that any given wrong will have both a public and a private dimension. In many cases it was up to jurists to determine what those dimensions were, the values at stake, and how best to resolve possible conflicts or contradictions.[6]

For instance, most readers will be familiar with the Islamic legal injunction against theft, namely amputation of the hand. This injunction is found in the Qur'ān itself. If A steals B's property, A may be subject to the punishment of hand amputation, so the argument goes. But even if A loses his hand, that does not make B whole. B suffers an ongoing loss that the corporal punishment does not redress. Does this seem fair, right, or good? Is it just? How might these natural-law-like questions find expression in technical legal reasoning? I suggest that juristic debates about the *huquq Allah* and *huquq al-'ibad* constitute such a site of reasoning.

For the Hanafis, the answer to the question of compensatory liability for theft came in the form of a *hadith,* where the victim could choose to claim compensatory damages instead. The victim enjoyed a claim against the regime, where the public interest served by the amputation was sacrificed to make the victim whole again. Whereas society could distribute the loss occasioned by the theft (e.g., social costs about reliable possession), the individual was not always in a position to redistribute his loss due to the theft. The Hanafis relied on a textual tradition to introduce a degree of choice and variance in the outcome for theft, based on the victim's capacity to sustain the loss or not.

But other Sunni schools of law considered the relevant *hadith* inauthentic. Consequently, they had *no source text to rely upon* to decide whether B must suffer his loss in silence, or somehow seek compensatory damages. As it turned out, jurists figured out B's fate by reference to the heuristic *huquq Allah* and *huquq al-'ibad.* They recognized that the Qur'ānic injunction on amputation reflected a *huquq Allah,* or claim of God that reflected a public interest in securing possession. Indeed, with-

---

6. For a detailed discussion about this legal heuristic and its operation across various areas of premodern legal debate, see Anver M. Emon, "Huqūq Allāh and Huqūq Al-'Ibād: A Legal Heuristic for a Natural Rights Regime," *Islamic Law and Society* 13, no. 3 (2006): 325–91.

out such security of possession, one could not have a reliable market for trade and exchange.[7] But security of possession was not merely a public matter that resonates at the macro-level. At the micro, individual level, theft meant that the victim suffers a direct and specific harm, the loss of which is not easily distributed to others, and so cannot be ignored. Indeed, according to the Shafiʿis and Hanbalis, to redress one sort of harm (e.g., the public harm via amputation) did not mean the other went away or could simply be ignored (e.g., the private harm of lost property). The private and public harms both coexisted at the same time; resolving one did not render the other irrelevant or resolved. Consequently—and importantly, *without reference to scriptural sources*—Shafiʿi and Hanbali jurists argued that the victim in theft has a claim against the thief for compensatory liability, even though the thief may also be subject to the corporal Qurʾānic sanction too.

Malikis also recognized that both claims coexist, but they went on to introduce a third claim, namely of the defendant. Malikis worried that imposing both forms of liability (i.e., punitive and compensatory) on a defendant might appear as a double punishment for a single underlying offense. It is not that the victim of the theft has no claim against the defendant, or that a choice must be made. Rather, the Malikis recognized that the public and the victim were not the only parties to consider in this equation; the defendant and his or her future well-being had to be considered as well. If the defendant-thief loses his hand through amputation, and must financially compensate the victim of his theft, the defendant-thief may end up in a form of involuntary servitude, having to pay off a debt that he cannot reasonably afford to pay. Indeed, it may be that to impose this dual form of liability would transform the defendant-thief into a ward of the regime, posing a different cost to the public weal than his original theft. In a pragmatic fashion, given these countervailing concerns, Malikis came up with a compromise position. The scope of the defendant's compensatory liability depended on his wealth between the moment he stole and the determination of his liability. If he was sufficiently wealthy to compensate the victim without suffering unduly, he was liable to pay. If he was too poor to compensate the victim, then no compensatory liability was imposed.

7. See, for instance, the Hanafi jurist Badr al-Dīn al-ʿAynī, *Al-Bināya Sharḥ Al-Hidāya*, ed. Ayman Ṣāliḥ Shaʿbān (Beirut: Dār al-Kutub al-ʿIlmiyya, 2000), 7:216–17.

How did jurists develop these rules? Their fiqh texts suggest that they simply reasoned to a range of values about property, possession, the public weal, and the interests of both victim and defendant-perpetrator. Whether we agree with their assessments is beside the fact. Rather, what we see is that moving from theology to jurisprudence and to legal doctrine, the capacity to reason signals different and distinct issues depending on the disciplinary field within which it is examined. If we focus only on theology, we miss something important about the plurality embedded within Islamic intellectual history, and in particular the disciplinary particularity of law as a field of debate and inquiry. Our challenge in the North Atlantic academy, whether in research universities or seminary contexts, is to scale our disciplinary approaches so as not to mistake a part for the whole.

CONCLUSION: DISCIPLINING THE ISLAMIC
IN THE STUDY OF LAW

In the field of Islamic studies, this particular understanding of Islamic natural law is subject to debate and some controversy. For instance, some argue that natural law is an inappropriate application of a phrase whose origins in the Latin West preclude application to the Islamic intellectual tradition. Rather, a more appropriate starting point might be, for instance, the Arabic term *tabi'a* (nature) in the field of Islamic natural philosophy. But the field of natural philosophy (*al-tabi'iyyat*) is not the same as legal philosophy. The debates between al-Ghazali, Ibn Sina and Ibn Rushd in philosophy (*falsafa*) reflected different questions than those that animated a legal theory about natural law. Indeed, when al-Ghazali, for instance, addressed natural philosophy, he focused his interventions on topics such as causation and miracles, and their implications for notions of truth and veracity, rather than reason and its authority for legal determinations. This criticism, therefore, relies on the priority of philology in the study of Islam. Since the nineteenth century, the academic study of Islam generally, and Islamic law specifically, has been done in fields characterized by the discipline/method of philology. Philology is variously defined, and in some quarters even out of fashion. At a minimum, it centers on textuality and diction in a way that is more linguistic and historical than legal and jurisprudential. To stand away from philology in order to identify a jurisprudential discussion of natural law in Islam therefore requires that we pay close attention (if not exercise disciplinary humility) about the intellectual standpoint that we occupy as scholars.

It is perhaps true that Muslim jurists did not have a term or phrase to denote "natural law." But the absence of such a term does not mean that the fundamental questions underlying natural law theories (e.g., reason and authority) were unknown to Muslim jurists or irrelevant to them. Nor does this lexical absence suggest they did not think or reflect on creation and its implications for how they might reason to norms and law to govern the infinite variations of human experience and conflict. Indeed, as scholars have shown already and extensively, these questions were at the forefront of their inquiries in legal theory manuals (usul al-fiqh). Consequently, to be able to speak of Islamic natural law theory is to recognize jurisprudence as a field of study distinct from other fields, such as theology, natural philosophy, and so on, all of which are vibrant areas of debate and scholarly research in Islamic legal studies.

Others might contend that this approach to Islamic natural law theories is simply a cover for what, at their root, are foundational debates about theology. To cast this theological debate in jurisprudential terms, one might argue, ignores the real stakes at play in this debate on reason. This view would lead us to frame debates on reason and authority in terms of theology, pitting the "heterodox" Mu'tazilites against the "orthodox" Ash'arites. But to frame the topic in that fashion presumes a content-laden notion of "orthodoxy" that gives primacy to a *disjunction* between reason and authority. A natural law approach to Islamic law, on the other hand, gestures to a *conjunction* of reason and authority, and thereby raises new and important questions about the relationship between knowledge and coercion, the indices of authority, the nature of reason, and the relationship between ethics, morality, and law.

In the Sunni Muslim world, the account of competing Islamic natural law theories raises some hackles because the jurisprudential approach is understood as circumscribing important theological views. To suggest that orthodox and heterodox theological camps ultimately came to a shared sensibility about the authority of reason in the law might be construed as dangerous to the primacy of a certain notion of orthodoxy. If the exclusionary force of theological heresy can be dulled by recourse to jurisprudence, the claim to orthodox belief loses its political force and effect.

Relatedly, Sunni Muslims committed both to a voluntarist theological orthodoxy and to modernist legal reform may find the limiting role of maqasid unacceptable. Some modern liberal or progressive Islamists look to maqasid and maslaha as ways to reform Islamic law and allow for greater reasoned deliberation.[8] The irony, though, is that the maqasid-maslaha was designed to limit the scope of reason's authority in the law. This is not to suggest that modern reformers cannot draw upon the maqasid tradition. Rather it is merely to suggest that the inefficacy of maqasid-based reform efforts to date may in part be due to the inability or unwillingness of reformers to reflect on the original design of maqasid as a narrowing, limiting device on reason's scope and sway.

This debate in the academy and among Muslim theologians and scholars is separate from our discussion here of what an Islamic perspective on natural law might offer. The promise of natural law lies in the ethereal universal ideal of common ground, whereby such values presumably transcend human difference, despite our differences in tradition and value systems. There is a paradox involved in locating the universal in particular traditions. Universals by their very nature are ahistorical, yet the traditions from which these universals are sought are nothing if not historical, rooted in time, space, and the practices of communities. In some sense, universals are not unlike the claim of something as "common sense." But as anthropologists have shown repeatedly, the construction of "common sense" is a process of cultural production.[9] Perhaps our search for natural law across traditions is to create a new cultural product—one that people of all traditions can contribute to and participate in. While this remains a highly laudatory goal, it may be best understood in terms of an eternal, agonistic struggle rather than a formal process of discovery (on the assumption that there is an end to that process). We can see this agonistic tendency in the history of human rights in the lat-

---

8. See, for instance, Jasser Auda, *Maqasid Al-Shariah as Philosophy of Islamic Law: A Systems Approach* (Herndon, Va.: IIIT, 2008). For a critical engagement between advocates and critics of maqasid-based reasoning, see Idris Nassery, Rumee Ahmed, and Muna Tatari, *The Objectives of Islamic Law: The Promises and Challenges of the Maqāsid Al-Shari'a* (Lanham, Md.: Lexington Books, 2018).

9. On the history of "common sense" as an idea, see Sophia A. Rosenfeld, *Common Sense: A Political History* (Cambridge, Mass.: Harvard University Press, 2011).

ter half of the twentieth century and into the twenty-first. The Universal Declaration of Human Rights, and the various subsequent instruments, articulate in the aggregate a universal set of values for all of humanity. But as many have already shown, these instruments do not promise the same freedom for everybody. As the European Court of Human Rights has shown repeatedly in its religious freedom cases (e.g., *Sahin v Turkey*, *Dahlab v Switzerland*, *Tautsi v Italy*), it cannot help but articulate the scope of freedom by reference to the demands of the state.[10] Indeed, if there is a universal at all, it is the agonistic character of debates about universals that seems constant. Perhaps, rather than trying to identify the content of a universal (which is little more than a claim of truth), the challenge is to create a space that maximizes the claims about what the universal might be. But to do so will require, in addition, a humility that has thus far evaded conversations about value, namely that no one can meaningfully claim, in this imagined expansive dialogic space, a monopoly on the truth.

---

10. Nehal Bhuta, "Rethinking the Universality of Human Rights: A Comparative Historical Proposal for the Idea of 'Common Ground' with Other Moral Traditions," in *Islamic Law and International Human Rights Law: Searching for Common Ground?*, ed. Anver M. Emon, Mark S. Ellis, and Benjamin Glahn, 123–43 (Oxford: Oxford University Press, 2012). This deference to the state takes shape in the form of the Court's jurisprudence on the "margin of appreciation." On this legal doctrine, see Yuval Shany, "Toward a General Margin of Appreciation Doctrine in International Law?," *European Journal of International Law* 16, no. 5 (2005): 907–40; Dean Spielmann, "Whither the Margin of Appreciation?," *Current Legal Problems* 67, no. 1 (2014): 49–65.

3 ∿ Natural Law and Byzantine Philosophy

This chapter aims to give a panoramic view of the reflection on natural law within Byzantine philosophy until the introduction of Thomas Aquinas's works into Byzantium, beginning in 1354. To this end, some preliminary clarifications are in order.

According to John Damascene (d. ca. 753), "a descriptive definition" is constituted by its "combination of essentials and non-essentials."[1] As Michele Trizio has shown, whether it is possible to provide a descriptive definition of Byzantine philosophy is a highly controverted issue.[2] For this reason, I take Byzantine philosophy in the broadest sense and view each of the six definitions, conveniently compiled by Damascene, as being equally applicable:

> [i.] *Philosophy* is knowledge of things which are in so far as they are, that is, a knowledge of the nature of things which have being. [ii.] And again, philosophy is knowledge of both divine and human things, that is to say, of things both visible and invisible. [iii.] Philosophy, again, is a study of death, whether this be voluntary or natural [...] [iv.] Still again, philosophy is the making of one's self like God [...] [v.] Philosophy is the art of arts and the science of sciences. This is because philosophy is the principle of every art, since through it every art and science has been invented. [...] [vi.] Philosophy, again, is a love of wisdom. But, true wisdom is God. Therefore, the love of God, this is true philosophy.[3]

1. John of Damascus, *Philosophical Chapters*, in *Writings*, The Fathers of the Church: A New Translation, 37, 3–110 (New York: Fathers of the Church, 1958), 27 [Ch. 7].

2. Michele Trizio, "Byzantine Philosophy as a Contemporary Historiographical Project," *Recherches de théologie et philosophie médiévales* 74, no. 1 (2007): 247–94.

3. John of Damascus, *Philosophical Chapters*, 11 [Ch. 3]. The numbering of the definitions is mine.

The reader may find these definitions too broad to distinguish philosophy as a discipline that is autonomous from theology. If so, then the reader has grasped the essential difficulties surrounding the notion of "Byzantine philosophy." At any rate, this paper will look at figures whose work is often classified under either theology or Greco-Roman jurisprudence.

A second point to bear in mind is that philosophical or theological speculation on *ius naturale* (in contradistinction to *ius positivum*) was not as extensive among Byzantine authors as it was in the arts and theology faculties of Latin-speaking medieval universities. Paul Babie sums up the literature until present: "Natural law in the Orthodox world has played nothing like the dominant role it has in the Christian West and this was true from the very earliest emergence of Christianity."[4] While Byzantines were content, for the most part, to conserve and repeat traditional axioms of the Roman juristic tradition, which was informed by Stoicism, the evidence available does not support such a negative judgment. Typically, Grecophone citizens in the Eastern Roman Empire wrote very brief descriptions of natural law, related it to some Roman institutions and certain precepts (like those of the decalogue), and then moved on to treat the *ius commune* or the written law of the state. Moreover, the second of Damascene's six definitions of philosophy coincides with what might be dubbed the official definition of Byzantine juristic science.

This definition of philosophy goes back to Ulpian and is reproduced in Justinian's sixth-century *Institutes*: "Jurisprudence is the knowledge of divine and human matters; the science (*scientia*) of what is just and unjust."[5] However, philosophy holds a more ancient claim to this definition than law on account of a tradition going back to the Stoic Chrysippus. Plato's *Republic* (335e1–4) defends the view that the true philosopher or sage is a just rewarder of deserts. Particularly following Chrysippus's intellectualistic reception of Socrates's teachings, as recorded by Plato, virtue is regarded as consisting essentially in knowledge (ἐπιστήμη).[6]

4. Paul Babie, "Natural Law in the Orthodox Tradition," in *Christianity and Natural Law: An Introduction*, ed. Norman Doe (Cambridge: Cambridge University Press, 2017), 37.

5. Justinian, *Imperatoris Justiniani Institutionum libri quattuor*, ed. Philipp Eduard Huschke, 4 vols. (Leipzig: B.G. Teubner, 1868), 1:3 [I, tit. 1, 1].

6. Christoph Jedan, *Stoic Virtues: Chrysippus and the Religious Character of Stoic Ethics* (New York: Continuum, 2009), 76.

The well-known tripartite division of intellectual virtue into dialectic, physics, and ethics might derive from Chryssipus. For Stoics in general, the mental virtue of reasoning assures that a human does not assent to what is false and so is never deceived. Early Stoicism seems to consider Plato's cardinal virtues to be merely representative of fields of action for theoretical wisdom.[7] Because Stoics standardly asserted that possessing one virtue means to possess them all, wisdom entailed a perfect possession of the virtues and their practice. In this vein, the Stoics teach, like Plato's representation of Socrates, that there is a practical law of the mind to do good by understanding nature and what ought to be done in accord with it. In short, Stoic epistemology—insofar as it can be reconstructed in its commonly held essentials—holds for infallible perception and judgments about the existence and essence of objects, which can be systematized into infallible knowledge out of so-called kataleptic impressions, resulting in the sage assenting to scientific knowledge and choosing the good therefrom.[8] In this vein, Stoic reflections on justice were ripe for absorption by jurisconsults of the Roman republic. Later, in his influential paraphrase of Ulpian's *Institutes*, Theophilus, one of Justinian's *antecessores* or law experts, acknowledges that sciences, moral philosophy and jurisprudence, all lay claim to the aforementioned philosophical definition.[9] After the rebranding of Byzantium as Constantinople (324), Greek-speaking citizens of the Roman Empire were continuously exposed to this topic and, from the fifth century onward, to discussion of it in the civil codes of Roman law; from the sixth century onward, to treatments of it in ecclesiastical *nomocanons*. Each source employs Roman terms to refer to natural law (*ius naturale*) or the law of peoples (*ius gentium*). The following epitome perfectly sums up the late Republican and early imperial theory of natural law as it existed prior to the law codes promulgated by Christians of the Roman East, which were thereafter absorbed into Byzantine jurisprudence.

7. Jedan, *Stoic Virtues*, 77.

8. See R. J. Hankinson, "Stoic Epistemology," in *The Cambridge Companion to the Stoics*, ed. Brad Inwood (New York: Cambridge University Press, 2009), 59–79.

9. Theophilus Antecessor, *Institutionum graeca paraphrasis*, ed. Contardo Ferrini and Karl Eduard Zachariae von Lingenthal (Berlin: S. Calvary, 1884), 4 [I, tit. 1, lin. 2–14]. *Nota bene*, while Byzantines knew this *incipit* from their Greek versions of the text, the most recent critical edition treats it as unoriginal. See Theophilus Antecessor, *Theophili antecessoris paraphrasis institutionum*, ed. J. H. A. Lokin et al. (Groningen: Chimaira, 2010), 956.

> Natural law [was] an ideal [of] an universally valid set of precepts, deriving from the principle of order which is manifest in the physical universe and which is represented in man by his reason, becoming a philosophical and rhetorical commonplace, particularly among the Stoics. [...] It appears first—and frequently—in Cicero [...] as [in] Gaius [...] as synonymous with *ius gentium*. In this sense the two terms represent two aspects of the same idea. The term *ius naturale* looks to the origin of this term in natural reason (which Cicero identifies with divine reason), and the term *ius gentium* to its universal application. Gaius expresses this compendiously when he says that "the law which natural reason establishes among all humankind is observed equally by every people [gens/ἔθνος]." There is here an illogicality. *Ius naturale* is law that ought to be observed by all humankind, whereas *ius gentium* is law which is in fact observed by all humankind; and one cannot logically proceed either from the fact that a rule is observed to the proposition that it ought to be preserved, or vice versa. The Roman, however, never made this clear distinction between positive law (i.e., law which is actually applied) and law as it ought to be. And similarly they never developed what may be called the revolutionary aspect of natural law as a higher law capable of invalidating the positive law.[10]

Greek-speaking Christians, both pre- and post-Byzantine, are convinced that Paul provides biblical support for a natural law that is itself a reflection of the divine law.[11] In particular, Byzantines carry on various themes from Roman thought. They argue that: divine reason undergirds what is enduring in human thinking on justice; there are natural structures common to all living creatures (e.g., preservation of life and physical reproduction) that justify certain human institutions (e.g., marriage and childbearing); some human institutions (e.g., contracts) are common a priori to all cultures. Moreover, Theophilus bequeaths to Byzantines a slightly augmented paraphrase of the *Institutes* and adds further examples to Gaius's description: of natural law (Gr. φυσικὸν νόμιμον/ φυσικὸς νόμος) in both its nonrational and rational sense: of its expres-

---

10. Barry Nicholas, *An Introduction to Roman Law*, 3rd ed. (Oxford: Clarendon Press, 1987), 54–55.

11. There is sparse literature on natural law in Byzantium. See Stanley S. Harakas, "The Natural Law Teaching in the Ante-Nicene Fathers and in Modern Greek Orthodox Theology" (PhD dissertation, Boston University School of Theology, 1964); Harakas, "Eastern Orthodox Perspectives on Natural Law," *Selected Papers from the Annual Meeting* (*American Society of Christian Ethics*) 18 (1977): 41–56; Harakas, "Eastern Orthodox Perspectives on Natural Law," *American Journal of Jurisprudence* 24 (1979): 86–113. The otherwise meritorious studies of Harakas lack a discussion of Roman law and, in particular, the *ius gentium*.

sion in the law of nations (Gr. ἐθνικὸς νόμος, Lat. *ius gentium*): and of the law of nations' relation to the common law of the city (Gr. πολιτικὸς νόμος, Lat. *ius commune*).[12]

Significantly, despite Roman Stoicism's moral reflections on slavery (e.g., Musonius Rufus, Epictetus), the Byzantines never try to resolve, whether philosophically or legislatively, the Roman aporia regarding slavery: although humans are born free by nature, the *ius gentium* or universal custom upholds institutional slavery. It appears that late Stoicism did not tempt Roman jurists to overturn existing institutions.[13]

At any rate, the Greek Fathers frequently refer to natural law, albeit mostly *obiter dicta*. This indicates that, in late antiquity, Greek-speaking Christians of the Eastern Roman Empire effortlessly assume the existence of natural law and regard its precepts as central for the development of ethics and law.

NATURAL JUSTICE FROM PLATO TO ROMAN STOICS

Scholarly studies have proved unable to link Romans 2:1–6 definitively to a concrete source from Greek Stoicism.[14] In the selections that follow, I propose that there is a link between Paul's Letter to the Romans and Ulpian's unnamed source in the *Institutes* for his description of juristic science and his definition of justice. This link is manifest by their similar lexical choices and shared syntactical structures. Martens's extensive study on the Greek vocabulary of natural law concludes that Paul's vocabulary in Rom 2:1–6 does indeed enjoy a Stoic flavor but that Paul's technical terms do not all derive from extant Greek literature, as combining gentile and natural law together. However, the Roman reception of Stoicism, as rearranged by Ulpian into Latin, coincides with some of Paul's syntax, not to mention thematic interest, to a surprising degree. For example, Ulpian refers to natural law in connection with the law of the nations: "*ius gentium est* [...] *quod a naturali recedere facile intellegere licet.*" This—unlike the Greek philosophical, lexical, and syntactical treatment of the natural law—can account for Paul's strange remark,

---

12. Theophilus Antecessor, *Institutionum graeca paraphrasis*, 2 [I, tit. 2, lin. 2–25].

13. Nicholas, *An Introduction to Roman Law*, 55.

14. See John W. Martens, "Romans 2.14–16: A Stoic Reading," *New Testament Studies* 40, no. 1 (1994): 55–67.

"Gentiles who have not the law do by nature what the law requires" (ἔθνη τὰ μὴ νόμον ἔχοντα [ἔγγραπτον] φύσει τὰ τοῦ νόμου ποιῶσιν [Rom 2:14]). In another example, Paul uses the genitive absolute (typically employed to render *ad verbum* Latin ablative absolutes into Greek), to speak of conscience justifying or condemning the goodness of acts by an internal law of nature. Finally, early Christians like Clement, writing decades before Ulpian, exegeted Paul's doctrine of natural law by recourse to a Greek source containing the same terms and content as Ulpian's Latin definitions. A chronologically ordered list of citations on natural justice, from Plato to Justinian, betrays overall diachronic constancy, despite some variation, in defining juristic science and justice.

> Tell me, then, you the inheritor of the argument, what it is that you affirm that Simonides says and rightly says about justice. That it is just, he replied, to render to each his due. In saying this I think he speaks well. (Plato, *Resp.* 331e)

> If, then, anyone affirms that it is just to render to each his due (τὰ ὀφειλόμενα ἑκάστῳ ἀποδιδόναι) and he means by this that injury and harm is what is due to his enemies from the just man and benefits to his friends (δίκαιον εἶναι, τοῦτο δὲ δὴ νοεῖ αὐτῷ τοῖς μὲν ἐχθροῖς βλάβην ὀφείλεσθαι παρὰ τοῦ δικαίου ἀνδρός, τοῖς δὲ φίλοις ὠφελίαν), he was no truly wise man (σοφός) who said it. (Plato, *Resp.* 335e)[15]

> Justice [...] is a distributive habit (ἕξις ἀπονεμητικὴ) [...] to each according to one's dignity (κατ᾽ ἀξίαν).[16]

> Justice (*iustitia*) decrees [...] to render to each what is his [right (*ius*)] (*suum cuique reddere*).[17]

---

15. Plato, *Republic*, in *The Collected Dialogues of Plato, Including the Letters*, ed. Edith Hamilton and Huntington Cairns (Princeton: Princeton University Press, 1961), 580, 585.

16. Chryssipus, *Fragmentum* 125, in Hans Friedrich von Arnim, *Stoicorum veterum fragmenta*, 4 vols. (Leipzig: Teubner, 1903), 3:30.

17. Cicero, *De re publica*, 3, 24. For the Latin text, see Marcus Tullius Cicero, *De re publica*, in *De re publica, De legibus, Cato Maior de Senectute, Laelius de amicitia*, ed. Jonathan G. F. Powell (Oxford: Clarendon Press, 2006), 1–154 at 104. See also Marcus Tullius Cicero, *De officiis*, ed. Michael Winterbottom (Oxford: Clarendon Press, 1994), 18 [I, 14, 42]: "Ut pro dignitate cuique tribuatur; id enim est iustitiae fundamentum."
Cicero introduces Romans to Platonic and Stoic accounts of justice. At times he stresses the Stoic concept of *dignitas*; at other times, the Roman notion of *ius*. This is subsequently imitated in: Seneca, *Epistulae morales ad Lucilium* 81, 7, in Lucius Annaeus Seneca, *L. Annaei Senecae opera quae supersunt*, ed. Friedrich Haase, 3 vols. (Leipzig: B.G. Teubner, 1898), 3:207. See also *Epistulae morales ad Lucilium* 89, 14, in Seneca, *L. Annaei Senecae opera quae supersunt*, 3:257.

And this arrangement is the right reason of nature (ὁ τῆς φύσεως ὀρθὸς λόγος), which in more appropriate language is denominated law (θεσμός), being a divine arrangement (νόμος θεῖος) in accordance with which everything suitable (τὰ προσήκοντα) and appropriate is assigned (ἀπενεμήθη) to every individual.[18]

When Gentiles who have not the law do by nature what the law requires, they are a law to themselves, even though they do not have the law. They show that what the law requires is written on their hearts, while their conscience also bears witness and their conflicting thoughts accuse or perhaps excuse them. (Rom 2:14–15)

Indeed it is appropriate for a king (προσήκει μὲν τῷ βασιλεῖ) [...] to decide on just things for subjects (τὰ δίκαια βραβεύειν τοῖς ὑπηκόοις), so that no one has more or less than his due (τὴν ἀξίαν) but the ones who are deserving receive both honor and punishment (καὶ τιμῆς καὶ τιμωρίας τυγχάνειν τοὺς ἀξίους).

How would anyone be just if he did not understand (ἐπιστάμενος) what sort of thing justice (δικαιοσύνην) is? So again a king must study philosophy. Indeed, it is appropriate for a king [...] to decide on just things for his subjects, so that no one has more or less than his due, but the ones who are deserving receive both honor and punishment. (Musonius Rufus)[19]

It is also characteristic of the rational soul to love its neighbors, to be truthful, to show reverence, and to honor nothing more than itself, which is also characteristic of the law. Thus, there is no difference between right reason (λόγος ὀρθὸς) and the reason embodied in justice (λόγος δικαιοσύνης). (Marcus Aurelius)[20]

The legislator (ὁ νομοθετικὸς) is accustomed to distribute (ἀπονέμωνε) what is due (τὸ προσῆκον) to each portion of the soul and to their works. (Clement of Alexandria)[21]

18. Philo of Alexandria, *The Works of Philo: Complete and Unabridged*, new updated edition, trans. Charles Duke Yonge (Peabody, Mass.: Hendrickson Publishers, 1993), 20B. For the Greek text, see Philo of Alexandria, *De opificio mundi*, in *Philonis Alexandrini opera quae supersunt*, ed. Leopold Cohn (Berlin: Georg Reimer, 1896–1930), 1:50, lin. 11–13 [50, 143].

19. Musonius Rufus, *Lectures and Sayings*, trans. Cynthia King, ed. William B. Irvine (Scotts Valley, Calif.: CreateSpace, 2011), 40; Musonius, *Dissertationum a Lucio digestarum reliquiae 8*, in *C. Musonii Rufi Reliquiae*, ed. Otto Friedrich Hense (Leipzig: Teubner, 1905), 33, lin. 6–16.

20. Marcus Aurelius, *The Meditations: Marcus Aurelius Antoninus*, trans. G. Grube (Indianapolis: Hackett Publishing Company, 1983), 110. For the Greek text, see Marcus Aurelius, *The Meditations of the Emperor Marcus Aurelius*, ed. Arthur Spencer Loat Farquharson, 2 vols. (Oxford: Clarendon Press, 1944), 1:214, lin. 17–20 [XI, 1, 3].

21. Clement of Alexandria, *Stromata I-VI*, ed. Otto Stählin (Leipzig: J.C. Hinrichs'sche Buchhandlung, 1906), 104, lin. 21–22 [I, 26, 167, 3].

Contrariwise, I think that what is properly is due (τὸ προσῆκον) to law and to right reason for each is to distribute (ἀποδιδόναι) and to share what is one's own. (Clement of Alexandria)[22]

The law of nations (*ius gentium*) is what human peoples (*gentes*) utilize. One can easily understand that it does not coincide with natural law, because whereas natural law is common to all animals, it is common to humans alone in their dealings with one another.… Civil law (*ius civile*) is that which neither departs entirely from the natural law or that of the nations, nor is subject to it in all regards. Hence, whenever we add some law of our own to the common law or remove it, we make it a civil law. Therefore, this law (*ius*) of ours (i.e., *ius civile*) is constituted from either what is written (*ex scripto*) or unwritten (*sine scripto*), as the Greeks say: "of laws some are written, others unwritten (τῶν νόμων οἳ μὲν ἔγγραφοι, οἳ δὲ ἄγραφοι.)." (Ulpian)[23]

Platonic speculations on natural justice provide the remote inspiration for Greco-Roman jurists in their definition of justice and law. Paul and Ulpian repeat axioms derived from common ancient sources. First, Paul's talk of the "Gentiles who have not the law do by nature" (ἔθνη τὰ μὴ νόμον ἔχοντα [ἔγγραπτον] φύσει) corresponds to Ulpian's statement: "The law of nations is what human peoples utilize" (*ius gentium est quo gentes utuntur*). Second, whereas Paul speaks of the gentiles who are without the written law, Ulpian appeals to an unwritten (*sine scripto*) law of gentiles. Third, Paul posits the unwritten law using the Hebraism "in their hearts" (ἐν ταῖς καρδίαις), while Ulpian supposes that it exists in all people (*illud omnibus…commune est*). Fourth, both use the same vocabulary to contrast this to the written law. Fifth, Paul identifies human conscience or reason as bearing witness to truth; Ulpian, in his definition of jurisprudence, appeals to an evident human science of understanding the just and unjust. Sixth, Paul links this conscience to a genitive prepositional phrase whereby some people are with sinful accusatory thoughts and others with justifying thoughts, whereas Ulpian's definition of jurisprudence speaks of a science, in the genitive, of what is just and unjust. The symmetry and vocabulary shared between the two is quite uncanny.[24] If, as Martens has already shown, Paul adjusts Roman Stoic vocabulary for his theological purposes, he nevertheless insists that

22. Clement of Alexandria, *Stromata I-VI*, 513, lin. 23–25 [VI, 17, 159, 3].

23. Justinian, *Digesta Iustiniani Augusti*, ed. Theodor Mommsen and Paul Krueger, 2 vols. (Berlin: Weidmann, 1870), 1:1–2 [1.1.4 and 1.6].

24. Tony Honoré, *Ulpian: Pioneer of Human Rights*, 2nd ed. (Oxford: Oxford University Press, 2002), 80: "It seems that Ulpian's outlook was predominantly Stoic."

natural reason automatically judges certain actions as either a good or evil. Interestingly, Luke records how Paul uses a *Stoic* theory of the existence of God when preaching in Athens.

> Paul then stood up in the meeting of the Areopagus and said: "People of Athens! I see that in every way you are very religious. For as I walked around and looked carefully at your objects of worship, I even found an altar with this inscription: 'To an unknown god.' So you are ignorant of the very thing you worship—and this is what I am going to proclaim to you." (Acts 17:22–23)

Here Paul uses a Stoic trope: that God's existence is known but people are ignorant of his essential attributes. He goes on to say:

> For what can be known about God is plain to them, because God has shown it to them. Ever since the creation of the world his eternal power and divine nature, invisible though they are, have been understood and seen through the things he has made. (Rom 1:19–20)

Once again, in line with Roman Stoicism, Paul assumes that natural reason intuitively grasps God's existence. Seneca makes virtually the exact same point.

> A god doth dwell, but what god know we not. If ever you have come upon a grove that is full of ancient trees which have grown to an unusual height, shutting out a view of the sky by a veil of and intertwining branches, then the loftiness of the forest, the seclusion of the spot, and your marvel at the thick unbroken shade in the midst of the open spaces, will prove to you the presence of deity. Or if a cave, made by the deep crumbling of the rocks, such spaciousness by natural causes, your soul will be deeply moved by a certain intimation of the existence of God.[25]

There are numerous overlaps between these passages from Seneca and Paul. Indeed, Paul attended a rhetorical school in Tarsus that almost certainly benefitted from the influence of the Augustan court-philosopher, Athenodorus Cananites (d. 7 AD), who would have exposed imperial Romans to the same Stoic sources that Cicero and Seneca employ. Likewise, these sources would have been the staple of the philosophical schools in Tarsus after Athenodoros's return as its governor.[26]

---

25. Seneca, *Epistulae morales ad Lucilium* 41, 1–3, in *L. Annaei Senecae opera quae supersunt*, 3:85. For the English translation, see Lucius Annaeus Seneca, *Epistles 1–65*, ed. Richard M. Gummere, Loeb Classical Library (Cambridge, Mass.: Harvard University Press, 1917), 273–75.

26. If Paul reflects an education based upon Athenodorus's influence, then the same line

Propitiously, Paul cites verbatim sources that the Stoic Epictetus valued when in Rome.[27] Additionally, Seneca's brother Gallio (Acts 18:12–17) —recipient of some of his brother's works—favored Paul in a legal action while governor of Achaia (connecting Paul to Seneca's family). Given these fortuitous circumstances and overlaps, it would not be unreasonable to suspect that Paul and Seneca may have drawn from similar sources for their respective proofs for the existence of God.

BYZANTIUM ON NATURAL LAW AND THE EXISTENCE OF GOD

A passage from Clement of Alexandria's *Stromata* was quoted above. It belongs to a section of the work in which Paul's talk of natural law is linked to Moses as a lawgiver and Christ as the new lawgiver. Furthermore, Clement applies to Christ his Ulpianic definition of justice: Christ is the giver of what is due. Clement's wider discussion of Christ's law incorporates Galatians and Romans into his reflections on Christ as quasi-Ulpianic legislator.[28] Ulpian's third-century definition of justice is nearly a verbatim repetition of Clement's second-century citation. This confirms Honoré's assertion that Ulpian's definition was drawn from an earlier source.[29] Clement also explicitly associates law (νόμος), when citing Moses and Paul, with Chrysippus's Stoic notion of justice. Byzantine Christians continue to assume that such connections exist. However, the Byzantine archbishop of Constantinople, Gregory Nazianzen (379–381), develops Paul's theory (Rom 1:19–20) *philosophically* in an innovative

---

of influence on Cicero (e.g., Posidonius) should be expected (see Rom 2:14). For Paul's possible connection to Athenodorus through his successor Nestor, see Jack Finegan, *The Archeology of the New Testament: The Mediterranean World of the Early Christian Apostles* (Boulder, Colo.: Westview Press, 1981), 54.

27. See, e.g., Galatians 4:1: "Yet, I declare that the heir, as long as he is a child, he differs not all from a slave (οὐδὲν διαφέρει δούλου), even while he is the lord of all [the estate]." Likewise, Epictetus cites the same source while discussing Roman citizens as historically slaves as sons sold three times by a paterfamilias in Epictetus, *Epicteti Dissertationes ab Arriano digestae, ad fidem Codicis bodleiani*, ed. Heinrich Schenkl (Leipzig: B.G. Teubner, 1916), 356, lin. 1–3 [IV, 1, 7]: "You speak to him truths; namely, that 'You do not differ at all with respect to being slave from those sold thrice over' (ὅτι 'τῶν τρὶς πεπραμένων οὐδὲν διαφέρεις πρὸς τὸ μὴ καὶ αὐτὸς δοῦλος εἶναι')."

28. Clement of Alexandria, *Stromate I*, Sources Chrétiennes, vol. 30 (Paris: Éditions du Cerf, 1951), 165–67 [I, 25, 166, 5 – I, 26, 169, 2].

29. Honoré, *Ulpian*, 76.

manner: "Both sight (ὄψις) and natural law (ὁ φυσικὸς νόμος) are the teacher that God—the creating and sustaining cause (αἰτίαν) of all—exists. On the one hand, sight alights upon things seen as beautifully fixed in their courses, borne along in motionless movement. On the other, natural law concludes from premises (συλλογιζόμενος) their first cause (τὸν ἀρχηγὸν) through the things both seen and through their arrangement."[30]

By appealing to apodictic arguments from physics (φυσικαὶ ἀποδείξεις), Gregory explicitly proposes an a posteriori approach to demonstrating God's existence, while retaining the notion of natural law.[31] This marks a departure from the Stoic view that we have implanted preconceptions of the *ens divinum*. Cicero sums up the classic Stoic position well: "Consequently, the sum of the matter is known to all nations everywhere. Indeed, it has been implanted at birth for all and has been as if inscribed upon their mind that gods exist. Of what qualities these [gods] be, there is ambiguity, but nobody denies that they exist."[32]

This appeal to "all nations" (*omnium gentium*) carried weight among Romans since universal customs or laws reflected the law of nature (*ius naturale*). The universal custom of the law of nations (*ius gentium*) (including religious custom in the Roman republic) reflects the law of nature. Later, Archbishop Proclus of Constantinople (434–46) takes up Gregory's a posteriori argument and supplements it by incorporating Paul's allusion to "natural law" (Rom 2:14–15).

> The first law is the natural law about which Paul says, "When the gentiles who have not the law do by nature what the law requires, they are a law unto themselves, even though they do not have the law." The second law is that which comes through sight, for the law proclaimed by the creator is confirmed by the sight of creation, for "from the greatness and beauty of created things comes a corresponding perception of their creator."[33]

30. Gregory Nazianzen, *Discours 27–31* (*Discours théologiques*), ed. Paul Gallay and Maurice Jourjon, Sources Chrétiennes, vol. 250 (Paris: Éditions du Cerf, 1978), 110, lin. 1–6 [orat. 28, 6].

31. Gregory Nazianzen, *Discours 27–31* (*Discours théologiques*), 111, lin. 15–16 [orat. 28, 6].

32. Marcus Tullius Cicero, *De natura deorum*, ed. Harris Rackham, Loeb Classical Library vol. 268 (Cambridge, Mass.: Harvard University Press, 1951), 134–37 [II, 4–5]. Three versions of the intuitive argument have been ably summarized in Joseph Edward Steineger, "The Naturally Implanted Knowledge of God's Existence: Two 13th Century Scholastic Interpretations of John of Damascus and Anselm of Bec" (Phd Dissertation, University of Chicago, The Divinity School, 2014), 25.

33. Nicholas Constas, *Proclus of Constantinople and the Cult of the Virgin in Late Antiquity: Homilies 1–5, Texts and Translations*, Supplements to Vigiliae Christianae, vol. 66 (Leiden: Brill,

Proclus maintains Gregory's vocabulary but reads him in a more Sto-icizing manner as opposed to a Neo-Platonic one: through an innate law of practical reason we intuit the deity. Clearly, natural law is not being taken in the strictest Stoic sense of an ethics of a noninferential insight into God's existence. Unlike Gregory's cosmological argument, Proclus recurs to another Christian vein of natural law theory, one which can be traced back to the apologist Athenagoras.[34] This emphasizes firstly that, properly speaking, natural law is unwritten and "untaught," and that it legislates for the human mind as it rationally encounters the world. Sec-ondly, natural law requires an a posteriori perception of the deity, as the cause of the beauty that we perceive in the world. Proclus also affirms an innate precept to choose good, even if humans seem to lack an im-mediate intuition of God as supreme good. To some extent, Proclus ac-cepts Gregory's view that we infer from created beauty the existence of its cause or organizing principle, but through an immediate intuition that occurs in the very act of perceiving the beautiful, an experience that provides premises leading to a syllogistic conclusion.[35]

This line of argument is also followed by an anonymous homilist in Constantinople, who rephrases Paul's statements in the vocabulary of Stoicism. This popular homily (449) argues that belief in God's existence is obligatory because the mind "stretches upwards" and cannot grasp anything beyond divine existence. Christians are said to admit only the proposition: "God exists," in accord with Scripture: "For by the great-ness and beauty of the creatures proportionately the maker of them is seen" (Wis 13:5). Due to the fall, however, human minds are darkened by sin and even become bestial. Even so, God does not neglect the human race but provides humans with a notion of the invisible Godhead, whom they know by means of visible creatures. As the homilist states, "He also placed inside us the natural law for the knowledge of good and evil (διὰ δὲ τοῦ φυσικοῦ νόμου, τῶν καλῶν τε καὶ κακῶν τὴν γνῶσιν ἡμῖν ἐνθείς)."[36]

2003), 175 [Homily 2, lin. 195–201]. For the Epicurean use of ἔμφυτος/*innatus*/ἐναργὴς γνῶσις to speak about Stoic preconceptions, see Steineger, "The Naturally Implanted Knowledge of God's Existence," 21–22.

34. Athenagoras, *Athenagorae qui fertur De resurrectione mortuorum*, ed. Miroslav Mar-covich, Supplements to Vigiliae Christianae, vol. 53 (Leiden: Brill, 2000), 37 [13, 1] and 62 [24, 4].

35. For the problems surrounding Stoic claims of *evidentia* or ἐνάργεια for gods' exis-tence—seemingly making demonstrations and expositions superfluous—see Steineger, "The Naturally Implanted Knowledge of God's Existence," 17–19.

36. For my citations and summations of the text, see Pseudo-Basil of Seleucia, *Oratio XXXIX: In sanctissimae Deiparae assumptionem*, in Patrologia Graeca, vol. 85, 425–52 (Paris:

Through the power of "imperial reasoning" (a reference to the reasoning of the Stoic sage) Christians reject the worship of creatures and honor the creator (cf. Rom 1:25). By violating the natural law of worship, pagans are said to have then turned to unnatural evil. Despite these errors, God provides written laws, which teach the true knowledge of God (θεογνωσίαν) and lead to the path of virtue.[37] This homily became a principal source for the monumental Marian hymnody of the *Akathistos*. It is simply a matter of course that Byzantines subsequently read Wisdom and Romans in this vein, though they remain divided as to whether God's existence enjoys self-evidence (ἐνάργεια). They tend to agree, though, that reason can be potentially mistaken about the nature or essential attributes of God.

Maximus the Confessor, who writes in the seventh century (633–56), is the first Byzantine to develop a theory or natural law with systematic arguments. He claims that this law is capable of infallibly guiding reason to choose the good and thereafter, a posteriori, to the existence of God.[38] In his commentary on Gregory of Nazianzus's *Oration* 28, he argues that God's existence can be demonstrated a posteriori, even though this is insufficient to describe or define the divine nature.[39]

The last significant proofs for God's existence in this vein, prior to the introduction of Aquinas's works into Byzantium, come from Gregory Palamas (d. 1357), who recapitulates a line of argument similar to Maximus's bipartite theory of law.[40] Palamas says, "After the natural law, the written law, and Christ's first coming, which is associated with the law of grace, it will clearly be time for Christ's second advent."[41]

Much like Philo, Palamas and Maximus regard Mosaic legislation as

---

Jacques-Paul Migne, 1964), 433C. For the translation, see George Dragas, "The Blessed Basil of Seleucia: The Great Antiochian Theologian of the 5th Century A.D. and His Homily 39 on the Annunciation of the Theotokos," *The Patristic and Byzantine Review* 25, no. 1–3 (2007): 183–86.

37. Pseudo-Basil of Seleucia, *Oratio XXXIX*, 433C.

38. Maximus the Confessor, *On Difficulties in Sacred Scripture: The Responses to Thalassios*, trans. Maximos Constas, The Fathers of the Church: A New Translation 136 (Washington, D.C.: The Catholic University of America Press, 2018), 305 [51.2].

39. Maximus the Confessor, *On Difficulties in the Church Fathers: The Ambigua*, ed. Nicholas Constas, 2 vols., Dumbarton Oaks Medieval Library, vols. 28–29 (Cambridge, Mass.: Harvard University Press, 2014), 1:362–65 [*Ambigua ad Ioannem*, 15, 1–4].

40. See John W. Martens, *One God, One Law: Philo of Alexandria on the Mosaic and Greco-Roman Law*, Ancient Mediterranean and Medieval Texts and Contexts, vol. 2 (Boston: Brill Academic Publishers, 2003), 95–98.

41. Greorgy Palamas, *Saint Gregory Palamas: The Homilies*, ed. Christopher Veniamin (Waverly, Pa.: Mount Tabor Publishing, 2014), 255 [Homily 32].

divine and as a natural law put down in writing, and they extend the Roman concept of the law of nations (*ius gentium*, νόμος ἐθνικός) to include the Mosaic law.[42] Palamas believes that both the Mosaic and the spiritual law of Christ contain precepts of divine and natural law. This means that both are superior to any merely philosophical demonstration of the existence of a divine being and to some few precepts discerned through the unwritten law of the mind.[43] Here Palamas is contesting a fellow Greek Orthodox, Barlaam of Calabria (d. 1348), whom he regards as giving excessive importance to the doctrines of Hellenic philosophy. This leads Palamas to rehash Gregory of Nazianzus's account of natural law as an a posteriori demonstration of God's existence:

> And now we know by those who are ignorant of God since every [so-called] knowledge of philosophy is not also true. But we suppose [...] and bring forward that people come to knowledge of God through knowledge of creatures. Wherefore, the contemplation and coming to know through the aforementioned is called "natural law." Due to this, too, before the patriarchs and prophets, and the written [Mosaic] law, the human race was called back and returned to God (who is also the aforementioned demiurge); by following the sages among the Hellenes; it is useful for those who depart from knowledge [obtained] by nature.[44]

By Palamas's time Constantinopolitans had become accustomed to a Neo-Platonic diet of cosmological arguments, which differed from Cyril of Alexandria (412–44), who insists that the mind intuits God's existence and, as a corollary, makes axiological judgments about what is morally good and to be done, or evil and to be avoided: "Consequently, a law of innate knowledge of God (τῆς ἐμφύτου θεογνωσίας), which is in us, called humans to the obligation of making thanksgiving offerings to the demiurge of all things and to God, the one who gives us every good."[45]

This is very similar to another famous, if alternative, first principle

---

42. For Roman and Byzantine collections comparing Mosaic law to Roman law, see Danilo Ceccarelli Morolli, *Il Diritto dell'Impero Romano d'Oriente. Introduzione alle fonti e ai protagonisti* (Rome: Lilamé, 2016), 71.

43. Gregory Palamas, Ἀντιρριτικος, ed. Panagiotis Chrestou, Γρηγορίου τοῦ Παλμᾶ Συγγράμματα, 3 vols. (Thessaloniki: 1970), 3:277, lin. 19–21 [4, 18, 48].

44. Gregory Palamas, Λόγος ὑπὲρ τῶν ἱερῶς ἡσυχαζόντων, ed. Panagiotis Christou (Thessaloniki: 2010), 1:578 (2, 3, 44, lin. 1–9).

45. Cyril of Alexandria, *Glaphyra in Pentateuchum*, ed. Jean Aubert, Patrologia Graeca, vol. 69 (Paris: Jacques-Paul Migne, 1864), 36. The translation is mine.

of practical reason: "*deus diligendus est.*" Cyril gives the example of Abel who, upon intuiting the existence of the deity, feels bound by reason to offer him gifts worthy of his majesty. In other words, we infer that there has been a cause of the goods which we have received, and that we ought to honor this benefactor. Furthermore, for Cyril, we necessarily intuit God's existence, not a posteriori but analytically, once we recognize that "good itself" underlies every other good. Hence, the good must exist, since the goods which surround us partake of it and presuppose its existence. Paul's exegesis culminates for Byzantines with John Damascene, whose discussion of God's existence prefers Cyril's line of argument to Gregory's a posteriori one, even though he supplements the former with the latter: "Nevertheless, God has not gone so far as to leave us in complete ignorance, for through nature the knowledge of the existence of God has been revealed by him in all humans. The very creation of its harmony and ordering proclaims the majesty of the divine nature."[46] A more accurate translation would be "the knowledge of the existence of God has been naturally implanted (φυσικῶς ἐγκατέσπαρται) by him in all humans."[47]

Joseph E. Steineger concludes that, in this regard, Damascene is probably guided by a Stoicizing approach.[48] Importantly, Damascene follows the Stoics in holding that, while humans might be mistaken about God's nature, they possess an a priori knowledge of his existence. Building on Steineger's study, I propose that Damascene's line of argument can be traced back to an Antiochene author.

> Now, if it [Psalm 1:1] mentions *law* (v. 2), it does not oblige us to think only of the written law but of the innate natural law, which is not coercive, as the Manichees say, but instructing the person prepared to learn. So do not allow the identity in terms to give rise to misunderstanding: law that is natural and linked to nature is referred to, which is not temporary, like a person's having a sense of humor, having two feet, going grey in old age. It is implanted in all people and in every individual person; it is not temporary or subject to alteration, being also called a natural law because by it we can learn and distinguish what is for the better, like knowing that God exists, that it is good to respect parents and not to harm others. It is nature, in fact, that teaches each

46. John of Damascus, *An Exact Exposition of the Orthodox Faith* (*De fide orthodoxa*), 165–66 [I, ch. 1].

47. John of Damascus, *Expositio fidei*, ed. Bonifatius Kotter (Berlin: Walter De Gruyter, 1973), 7, lin. 14–15.

48. Steineger, "The Naturally Implanted Knowledge of God's Existence," 61–66.

person this as if giving orders not to do to another what one would not want to suffer from someone else.[49]

In their writings, both Diodorus and John Damascene single out the Manicheans, who are peculiarly opposed to natural law theory. What is more, John's philosophical comments commonly link the internal law of nature to human reason, of which risibility is its principal property.[50] Finally, knowledge of God's existence is put on par with other precepts like intuition of the golden rule. Damascene's legacy would appear to have put to rest Greek speculations on natural law and the knowledge of God, for the most part, until the aforementioned Barlaam-Palamas controversy broke out in 1334.

BYZANTINE JUSTICE, VIRTUE ETHICS, AND PRECEPTS

Paul's teaching on how human reason is capable of identifying the good to do and the evil to avoid appealed to Byzantine writers. Damascene summarizes it as "the law of the mind, i.e., the conscience (συνείδησις)."[51] Although Paul never describes conscience (viz., συνείδησις) explicitly as a habit (ἕξις/*habitus*), authors like Clement of Alexandria and Gregory Nyssa stress and expand upon its underlying habitual nature. Furthermore, Gregory uses the Stoic definition of justice to describe divine justice: "The just judgment of God comes to distribute to each according to one's dignity."[52] In addition to several citations from Gregory, the *Thesaurus Linguae Graecae* cites Eusebius, Epiphanius, and other authors who endorse this definition of divine justice. Thereafter, it became standard among literary figures in Byzantium. Byzantines tended to supplement Paul's terse words with a typically Stoic definition of justice to develop

49. Diodore of Tarsus, *Diodore of Tarsus: Commentary on Psalms 1–51*, trans. Robert C. Hill (Atlanta: Society of Biblical Literature, 2005), 5. See Diodore, *Commentarii in psalmos*, ed. Jean-Marie Olivier, 2 vols., Corpus Christianorum Series Graeca, vol. 6 (Turnhout: Brepols, 1980), sec. 1, preface.

50. John of Damascus, *Philosophical Chapters*, 19 [Ch. 5].

51. John of Damascus, *Expositio fidei*, 23, lin. 18 [95].

52. Gregory of Nyssa, *In sextum psalmum*, in *Gregorii Nysseni In inscriptiones psalmorum In Ecclesiasten homiliae*, ed. James McDonough and Paul Alexander, Gregorii Nysseni Opera, vol. 5, 87–93 (Leiden: E. J. Brill, 1962), 190, lin. 5–6.

Paul's notion of συνείδησις as a practical faculty discerning the merited and final good for oneself and others.[53] For example, citing Rom 2:12–16, Maximus argues that the Word judges all human acts by how they conform to the τέλος of all law: the divine essence. Using the Stoic definition of justice, Maximus explains that the Word distributes rewards in accord with one's dignity, which depends on how one conforms through right reason to the final end underlying every precept.[54] Justice is predicated primarily of the divinity, who orders and judges. However, justice also designates a human habit. Later, Medieval scholiasts on the *Nicomachean Ethics* interpret Aristotle's account of justice against the backdrop of Maximus's remarks: "Justice, according to common coin, is a *habit* (ἕξις) [...] distributive of what is equitable according to one's dignity."[55]

This literary and philosophical definition of natural justice differs from the juristic and ecclesiastical one only in its wording. Theophilus conserves the legal tradition in his paraphrase of Justinian's *Institutions* (c. 533). He describes it as a habit of the will: "Justice is a solid and constant will of distributing to each what is properly one's right (δικαιοσύνη ἐστι σταθερὰ καὶ διηνεκὴς βούλησις τοῦ ἀπονέμειν ἑκάστῳ τὸ ἴδιον δίκαιον)."[56] The great civil law codes (*Ecloga, Epanagoge, Basilica,* and *Procheiron*) employ a variant of this definition. The same is true of Matthew Blastares's *Syntagma* or *nomocanon* (1335), whose ecclesiastical authority was second to none.[57]

Both philosophers and jurists assume that *ius divinum* is in harmony with natural law. Still, few Byzantines philosophize extensively on divine law in relation to natural law and how it may constitute a standard

53. Stoic rationality is a "δεκτικὴ ἕξις" or intellectual virtue (ἀρετή) defined as "the ἐπιστήμη of distributing what is due to each." See Jedan, *Stoic Virtue,* 52, 57, 67, 69.

54. Maximus, *On Difficulties in Sacred Scripture,* 138–39 [19.2].

55. *Eustratii et Michaelis et anonyma in ethica Nicomachea commentaria,* ed. Gustav Heylbut (Berlin: Reimer, 1892), 138.

56. Theophilus Antecessor, *Institutionum graeca Paraphrasis Theophilo Antecessori vulgo tributa,* ed. Contardo Ferrini and Karl Eduard Zachariae von Lingenthal, 2 vols. (Berlin: S. Calvary & Associates, 1884), 1:3 [I, tit. 1, lin. 1–2]. This hypothetical restoration is drawn from *marginalia* that attempted to fill in missing Title I by recourse to the later *Basilika.* The newer critical edition omits the plausible reconstruction in fidelity only to the extant text in the best manuscripts.

57. For the history and importance of this text in the Eastern Churches, see Victor Alexandrov, *The Syntagma of Matthew Blastares: The Destiny of a Byzantine Legal Code among the Orthodox Slavs and Romanians, 14–17 Centuries* (Frankfurt am Main: Löwenklau-Gesellschaft, 2012).

for adjudicating the validity of civil law. Nonetheless, one of the principles enshrined in the Byzantine law codes is that even the emperor, who embodies the Stoic philosopher-king or *lex animata*, is unable to promulgate any valid law that is contrary to divine law or "the ecclesiastical canons."[58] Contextually, both the Stoic theory of divine-human participation in cosmic reason and Philo's theory of God as author of the natural law (embodied principally in the Mosaic law) influences Byzantine discussion of the nature of law. Eusebius (d. ca. 339), notwithstanding his reputation of heterodoxy, is the first to popularize Philo as a putatively Christian philosopher.[59] In all this, Byzantines remain characteristically "Roman." They are content to cling to pithy and concrete axioms about natural law. Maximus the Confessor is the first to develop a truly philosophical natural law theory: "The Word of God, Jesus Christ, as the demiurge of all, is also the maker (ποιητής) of the natural law. As provider (προνοητὴς) and lawgiver (νομοθέτης), he clearly is also the giver of both the written law (ἐν γράμματι) and the spiritual law (ἐν γράμματι), the latter of which is the law in grace (ἐν χάριτι)."[60] Secondly, God is said to establish three laws in creation:

> The Word of God, Jesus Christ, as the creator of all things, is also the maker of the natural law. As provider and lawgiver, he clearly is also the giver of both the written law and the spiritual law, which latter is the law of grace [...] For the Word of God is the author of every nature, and of every divine law, regulation, and order, from which it follows that he is the judge of those who live under nature, law, regulation and order [...].[61]

This passage relates *ius naturale* to the *ius divinum*, which comprises "written law" and the Gospel, and is superior to, but in accord with, natural law. Maximus goes on to call these three laws: "the more general laws (οἱ νόμοι γενικώτεροι)."[62] While, in itself, this phrase is ambiguous, following the Stoic and Roman distinction between written and unwritten law, it includes Mosaic law since its precepts often reflect either the *ius gentium* or the higher divine precepts. All three laws "illumine hu-

---

58. Morolli, *Il Diritto dell'Impero Romano d'Oriente*, 29.

59. For Philo's reception in Byzantium, see David T. Runia, *Philo in Early Christian Literature: A Survey* (Assen, Netherlands: Uitgeverij Van Gorcum, 1993), 212–74.

60. Maximus the Confessor, *On Difficulties in Sacred Scripture*, 138 [19.2].

61. Maximus the Confessor, 138–39 [19.2].

62. Maximus the Confessor, 226 [39.3].

man nature" by filling "the intellective eyes of the intelligible soul with light."[63] Yet, each law is present to human nature differently. Natural law enlightens through the very principles of reasoning.[64] The knowledge provided by reasoning accords with the Gospel in that both command the same natural virtues to be pursued.[65] So, Maximus claims that the natural law of practical reason performs "natural activities" that lead toward the resurrection first promised in the garden of paradise. In fact, both natural law and written law of Christ are equal in their uniform virtues and accord with reason.[66] Preference for the new and written law of Christ over natural law is due to, or justified by, the fact that our nature currently suffers from passions that prevent us from fulfilling the commandments by our own exertions.[67] Lastly, Maximus concludes his main discussion of natural law by noting that the mind can reflect on the principles of knowledge to discover their first cause, who must be a divine light in whom natural law is seen.[68] Observing natural law brings us back to virtue, which establishes inhering relations or habits that exclude all activities not in conformity with proper human praxis.[69]

St. Paul is well-known for repeatedly using Hellenic lists of virtues, which, as is the case with the so-called cardinal virtues, were already being absorbed into Judaism. Following the precedent set by Judeo-Christians, the Byzantines take up Hellenic virtue ethics and see it as intimately connected to natural law. Following Wisdom (1:13–14; 13:1–9) and under the influence of Stoicism, they expound on the cardinal virtues as a central part of their ethics. The New and the Old Testament encourage Byzantines to use Stoic virtue theory to articulate their moral teaching.

In pre-Byzantine times, Greek Christians had already embraced virtue ethics, particularly by affirming the cardinal virtues. Greek Christians were principally attracted to the Roman Stoic school, as attested by editions of Epictetus's works that are tailored to reflect monotheism and other Christian beliefs. In late antiquity, the numerous mo-

---

63. Maximus the Confessor, 227 [39.3].

64. Maximus the Confessor, 226 [39.3].

65. Maximus the Confessor, 227 [39.3].

66. Maximus the Confessor, *Difficulties in the Church Fathers*, I: 238, 240 [*Ambigua ad Ioannem* 10.2–5].

67. Maximus the Confessor, *On Difficulties in Sacred Scripture*, 179 [26.12].

68. Maximus the Confessor, 227 [39.3].

69. Maximus the Confessor, 228 [39.4].

nastic texts generally prefer to develop ethical discourse by drawing, without acknowledgements, on Stoicism. During the Byzantine period, σχολαστικοί (i.e., *iuris periti*) and authors with Stoic affinities predominate. Even so, there is also the odd treatise that draws on Peripatetic ethics. John Damascene, on the other hand, is a well-known synthesizer of the Peripatetic and Stoic ethical traditions. Such recourse to the Peripatetic tradition is not a major influence on natural law discourse, though. After all, Aristotle only touches upon natural law theory briefly.[70]

Of course, in both antiquity and late antiquity, quite a number of authors, including some Christians, write commentaries with a prevalently ethical thrust on Platonic, Aristotelian, and other philosophical texts. However, natural law is not a theme in which Neoplatonists are generally interested. The notable exception is the monumental figure of Maximus the Confessor.

Like his predecessors, Maximus embraces the four "general virtues" and describes them as the "inner principles of truth" obtained by power of free choice. However, he also tries to show that justice is closely connected to conscience and natural law (Rom 2:14–16). The virtues of prudence and justice constitute the wisdom or overarching knowledge of the good, of which Paul speaks. Prudence is the scientific and theoretical contemplation of means to attain some proper end; justice, on the other hand, as the Stoic definition shows, regards the rational beings, who constitute the ends, according to the proper order of things. Furthermore, humans who understand the principles of all four cardinal virtues can detect God as their source.[71]

After Maximus's apotheosis, Byzantine tradition (as attested in Byzantine liturgical offices) effectively canonized the cardinal virtues by attributing them to Maximus's spiritual father in the liturgical text for his feast, on March 11: "You [Sophronios] whose nickname is from temperance (σωφροσύνης), already called Sophronios by divine providence, have become temperate (σώφρων), and just, courageous, and prudent in your works; you are crowned by way of genus with the generic virtues

---

70. Aristotle, *Ethica Nicomachea*, ed. Ingram Bywater (Oxford: Clarendon Press, 1963), 1129a1–17; Aristotle, *Ars rhetorica*, ed. William David Ross (Oxford: Clarendon Press, 1959), 1372b2–8.

71. Maximus the Confessor, *Difficulties in the Church Fathers*, 424–25 [21.5]; 430–33 [*Ambigua ad Ioannem* 21.8].

(ἀρεταῖς ταῖς γενικαῖς γενικῶς), and as the most exacting judge you naturally distribute [them] by attachment, each one to soul and body."[72]

These general virtues, in Stoic thinking, are primary and in some way principles of numerous subordinated virtues.[73] They stand to these other virtues as genera do to their various species. At any rate, the Stoic theory of four naturally acquired and generic virtues became the inheritance of the late-Byzantine period as in Damascene's *Philosophical Chapters* and in the akolouthies of the Byzantine rite.

Later, Medieval Byzantine hymnographers likewise incorporated (the literary) definition of natural justice into hymnody. For example, on the feast of St. Makarios of Egypt (19 January), there is sung: "O Father, I will bring the crown of justice (δικαισούνης) that Jesus prepared you; he distributes rewards according to one's dignity (ὁ κατ'ἀξίαν νέμων τὰ ἔπαθλα)."[74] As with the aforementioned citation from Plato and Roman Stoics (e.g., Musonius Rufus), this axiom supposes that the Stoic image of the philosopher (who as a rational legislator is an eponymous king) rewards people according to right reason, long applied to Christ as the sage-king by Stoicizing Christians in pre-Byzantine times. Later, the philosopher-king (νόμος ἔμψυχος), or Stoic sage, was formalized as the *ex officio* function of the Byzantine emperor who legislates according to reason for the good of his people.

Some scholars emphasize that natural law plays almost no formal role in judicial processes of the period. Still, certain principles are thought to be always in force. The prince, for example, does not have the power to legitimize something that is contrary to the law of nature.[75] Be that as it may, no exhaustive list or theory of axioms—based on nature law—ever became part of Byzantine jurisprudence, whether in Latin or Greek. Byzantium, nonetheless, passes on, as part of its legacy, is summation of

72. Ἀνθολόγιον τοῦ ὅλου ἐνιαυτοῦ (hereafter, *Anthologion*), 3 vols. (Rome: Sacra Congregatio Ecclesiarum Orientalium, 1974), 2:1490.

73. Matthew Sharpe, "Stoic Virtue Ethics," in *The Handbook of Virtue Ethics*, ed. Stan Van Hooft (Durham, UK: Acumen, 2014), 28–41 at 38.

74. *Anthologion*, 1:1487.

75. However, the singular example is limited to unnatural marriage in legislation dating from Justinian, *Novellae*, ed. Rudolf Schöll and Wilhelm Kroll, Corpus Iuris Civilis, vol. 3 (Berlin: Weidmann, 1895), 95, lin. 13–15 [Nov. XII, c. 1]. For example, incest would be an example of unnatural marriage by law. Simultaneously, the principle was left unapplied by civil law to slavery as witnessed in Theophilus Antecessor, *Institutionum graeca paraphrasis*, 1:8 [I, tit. 2, 2, lin. 16–21].

republican and imperial jurists, such as Cicero and Gaius. In effect, natural law remained the universal criterion by which Byzantine civil laws were deemed valid and natural law theory was incorporated into ecclesiastical collections of law up until the fall of the Polis. In line with Philo's theory on the Mosaic law, Byzantines typically assume, along with proto-canonical texts like the *Apostolic Constitutions*, that the decalogue reflected the basic precepts of the natural law.[76] Tellingly, however, many patristic lists of moral commandments mention other precepts from Roman law, such as the *lex talionis* for murder, punishments for adultery and thievery, and the rewarding of a favor in time of need, as well as human contracts, bestowal of gifts, and even the making of wills.[77]

CONCLUSIONS

Paul Babie has noted a *general* paucity of modern Orthodox studies on natural law, not merely on the Eastern patristic tradition.[78] He has also underlined that there is virtually no extant Byzantine literature on natural law after Maximus the Confessor. What does exist is a large collection of excerpts from pre- and post-Byzantine authors of the first millennium collected by Stanley Harakas. The Three Holy Hierarchs (Gregory of Nazianzus, Basil the Great, and John Chrysostom) and Gregory of Nyssa account for much of the Orthodox literature on natural law that Harakas surveys.

This study, given its limits of space, has provided a panoramic view of natural law during ten centuries of Byzantine rule over the Roman East. The concerns are much the same as those of the Latin West: the derivation of moral precepts from reflection on living (created) structures; establishing a first principle of practical reason and an order of rational thought for scientifically inferring moral truths about human ends; natural marriage (as opposed to incest, for example); the just reward for actions. Furthermore, the architectonic precept, "to do good and avoid evil," constitutes the point of departure for moral reasoning among many Byzantines. The only rival first principle (of practical reason) may have been that regarding the worship of God. This is hinted at

---

76. Harakas, "Eastern Orthodox Perspectives on Natural Law," 46–48.

77. See Theophilus Antecessor, *Institutionum graeca paraphrasis*, 1:3–5 [I, tit. 2, 1, lin. 5–15].

78. Babie, "Natural Law in the Orthodox Tradition," 37.

by Byzantines who thought the *ens divinum* to be a priori self-evident. Although a systematic treatise on natural law was never penned in Byzantium, Maximus the Confessor wrote a number of lengthy comments on its structure and application. By and large, Byzantines in the fields of philosophy, law, and theology were content to accept the Stoic, Roman, and pre-Byzantine suppositions about natural law, namely: that it is eternal since it is a participation in divine reason; that it is capable of both supplying moral precepts and grounding proofs for the existence of God; that, prior to the Mosaic and Christian written law, observing it renders humans just before God. Consequently, the topic was important enough to demand regular mention and affirmation by a plethora of Byzantine writers throughout its millennial history prior to the reception of the Greek translations of about sixteen of Aquinas's works in the fourteenth and fifteenth centuries.

Dominic Farrell, LC

4 ∽ Aquinas and the Central Question of Medieval Theories of Natural Law

One way of comparing the Latin tradition's conception of natural law with those of the other religious traditions of medieval thought is to focus on Thomas Aquinas. This strategy is recommendable for several reasons.

On the one hand, he is the main natural law theorist of the Latin tradition. He is repeatedly credited with developing the first fully systematic natural law theory and, as a result, the one that has become paradigmatic for subsequent reflection.[1] On the other hand, he expects that his views on natural law should be compared with those of the other traditions of medieval philosophy. Although he writes as a Catholic theologian, he engages extensively with various medieval Greek, Jewish, and Muslim thinkers, often inviting the reader to compare his views with theirs. Sometimes he criticizes them. At other times, he believes that they are right about some matter and draws on them. He may even engage them and draw on them in developing his own account of natural law. In comparing his conception of natural law to that of the other traditions of medieval philosophy, therefore, it is necessary to determine whether he does so. Even if he does not, his account of natural law is still addressed to people of all religions and non-believers. It purports to individuate universally valid reasons for action that are accessible to anyone who gives due consideration to the relevant facts. It is worth clarifying, therefore,

---

1. Michael Bertram Crowe, *The Changing Profile of the Natural Law* (The Hague: M. Nijhoff, 1977), xii, 111; John Finnis, *Natural Law and Natural Rights*, 2nd ed. (Oxford: Oxford University Press, 1980, 2011), 28; Mark C. Murphy, *Natural Law in Jurisprudence and Politics* (New York: Cambridge University Press, 2006), 1.

to what extent and on what grounds Aquinas expects right-thinking people from other traditions to agree with his account of natural law.

There are several reasons, then, for examining the ways in which Aquinas's account of natural law may be related to that of the other religious traditions of medieval philosophy. This essay attempts such a study.

First, it is necessary to establish whether Aquinas's account of natural law is comparable and commensurable with some feature of the other traditions. The notion of "natural law" does not feature in Jewish and Islamic thought of the period. A comparison is still possible. Medieval Jewish and Islamic thought grapples to some extent with the same question that is central to the Byzantine and Latin doctrine of natural law (section 1). This question can be formulated as follows.

> Can reason, working independently of (prophetic) Revelation, dictate authoritatively what we must do to attain our ultimate end, and, if so, can we attain that end by living in accord with reason?

By knowing how each tradition addresses this question, it is also possible to see where Aquinas agrees or disagrees with each on the issue of natural law. Indeed, it is even possible to detect some influence, or lack thereof, of each of these traditions on his natural law theory (section 2). However, it is also important to unpack and assess his own puzzling and possibly inconsistent answer to the central question (section 3). On the one hand, he only gives a qualified yes to the first part of the question. Reason can work out what is virtuous, but normally needs Revelation to gain a reliable understanding of right and wrong. On the other hand, he answers no to the second part of the question. In his view, our ultimate end is supernatural and only attainable through grace. By holding this view, he appears to render the first part of the question otiose and natural law with it. A natural law theory is meant to explain how reason, working by its own lights and independently of Revelation, can discover what we must do to attain our ultimate end. There does not seem to be much point to a natural law theory, though, if we cannot attain our ultimate end by acting according to reason and practicing the acquired virtues. Upon closer examination, though, Aquinas's answers to each part of the central question prove to be consistent with one another. He provides an account of how natural law is still necessary and not at all otiose. Natural law is right practical reason prescribing the exercise of the various acquired moral virtues. As such, it constitutes an ethico-political standard that right-thinking persons from different traditions have reason to accept. However, it also constitutes the framework of our understanding of Revealed moral teaching.

THE CENTRAL QUESTION OF MEDIEVAL NATURAL LAW THEORIES

Medieval philosophy is religious in inspiration. Consequently, each of the various medieval traditions of "natural law" can be construed as addressing the same central question to some extent. In the introduction, I proposed a generic formulation of it.

Generally, this question is not central to modern discussions of natural law. Currently, most theoretical contributions to the natural law tradition are philosophical rather than theological. They may be influenced by a religious tradition, but, unlike medieval theories of natural law, generally treat theological issues as peripheral rather than central. Their main concern is to articulate and defend a universalist, non-consequentialist moral philosophy that grounds moral judgments in a teleological conception human nature. To this end, they take pains to defend not only robust moral cognitivism and realism, but, above all, a non-consequentialist normative ethics that is grounded in some conception of natural teleology and its normativity for practical reason. Medieval natural law theories are normally just as committed to these positions. However, given the religious setting of medieval philosophy, even more fundamental are the theological issues expressed in the abovementioned question. Does the possession of reason put non-believers under the same moral demands as believers, and can they, through the practice of moral virtue, attain what is promised to the faithful? This in turn raises the question as to whether morality is grounded in creation or in further decisions of the divine will.

There is reason to believe that medieval thinkers of each religious tradition, in broaching the issue of "natural law", are addressing the same central question to some extent.

First, there is the Christian tradition. From early Patristic theology on, the concept of natural law is central to both its Greek and Latin branches.[2]

---

2. A number of ante-Nicene Church Fathers associate the Decalogue with natural law. Tertullian, *Adversus Iudaeos*, in *Opera*, ed. Emil Kroymann, 2 vols., Corpus Christianorum Series

However, the Byzantines do not appear to reflect as systematically and extensively on natural law as the Latins. Two reasons are normally adduced. First, Byzantine theology is influenced much less than Western Christianity by legal theory.[3] Second, it views nature, not as an autonomous domain, but from the perspective of man's divinization in Christ.[4] In this case, it may not attach as much importance to the central question as the Latins. Still, by defending and invoking natural law, it answers yes to the first part of the central question. Furthermore, by insisting that man's divinization requires a synergy between human freedom and grace, it answers no to the second part.

On the other hand, it could be argued that Maimonides, the most important medieval Jewish thinker, answers yes to both the first part and, with qualifications, to the second. David Novak's reconstruction of Maimonides's "natural law theory" supports this reading.

For Maimonides, the gentiles can recognize "the seven commandments of the children of Noah" (*sheva mitsvot bnei Noah*) and observe them on rational grounds. He thereby answers yes to the first part of the central question. However, there may even be some gentiles who acknowledge the divine authority of the Torah and so follow the seven commandments precisely because God bids them to. For Maimonides, this last group constitutes "the pious of the nations of the world" and will share in the world-to-come, albeit with a lower status than that of observant Jews.[5] He thereby gives a qualified yes to the second part of the central question. He also distinguishes, as Novak puts it, between gentiles who recognize natural law and those who see it as a divine law.[6]

Latina, vols. 1–2 (Turnhout: Brepols, 1954), 2:1341 [II, 2]; Tertullian, *De corona*, in *Opera*, 2:1046–47 [VI]; Irenaeus of Lyons, *Contre les Hérésies*, 5 vols., Sources Chrétiennes, vols. 100, 152–53, 210–11, 263–64, 293–94 (Paris: Éditions du Cerf, 1965–82), 1:524–27 [IV, 13, 1] and 1:534–35 [IV, 13, 4]; Justin the Martyr, *Dialogus cum Tryphone*, in Die ältesten Apologeten, ed. Edgar John Goodspeed, 90–265 (Göttingen: Vandenhoeck & Ruprecht, 1914), 207 [93, 1]; Origen, *Contre Celse*, ed. Marcel Borret, 5 vols., Sources Chrétiennes, vols. 132, 136, 147, 150, 227 (Paris: Cerf, 1967–76), 3:110–13 [V, 37, lin. 1–11].

3. Christiaan Kappes's contribution to this volume suggests otherwise: that Roman law played a central role in Byzantine natural law theory.

4. Stanley S. Harakas, "Eastern Orthodox Perspectives on Natural Law," *American Journal of Jurisprudence* 24, no. 1 (1979): 97–98; Georgios I. Mantzaridis, *Grundlinien christlicher Ethik* (St. Ottilien, Ger.: EOS Verlag, 1998), 75–83; Basilio Petrà, "La legge naturale nella teologia ortodossa," *Rivista di teologia morale* 40, no. 159 (2008): 325–32.

5. See Maimonides, *The Book of Judges*, trans. Abraham M. Hershman, The Code of Maimonides 14, Yale Judaica Series 3 (New Haven: Yale University Press, 1949), 230 [ch. 8, 11–12].

6. David M. Novak, "Maimonides and Aquinas on Natural Law," in *St. Thomas Aquinas*

Within Islamic thought of the period, there are various answers to the central question. Anver Emon has argued that the pre-modern Sunnite debate on reason as the source of Shariʻa can be construed as one about natural law. There are two main positions in this debate. Some, such as al-Jaṣṣāṣ (d. 981), al-Qāḍī ʻAbd-al-Jabbār (d. 1025), and Abū al Husayn al Baṣrī (d. 1044), claim that, since God only creates that which is good, human reason can know God's will through the medium of nature, independently of Shariʻa. In this case, they answer yes to the first part of the central question. Others reject this view. They do believe, however, that when it comes to matters on which Shariʻa is silent, human reason can discover God's will from nature, but only because God in his grace (*faḍl, tafaḍḍul*) has willed that nature be so and could alter its contingent arrangement. They are more inclined to say no to the first part of the central question. Due to their belief in divine voluntarism, they propose what Emon calls a soft as opposed to a hard conception of nature, and so, a soft theory of natural law as opposed to the hard alternative.[7]

If the preceding overview is correct, each religious tradition of medieval thought has a theory of natural law, either explicitly or, if not, by taking a position on the central question that underlies such a theory. In this case, there are grounds to think that Aquinas's reflection on natural law may be influenced by that of the Byzantine, Jewish, and Islamic traditions. Is this the case?

BYZANTINE, JEWISH, AND ISLAMIC INFLUENCES ON AQUINAS'S THEORY OF NATURAL LAW

Aquinas's account of natural law has its roots in the Church Fathers. The Stoic concept of natural law is adopted, transmitted, and in the process adapted, by the Church Fathers. During the twelfth century, with the renewed study of Roman law in Latin Christendom, civil and canon lawyers initiate a more detailed reflection. The more systematic and theolog-

---

and the Natural Law Tradition: Contemporary Perspectives, ed. John Goyette, Mark Latkovic, and Richard S. Myers (Washington, D.C.: Catholic University of America Press, 2004), 43–65 at 48–54. For the opposite view, see Marvin Fox, *Interpreting Maimonides:Studies in Methodology, Metaphysics, and Moral Philosophy* (Chicago: University of Chicago Press, 1990), 130–39.

7. Anver M. Emon, *Islamic Natural Law Theories* (New York: Oxford University Press, 2010).

ical treatment of the canon lawyers is taken up in turn by the *magistri sacrae paginae*, such as Aquinas.[8]

In thinking about natural law, Aquinas not only draws on the same four main sources as the Byzantines—Scripture, Patristic theology, ancient philosophy, and Roman law—but also their reflection on the matter.

Aquinas becomes acquainted with aspects of Roman law from the important literature on canon law that develops in the Latin West from the early twelfth century on.[9] In using Roman law, he is in turn indebted to Byzantium: to Justinian I's initiative to draw up the *Corpus Juris Civilis*.

A further trace of Byzantine influence is his use of post-Constantinian Greek patristic theology to articulate his account of natural law. A full survey of how he uses the Greek theologians in this regard falls outside the scope of this paper. For present purposes, it suffices to consider the section dedicated to natural law in the *Summa theologiae* (I-II, q. 94). There, Aquinas cites Basil of Caesarea and John Damascene. Basil, he states, claims that conscience or synderesis is the "law of our intellect." In the passages referenced, Basil argues that not only is the good to be done and evil avoided, but that we also have an innate capacity to discern both good and evil. He calls this capacity natural reason (*phusikos logos*) or natural judgment (*kriterion phusikon*).[10] However, contrary to what Thomas states, it is not Basil but John of Damascus who uses the expression "law of our (my) intellect" to refer to conscience (*suneidesis*).[11] Thomas cites John on two more occasions. First, to explain how the virtues are natural to us.[12] Second, to explain how sin is related to our twofold nature: the rational and the purely biological.[13]

8. See Crowe, *The Changing Profile of the Natural Law*, 1–81. In this line, Aquinas employs notions and statements from Roman law, certain arguments of Cicero, but above all Aristotle. The evidence is presented in Patrick M. Farrell, "Sources of St. Thomas' Concept of Natural Law," *The Thomist* 20, no. 3 (1957): 237–94.

9. For a list of the passages in which Aquinas cites Roman law when discussing the just (*ius*), the law of nations (*ius gentium*), natural right (*ius naturale*), and law, see Jean-Marie Aubert, *Le droit romain dans l'œuvre de saint Thomas* (Paris: Vrin, 1955), 19–20.

10. In *Summa theologiae* (hereafter, *ST*), 5 vols. (Ottawa: Harpell's Press, 1941–45), I-II, q. 94, a. 1, obj. 2. See Basil of Caesarea, *Homélies sur l'Hexaéméron*, ed. Stanislas Giet, Sources Chrétiennes, vol. 29 (Paris: Éditions du Cerf, 1949), 414–17 [Hom. 7.5]; Basil, *Homilia in principium Proverbiorum*, Patrologia Graeca, vol. 31 (Paris: Jacques Paul Migne, 1885), 385–424 at 406.

11. John of Damascus, *Expositio fidei*, ed. Bonifatius Kotter (Berlin: Walter De Gruyter, 1973), 222–23 [ch. 95].

12. *ST* I-II, q. 94, a. 3, s.c.: John of Damascus, *Expositio fidei*, 144 [ch. 58, lin. 168–69].

13. *ST* I-II, q. 94, a. 3, ad 2. Here Thomas appears to be referencing John of Damascus, *Expositio fidei*, 75–80 [ch. 26].

Thomas, therefore, draws whenever possible on the Greek Fathers and Byzantine theologians, such as Theophylact of Ohrid (c. 1055–c. 1107), who discuss natural law and conscience.[14] They may not influence his thought on natural law as deeply as the Augustinian tradition, even though he is reasonably well read in the Greek Fathers and Byzantine theology.[15] This is mainly because Eastern theology does not develop as explicit and systematic an account of natural law as the Latins. Still, by citing it freely on the matter and without any qualifications, he clearly takes the Churches of the East to hold the same conception of natural law.

Indeed, there is at least one instance in which a Byzantine's virtue theory contributes significantly to Aquinas's account of natural law.

Thomas is acquainted with some of the medieval Greek commentaries on Aristotle's *Nicomachean Ethics*. Robert Grosseteste translates these along with that work. Albert uses these translations in his first commentary on the *Nicomachean Ethics*, dictated when Thomas is his student at Cologne (1248–1252). Aquinas takes away from these lectures an observation made by Michael of Ephesus, a scholar active at Constantinople during the first half of the twelfth century and the author of a both commentary on Book V of the *Nicomachean Ethics* (hereafter, *EN*) and some *scholia* on Books IX–X.[16] For Aristotle, says Michael, the principles of practical wisdom (*phronēsis, prudentia*) do not merely accord with the moral virtues (*EN* X, 8, 1178a17–18), but constitute the ends of the moral virtues (VI, 12, 1144a6–9).[17] Thomas develops this insight to explain two matters. On the one hand, he uses it to explain how the Aristotelian account of *phronēsis* and the virtues is grounded in a precept of natural

---

14. He cites Theophylact in connection with natural law in Thomas Aquinas, *Catena aurea in quatuor Evangelia*, ed. Angelico Guarienti, 2 vols., 2nd ed. (Turin: Marietti, 1953), 1:556, 2:44, 2:195, 2:336.

15. A useful survey of the literature on Aquinas's use of the Greek Fathers can be found in Marcus Plested, *Orthodox Readings of Aquinas* (Oxford: Oxford University Press, 2012), 15–21.

16. Katerina Ierodiakonou, "Some Observations on Michael of Ephesus' Comments on *Nicomachean Ethics* X," in *Medieval Greek Commentaries on the Nicomachean Ethics*, ed. Charles Barber and David Jenkins, 185–201 (Leiden: Brill, 2009); H. P. F. Mercken, "The Greek Commentators on Aristotle's *Ethics*," in *Aristotle Transformed: The Ancient Commentators and Their Influence*, ed. Richard Sorabji (London: Duckworth, 1990), 407–43 at 429–36.

17. Michael of Ephesus, *In Ethica nicomachea IX–X Commentaria*. In *Eustratii et Michaelis et Anonyma in Ethica nicomachea Commentaria*, ed. Gustav Heylbut (Berlin: Reimer, 1892), 461–620 at 594, lin. 2–5, lin. 8. This text is cited in Albert the Great, *Super Ethica: Commentum et Quaestiones*, Opera Omnia 14/1–2 (Münster Westphalia: Aschendorff, 1968–72), 762, lin.15–22 [X, c. 13].

law. On the other hand, he deploys it to show how we begin our practical reasoning by recognizing the end of the virtues and that we should practice the various moral virtues.

The end of the moral virtues is acting or living according to reason. Moreover, one's reason indicates that living according to reason is a fundamental end we should pursue. One does not become aware of this normative end only with the acquisition of the intellectual virtue of practical wisdom. Rather, the practical reason of any person capable of responsible action recognizes and prescribes this end. Setting this end, therefore, is an act of synderesis, the intellectual *habitus* of the first principles of practical reasoning and *phronesis*. Furthermore, practical reason's prescriptive setting of this end amounts to a common precept of natural law. Indeed, this common precept prescribes the end of the moral virtues. Any moral virtue is a good operative *habitus* that disposes one to adhere affectively to right reason. Hence, acting in accord with reason is the end of the moral virtues.[18] Expanding in this way upon Michael's observation, enables Aquinas to explain how the doctrine of natural law and Aristotelian virtue theory designate and describe one and the same process of practical reasoning.

While Aquinas has every reason to look to Byzantine authors for guidance on natural law, he has less motives to do so when it comes to medieval Jewish and Islamic literature. The Hellenic term "natural law" does not figure explicitly in either tradition at that time. Then again, these two traditions can be said to have a theory of natural law. Each has an explanation of how authoritative reason is on moral matters when it is not informed by divine law. However, Aquinas's engagement with medieval Jewish and Islamic "natural law theories" is limited. This is inevitable. Like almost any scholar, he is not equipped to engage with each tradition in a fully adequate way. Furthermore, he is not familiar with most of the relevant literature. On the one hand, he has no knowledge of Islamic legal writings of the period.[19] On the other hand, his engage-

---

18. See *ST* II-II, q. 47, aa. 6–7. For a study of the background of these articles and their bearing on Aquinas's natural law theory, see Dominic Farrell, *The Ends of the Moral Virtues and the First Principles of Practical Reason in Thomas Aquinas*, Analecta Gregoriana 318 (Roma: Gregorian & Biblical Press, 2012).

19. On Aquinas's knowledge and understanding of Islam, see Louis Gardet, "La connaissance que Thomas d'Aquin put avoir du monde islamique," in *Aquinas and the Problems of His Time*, ed. Gerard Verbeke and Daniel Verhelst, 139–49 (Louvain: Leuven University Press

ment with medieval Jewish thought is limited to *The Guide of the Perplexed*, and he shows no signs of having read the *Misneh Torah*, the work in which some scholars believe Maimonides gives his fullest statement of a "natural law theory."[20]

Despite his limited knowledge of Maimonides, Thomas does not take him as a guide on natural law. He cites Maimonides frequently during his discussion of Mosaic law (*lex vetus*). Moreover, the texts cited are from the third part of *The Guide*. This part as, David Novak has pointed out, is on "the reasons of the commandments" (*ta ʿamei ha-mitsvot*), or what the Rabbinic tradition calls "the reasons of the law" (*ta ʿamei torah*).[21] Nevertheless, Thomas only relies on Maimonides when it comes to articulating the reasons behind the ceremonial and judiciary precepts.[22] He never cites him to clarify the moral precepts. Indeed, in an early work, Thomas charges Maimonides with misinterpreting Scripture's testimony to natural law on at least one point. Maimonides claims that, prior to the giving of the Torah, it was permissible to hire a prostitute for sexual intercourse, as Judah does with Tamar, and that this was analogous to the payment of a divorced wife's dowry.[23] Thomas objects that extra-matrimonial sexual relations are against natural law, and so can never have been licit, not even by way of dispensation.[24]

Aquinas, therefore, is not influenced by the "natural law theories" of medieval Jewish and Islamic philosophy. However, there are points at which his engagement with medieval Islamic philosophers carries over into his discussion of natural law.

Nijhoff, 1976); Simone van Riet, "La *Somme contre les Gentiles* et la polémique islamo-chrétienne," in *Aquinas and the Problems of His Time*, 150–60; James Waltz, "Muảmmad and the Muslims in St. Thomas Aquinas," *The Muslim World* 66, no. 2 (1976): 81–95; Dietrich Lorenz Daiber, "Santo Tomás de Aquino y el Islam en la *Suma contra los gentiles*," *Philosophica* 24–25 (2001–02): 123–37.

20. Novak, "Maimonides and Aquinas on Natural Law," 48–56.

21. Novak, 46.

22. In discussing the ceremonial precepts, he cites *The Guide of the Perplexed* (hereafter, *GP*) III, ch. 28 at *ST* I-II, q. 101, a. 1, obj. 4; *GP* III, ch. 32 at *ST* I-II, q. 101, a. 3, ad 3; *GP* III, ch. 37 at *ST* I-II, q. 102, a. 6, ad 5 et ad 6; *GP* III, ch. 45 at *ST* I-II, q. 102, a. 4, ad 2, ad 5, et ad 7 and a. 5, obj. 10; *GP* III, ch. 46 at *ST* I-II, q. 102, a. 3, ad 4 et ad 11; *GP* III, ch. 47 at *ST* I-II, q. 102, a. 5, ad 4; *GP* III, ch. 48 at *ST* I-II, q. 102, a. 3, ad 6 and I-II, q. 102, a. 6, ad 1; *GP* III, ch. 49 at *ST* I-II, q. 102, a. 6, ad 8.

In discussing the judiciary precepts, he cites *GP* III, ch. 40 at *ST* I-II, q. 105, a. 2, ad 12.

23. *GP* III, ch. 49.

24. Thomas Aquinas, *Scriptum super libros sententiarum magistri Petri Lombardi* (hereafter, *Scriptum*), ed. Pierre Mandonnet and Marie-Fabien Moos, 4 vols. (Paris: Lethieilleux, 1929–56), IV, d. 33, q. 1, a. 3, q.la 3, co.

On the one hand, he believes that some Islamic philosophers interpret Aristotle's philosophy of human nature in a way which is inimical to natural law. According to the reading which he and his Latin contemporaries make of Ibn Rushd, Averroism holds a controversial and problematic view on our power to understand the essence of a thing (the agent intellect). This is the power to form thoughts. It is to be distinguished from our power to hold thoughts (possible intellect). Rather, it allows us to understand what something is. It does so by setting aside the individuating features apprehended by the senses and laying bare its essential nature. According to Averroism, however, the agent intellect is not an interior principle of the individual capable of thought. Rather, it is either a substance or belongs to an individual who acts upon the minds of all humans engaged in thought. Aquinas objects that treating the agent intellect as a single substance, which operates simultaneously on every human engaged in thought, is at odds with the very conditions of possibility of morality and political life.

Individuals are the subjects of moral and political agency. To exert such agency, they need to possess the capacity for free choice. However, to be capable of free choice, an individual must perform his or her own acts of understanding. Were humans to share a single agent intellect, no individual would be performing his or her own acts of understanding. Rather, the collective agent intellect would be responsible. Under those conditions, therefore, no individual would possess free choice or moral agency.[25] This makes the Averroist conception of the human intellect inimical to natural law: the way in which human beings assimilate God's will through their own practical reasoning. In a certain sense natural law is simply, as Aquinas argues, the individual's own agent intellect: the capacity to understand for oneself what we should do.[26] In this case, denying that each human possesses an agent intellect which is entirely one's own amounts to a denial of the existence of natural law.

On the other hand, Thomas owes to Ibn Sīnā a central component of his natural law theory: the theory of first concepts.[27] This theory is

25. Thomas Aquinas, *De unitate intellectus contra Averroistas,* in Editio Leonina, vol. 43, ed. Hyacinthe-François Dondaine (Rome: Editori di San Tommaso, 1976), 308 [c. 4, lin. 76–95].

26. Jean-Pierre Torrell, "Les 'Collationes in decem praeceptis' de saint Thomas d'Aquin. Édition critique avec introduction et notes," *Revue des sciences philosophiques et théologiques* 69, no. 2 (1985): 24 [I, lin. 6–15].

27. See Avicenna, *Liber de philosophia prima sive scientia divina, I-IV*, ed. Simone van Riet,

an extension of Aristotle's reduction of all propositions to the principle of non-contradiction.[28] Ibn Sīnā argues that Aristotle's account of the principle of non-contradiction and its fundamental epistemological status has two further implications. First, there must be not only first propositions but also first concepts. These are the concepts out of which a first proposition, such as the principle of non-contradiction, is composed. Moreover, since they are the constituents of a first proposition, they are logically or conceptually anterior to it. Second, if the principle of non-contradiction is conceptually anterior to any of the propositions classified according to the ten categories, then the first concepts must also be conceptually anterior to the categories.

This theory of first concepts provides Aquinas with a key piece of his moral epistemology and natural law theory. He invokes it in his best-known discussion of natural law (*ST* I-II, q. 94, a. 2). It permits him to argue that, just as the notion of being grounds all thought and underlies the principle of non-contradiction, so too does the concept of the good ground all practical reasoning. It also allows him to explain how, once we start to think about the good in the realm of human action, we also grasp the first principle of practical reason and the first precept of natural law: "The good is to be done and pursued; evil avoided."

Three conclusions can be drawn, I submit, from this brief survey of how the various traditions of medieval philosophy feed into Aquinas's account of natural law. First, the "natural law theories" of the Jewish and Islamic traditions do not contribute to Aquinas's own. Second, Byzantine reflection on natural law does contribute to it in various ways. Third, Aquinas draws important elements of his Aristotelian account of practical reason from both medieval Byzantine and Islamic philosophy.

This last point has two possible implications. On the one hand, it

---

3 vols. (Louvain: E. Peeters, 1977), 1:31–42 [I, c. 5]. On the medieval reception of this aspect of Avicenna's thought, see Jan A. Aertsen, "Avicenna's Doctrine of the Primary Notions and Its Impact on Medieval Philosophy," in *Islamic Thought in the Middle Ages: Studies in Text, Transmission and Translation, in Honour of Hans Daiber*, ed. Anna Akasoy and Wim Raven, 21–42 (Leiden: Brill, 2008).

28. Aristotle argues that the principle of non-contradiction is indemonstrable and the surest of all principles, and that there must be first principles due to the impossibility of an infinite regress in our reasoning. See Aristotle, *Metaphysica*, ed. Werner Jaeger (Oxford: Clarendon Press, 1957), IV [Γ], 4, 1005b35–1006a11. See also Aristotle, *Analytica posteriora*, in *Analytica priora et posteriora*, ed. William David Ross and Lorenzo Minio-Paluello (Oxford: Clarendon, 1964), I, 3, 72b5–15.

suggests that there may exist a convergence between the virtue ethics of the various traditions of medieval philosophy. If their respective "natural law theories" are simply accounts of how the life of virtue is grounded in divine law, there may still exist a substantial amount of agreement among them regarding the nature and classification of virtue, even when they disagree over the nature of divine law. In this regard, it is significant that al-Fārābī, Ibn Rushd, Maimonides, Solomon ibn Gabirol, Eustrasios of Nicea, Michael of Ephesus, and Thomas Aquinas, endorse much of Aristotle's *Nicomachean Ethics*.[29] On the other hand, if the content of natural law can be articulated in terms of virtue ethics, then substantive moral disagreements between traditions should be addressed through philosophical debate over the nature of the virtues, their classification, and how they contribute to our flourishing. That, however, entails a bracketing of the central question of natural law theories in favor a virtue-ethical approach.

Whether Aquinas would approve of such a strategy will depend on how he answers the central question.

AQUINAS'S ANSWER TO THE CENTRAL QUESTION

Whereas virtue ethics centers on human goodness, the concept of natural law refers to God and the central question. In claiming that there is a natural moral law, Aquinas is pointing to how right practical reason expresses God's will and brings us under his direction.

He defines natural law as the rational creature's participation in eternal law.[30] This definition evokes man's condition as a creature made in God's image and likeness (Gen 1:27) and the creator's providential design over creation (*lex aeterna*).

A law consists of the reasoned ordinances which those in charge of a community issue to secure its common good.[31] In this case, God's providential design over creation has the character of a law. Not only is this providential design a reasoned plan, but, through it, God governs creation

---

29. al-Fārābī is said to have written a commentary, no longer extant, on the *Nicomachean Ethics*. In his *Selected Aphorisms* (*Fuṣil muntazaʿa*) he deploys Platonic and Aristotelian teaching on the virtues as the basis for ordering a soul well, the knowledge of which is necessary to order a polity well. Ibn Rushd (Averroes) too wrote a commentary on the *Nicomachean Ethics*.

30. *ST* I-II, q. 91, a. 2, co.

31. *ST* I-II, q. 90, aa. 1–4.

and leads it toward its common good. This law is described as "eternal" to distinguish it from other kinds of law. It receives this name because God, who is immutable, does not devise it at some point in time. Rather, it is an aspect of the eternal God himself.[32]

All creatures participate in this eternal law—that is, they fall under it and its direction—but in irreducibly different ways. A non-rational creature partakes of it by deterministically performing the acts and pursuing the ends to which its nature directs it. A human, on the other hand, does not fall under and follow God's providential design in an utterly deterministic way, but mainly through reasoned action. This way of participating in the eternal law is specific to humans, the only creature in the physical world that is endowed with reason.

Moreover, due to our capacity for practical reasoning and action, we participate not only in the eternal law but also in God's providence and reason. We do so by rationally directing our own actions to their due end and other people to theirs. This more excellent and irreducible mode of partaking of the eternal law—through one's own intellect and reasoning—constitutes a new kind of law: natural law.[33] Calling it a "law" refers to the way in which right practical reasoning is our way of participating in God's eternal law.

For Aquinas, therefore, the notion of natural law adds something to the concepts dealt with in Aristotle's virtue ethics. In fact, the *Summa theologiae* analyzes and endorses those concepts prior to its discussion of natural law. With its section on natural law, it is introducing a new perspective and going beyond the characteristic confines of Aristotelian virtue ethics. Having examined the interior principles of this movement toward the good (will, passions, *habitus*, virtues), the focus of Aristotelian virtue ethics, Aquinas turns his attention to God, the exterior principle.[34]

God moves us to the good by either instructing us through the law or aiding us through grace. Contrary to what we might assume, the "law" in question is not merely the sum of the precepts contained in Sacred Scripture. Rather, Aquinas is claiming that God moves us through each of the complementary varieties of law: his providential design over cre-

---

32. *ST* I-II, q. 91, a. 1.

33. *ST* I-II, q. 91, a. 2, co. et ad 3.

34. *ST* I-II, q. 90, prol. Aquinas deals with man's interior principles in *ST* I-II, qq. 6–89; God, the exterior principle, in qq. 90–114. On the general theme of the second part (*Secunda Pars*) of the *Summa theologiae*, see *ST* I, q. 2, prol., and I-II, q. 1, prol.

ation (*lex aeterna*), our participation in it as rational creatures (*lex naturalis*), the laws which we make to govern our polities (*lex humana*), and, finally, Revelation (*lex divina*), whereby God directs us to our ultimate, supernatural end.[35] Each variety of law is one of the forms in which divine providence directs us to our common good and end. In the case of natural law, God directs individuals providentially through their capacity and exercise of right practical reasoning. Right reason is not opposed to God's will, or above it, but expresses and enacts it.

Nevertheless, the natural law picture of practical reason is not opposed to the virtue-ethical one. For Thomas, the first principle of practical reason, "the good is to be done and pursued; evil avoided", is also the first precept of natural law.[36] Anyone who exercises practical reason is thinking about goods to be pursued and so is already acting under the impulse of natural law, even if such a person is not necessarily acting in accord with it, nor identifies the deliverances of his or her practical reason as a testimony to God's will. Moreover, in Aquinas's analysis, the precepts of natural law are practical reason's dictates to practice the various kinds of virtues.[37] His account of natural law, therefore, is not opposed to the Aristotelian, virtue-ethical conception of practical reason but endorses and supposes it. Rather it expands this conception of practical reason by considering it from a theological perspective.

For Aquinas, therefore, "natural law" is a theological notion. It refers to God. Specifically, it refers to one of the ways in which God is the exterior principle of human action. As such, it needs to be understood against the backdrop of the central question. This question is brought to the attention of Christian theologians mainly by Romans 2:12–16.[38] There Paul teaches that even though the Gentiles have not received the law (Torah), they are aware of it through their conscience and in their heart. As a result, Paul concludes, they will be judged on how they have observed it. Like the Church Fathers, Aquinas adopts the concept of natural law to articulate this teaching of the apostle.

In one regard, though, "natural law" is not a theological notion. The "theological" can be construed narrowly as the domain of truths

---

35. *ST* I-II, q. 90, aa. 1–4.

36. *ST* I-II, q. 94, a. 2, co.

37. *ST* I-II, q. 94, a. 3.

38. In determining whether there is a natural law, he appeals to Rom 2:14: *ST* I-II, q. 91, a. 2, s.c.

that are intrinsically indemonstrable on rational grounds and can only be accessed and accounted for through Revelation. Natural law is not a theological notion in this sense. After all, Romans 2:12–16 claims that the moral demands of the Torah are accessible to reason, independently from Revelation. That does not necessarily mean that their character as a law is ascertainable to reason. However, following Romans 1:19–20, Aquinas believes that we can demonstrate with philosophical arguments that "God" exists, that he has created the universe, and that he is provident.[39] In that case, it is also possible to appreciate the validity of such a metaphysics of creation on rational grounds and recognize, independently from Revelation, that there is a natural law: that the order of moral virtue, namely, right practical reasoning, expresses a divinely established law.[40] This, however, only amounts to a recognition of right practical reason's legal character. It tells us virtually nothing about the content of natural law.

While the recognition of the legal character of right practical reason requires a commitment to theism, Aquinas's own way of working out the content of natural law is essentially that of virtue ethics. The acquired moral virtues constitute the field and content of right practical reason.[41] It is possible to engage in shared rational inquiry into the content of natural law by inquiring into the requirements of human nature and flourishing. It is on these grounds that the content of natural law is accessible to reason.

Generally, though, Christians do not work out all the details of natural law by themselves but rely on Revelation for guidance. Still, revealed moral teaching qualifies as instruction on natural law if and only if it is accessible to reason on its own terms. Otherwise, it would be different in content from natural law.

Now, Aquinas believes that Sacred Scripture does contain a divinely revealed teaching on the content of natural law. Not only that. He argues that all of Scripture's moral teaching belongs to natural law and so is accessible to reason working on its own terms.

---

39. See, *ST* I, qq. 2, 22, 45.

40. Aquinas states quite clearly that God, rather than a human reason, is the legislator behind natural law: *ST* I-II, q. 97, a. 3, co.

41. See *ST* I-II, q. 94, a. 3; I-II, q. 100, aa. 1–2. In the last of these articles, he explicitly identifies the "order of reason" (*ordo rationis*) with the "order of virtue" (*ordo virtutum*).

This is a point which Aquinas makes at the beginning on one of his most detailed discussions of the content of natural law and our discovery of it (*ST* I-II, q. 100, a. 1). Significantly, the passage in question does not belong to the *Summa*'s discussion of natural law (*ST* I-II, q. 94), but to that of the Old Law (the Torah) (I-II, qq. 99–105). Indeed, for Aquinas, the Torah plays an indispensable role in transmitting natural law.

In the article under consideration, Aquinas ponders whether all the moral precepts of the Old Law belong to natural law. He concludes that they do, but only after working out a far-reaching argument on how a sacred text's moral teaching is related to reason.[42]

The biblical record of the Old Law contains three kinds of precept: moral, liturgical (*caeremonialia*), and civil (*iudicialia*) (see Dt 4:13–14; 11:1). Each group regards a different one of the three areas in which the Old Law should direct the chosen people: virtue, worship, and justice, respectively. Moreover, the ceremonial and judicial precepts are grounded in the moral precepts. They provide the necessary specifications on how certain moral precepts should be practiced within the community.[43]

This threefold categorization of the various kinds of precepts contained in the Old Law highlights that Scripture and religion cannot be reduced to morality. There is more to divine law than the moral precepts, more to a sacred text than its moral teaching. There are also norms on how God's people should put morality into practice within its worship and civic life.

Nevertheless, on the authority of Paul (Rom 2:12–16), Aquinas claims that all the moral precepts of the Old Law belong to natural law. If the gentiles do by nature what the Torah requires (Rom 2:14), this can only be the case with the moral, rather than the ceremonial and judicial precepts. Furthermore, Thomas appears to assume that, since Paul does not specify any limits in this regard, all the moral precepts of the Old Law

---

42. In what follows, I am drawing on part of a previously published paper: Dominic Farrell, "Two Visions of Moral Virtue? Aquinas on Moral Virtue in Revelation and Reason," in *The Virtuous Life: Thomas Aquinas on the Theological Nature of the Moral Virtues*, ed. Harm Goris and Henk Schoot (Louvain: Peeters, 2017), 221–43 at 232–43.

43. *ST* I-II, q. 99, aa. 2–5. Nevertheless, the judicial precepts, unlike standard civil law, are revealed and always religious in character. See Johannes Petrus Maria van der Ploeg, "Le traité de saint Thomas de la loi ancienne," in *Lex et Libertas: Freedom and Law according to St. Thomas Aquinas*, ed. Leo Elders and Klaus Hedwig (Vatican City: Libreria Editrice Vaticana, 1987), 185–99 at 189.

must be accessible to the gentiles, without Revelation. In that case, all of them belong to natural law.[44]

This is not the only reason for believing that all the moral precepts of the Old Law are coextensive with natural law. Any moral precept belongs to natural law. Whenever we talk of "moral" precepts or virtues, we are not referring to any behavior whatsoever. Instead, we are referring to rational action: the mores proper to humans. Furthermore, reason is not only the principle but also the standard of human action. Our mores are good when they are in accord with reason, bad when they go against it.[45] Any moral precept contained in Scripture, therefore, indicates a certain kind of act that it is rational and fitting for humans to perform.[46] It may be divinely revealed and promulgated. Even then, it merely commands something that right practical reason, working by its own lights, also requires.[47] On these grounds, Aquinas answers yes to the first part of the central question.

This argument has a further implication. It entails that any revealed moral teaching belongs, by its very nature, to natural law. All revealed moral teaching is accessible to reason and rationally justifiable on grounds external to religion.

This does not mean that all the moral precepts belong to natural law in the same way. Indeed, Aquinas distinguishes three ways in which they belong to it. What distinguishes one way of belonging from another is the degree of reasoning required to infer the moral precept from the naturally (i.e. non-syllogistically) known, common principles of practical reason [or common precepts of natural law] (*ST* I-II, q. 100, a. 1).[48] The proposition expressed in a moral precept is inferable either:

> A. through a minimum of consideration, because it is an obvious entailment of some common principle [e.g., the fourth, fifth and seventh commandments of the Decalogue are obvious entailments of what it means to love one's neighbor or non-malfeasance];

44. *ST* I-II, q. 100, a. 1, s.c.

45. *ST* I-II, q. 100, a. 1, co.

46. *ST* I-II, q. 104, a. 1, co. et ad 2.

47. *Scriptum* IV, d. 1, q. 2, a. 5, q.la 4, co.; IV, d. 2, q. 1, a. 4, q.la 1, ad 2; IV, d. 2, q. 1, a. 4, q.la 3, ad 2; *ST* I-II, q. 100, a. 1; q. 100, a. 11, co. et ad 2; q. 104, a. 1, co.; q. 108, a. 2, co.

48. These common principles are what Aquinas calls the common precepts of natural law. See, *ST* I-II, q. 94, a. 6, co.; I-II, q. 100, a. 3, ad 1. They are the commandments to love God, to love oneself by acting according to reason, and to love one's neighbor. For this classification of the common precepts, see Farrell, *The Ends of the Moral Virtues*, 156–63.

B. through extensive, careful consideration [e.g., "You shall rise up before the hoary head, and honor the face of an old man" Lv 19:32];

C. through divine instruction [e.g., the first and second commandments].

All with use of reason tend to reach A. The wise are usually the only ones who reach B on their own lights and even they normally need the aid of Revelation to reach C. On these grounds, Aquinas claims that A is the only set of moral precepts that belongs to natural law absolutely.[49] These are the only moral precepts which all people, both the imperfect and the perfect, recognize.[50] They are the only ones, therefore, that actually act as principles in the practical reasoning of all. Even so, the moral precepts of both B and C still belong to natural law. They are accessible to reason. True, divine instruction is necessary for those that belong to C. This is because they regard God, whom even the wise have difficulty in understanding.[51] We need divine instruction whenever a truth is not only accessible to natural reason in principle, though not in practice, but also particularly important for our salvation.[52]

For Aquinas, therefore, natural law needs to be supplemented by divine law. It is of vital importance for our salvation that we should know how we should conduct ourselves. We have the natural capacity to figure out how we should act, but very few of us are in the position to do so reliably. In practice, few of us are able to develop this capacity sufficiently and exercise it satisfactorily.[53] God cannot leave us to our own devices when the stakes are so high and the prospects of success so low. We need his instruction. We also need it, if we are to overcome the distortions in practical reasoning that derive from our disordered, sin-induced desires.[54]

It would be mistaken though to reduce divine law to a revealed teaching on the content of natural law. Not only does divine law contain more than moral precepts. It also regards a higher end than that of natural law.

<hr>

49. *ST* I-II, q. 100, a. 1, co.

50. *ST* I-II, q. 91, a. 5, ad 3.

51. Thomas Aquinas, *Liber de veritate catholicae fidei contra errores infidelium seu Summa contra Gentiles* (hereafter, *ScG*), ed. Ceslao Pera, Pierre Marc, and Pietro Caramello, 3 vols. (Turin: Marietti, 1961–67), III, c. 38 [2163]; *ST* I, q. 1, a. 1, co.; II-II, q. 2, a. 4, co.; Thomas Aquinas, *Super Evangelium S. Ioannis Lectura*, ed. Raffaello Cai, 6th ed. (Turin: Marietti, 1972), c. 17, lect. 6 [2265].

52. *ST* I, q. 1, a. 1, co.; I-II, q. 91, a. 4, co.

53. *ST* I, q. 1, a. 1, co.

54. *ST* I-II, q. 98, a. 6, co. et ad 1; I-II, q. 99, a. 2, ad 2; II-II, q. 22, a. 1, ad 1.

Aquinas makes this clear in the first of the four reasons he gives for why we need it: to attain our ultimate end.[55]

> I reply by saying that it was necessary for the direction of human life to have, besides natural law and human law, a divine law. There are four reasons. First, humans are directed to their proper acts, in line with their ultimate end. Were humans ordered solely to an end which was not disproportionate to man's natural capacity, there would be no need for them to have any further direction on the part of reason, above and beyond natural law and the law laid down by man, which is derived from the former. But the end to which man is ordered is eternal beatitude, which, as was explained above [i.e. *ST* I-II, q. 5, a. 5], exceeds the proportions of man's natural capacity. Consequently, it was necessary that, in addition to natural and human law, humans be directed to their end by a divinely issued law as well.

It is not clear from this passage whether we are ordered to beatitude by nature or by some further gratuitous divine decision. Aquinas clarifies his thought on the matter elsewhere. Beatitude is the ultimate end of human nature but unattainable if we are left to our own resources. Although we have been created for it, we do not deserve it and can only reach it if God gratuitously empowers us. At any rate, Aquinas's answer to the second part of the central question is clearly no. He is neither a Pelagian nor Semi-Pelagian but, in this regard at least, an Augustinian.[56]

Nevertheless, his answer to the second part of the central question is problematic. Ostensibly, it deprives natural law of any real importance. After all, what is the point of natural law if, when all is said and done, we need Revelation to know it and make us capable of beatitude?

It is not rendered redundant by divine law because, as Aquinas argues, we have a twofold end and standard of action. Under these conditions, natural law continues to perform two important functions. First, it provides us with the direction necessary for forming well-ordered polities and thereby attaining a certain level of happiness in this life. We can call this its ethico-political function. Second, in bringing us to un-

---

55. *ST* I-II, q. 91, a. 4, co.

56. Early on, Aquinas argues that we can freely choose to orient ourselves toward God, without habitual grace (*Scriptum* II, d. 28, q. un., a. 4), but after studying the decrees of the Council of Orange, he abandons this view, insisting instead that God moves us to make said choice through the infusion of grace (*ST* I-II, q. 113, a. 7, co.). See Henri Bouillard, *Conversion et grâce chez Saint Thomas d'Aquin: étude historique* (Paris: Editions Aubier-Montaigne, 1944).

derstand the order of the acquired moral virtues, it provides us with the framework we need to understand the moral teaching of Scripture.[57] We can call this its religious function.

Let us assume, with Aquinas, that our ultimate end is supernatural. In this case, we need to explain how we are empowered to attain it. Thomas's theological explanation can be summed up as follows. Through the grace that Christ has merited for us, the individual partakes of the divine nature and, as a result, the will is filled with charity: love for God insofar as he gives us a share in his blessed life. Under these conditions, we are acting according to God's direction and standards, rather than those of mere reason.[58] Furthermore, grace and charity bring other virtues with them. Charity orients all our desires and choices toward God. It does so through the moral virtues. However, these are God-directed moral virtues and have their source in grace and charity rather than our natural capacity for practical reasoning. They are divinely infused rather than acquired through our own exertions.[59]

What I have just described is a specifically Christian anthropology. In the *Secunda Pars* of the *Summa theologiae*, Aquinas is attempting to articulate such a theological anthropology, rather than a narrowly construed natural law ethics.[60] He still needs to address the central question, though. To do so, he must account for the status of the moral virtues of the ungraced.[61]

57. Arguably, it has a third function: that of disposing us toward grace. I shall skip this function since I do not believe that it is relevant to the theme of this essay. On Aquinas's nuanced views of how the acquired moral virtues dispose us toward grace, see *Scriptum* II, d. 28, q. un., a. 1, ad 5; *ST* I-II, q. 68, a. 8, ad 2; *ST* I-II, q. 112, a. 2, ad 2; I-II, q. 113, a. 7, co.

58. Aquinas describes the twofold rule in various ways: *ST* I-II, q. 21, a. 1, co. et *ST* I-II, q. 71, a. 6, co. [reason and eternal law]; I-II, q. 95, a. 3, co. [natural law and divine law]; II-II, q. 23, a. 3 et 6, co. [reason and God].

59. *ST* I-II, q. 64, a. 4; I-II, q. 65, aa. 3–4.

60. Various Thomists have deployed his account of natural law to address issues of moral, legal, and political philosophy, sometimes bracketing the related theological issues. In stressing the theological character of the *Summa*'s treatment of natural law, I am not taking issue with this approach. It is consistent with the ethico-political function that Aquinas ascribes to natural law. Nevertheless, Aquinas's views on natural law would be misrepresented if, in taking this approach, one brackets his claims about: the supernatural character of the end we naturally desire; our need of divine law, both to know natural law in practice and to attain our ultimate end. Aquinas gives philosophically articulable arguments for these claims. Bracketing these claims as theological ones makes reason appear capable of achieving more than Aquinas believes it can, even on philosophical grounds.

61. *ST* I-II, q. 65, a. 2; II-II, q. 23, a. 7.

Here Aristotle's distinction between perfect and imperfect happiness proves useful. Aristotle argues that perfect happiness consists in a life centered on the most perfect of the virtues, wisdom; imperfect happiness, in dedication to the practice of the moral virtues.[62] Thomas believes that this is right if we are dealing with the restricted scope of Aristotle's ethics, which is concerned with the ultimate end attainable in this life.[63] For the Christian theologian, however, perfect happiness consists in beatitude. Thomas, therefore, believes that Aristotle's classification of the degrees of happiness needs to be overhauled. Aristotle is right to distinguish between perfect and imperfect happiness when discussing the happiness attainable in this life through our own exertions. It is simply that the two degrees of happiness which Aristotle identifies are, ultimately, both imperfect. Although each constitutes an authentic form of happiness, neither is unqualifiedly our ultimate end. On this basis, Aquinas can claim that we have a twofold end and good.[64] On the one hand, there is our ultimate end, beatitude, which we attain through divine law, charity, and the infused moral virtues. On the other hand, there is the happiness which, in principle, we can attain in this life and through our own, ungraced exertions: through natural law, human law, and the acquired moral and intellectual virtues.

Thomas brings this out in one of his explanations of the infused moral virtues. To distinguish these from the acquired moral virtues, he extends a point made in Aristotle's *Politics.* A citizen of polity P requires the kind of virtue that is suited to the constitution of P.[65] We should distinguish infused moral virtues from acquired ones, therefore, if and only if each is suited to a different polity and we can belong simultaneously to each community. Aquinas argues that both conditions can be satis-

62. Aristotle, *Ethica Nicomachea*, ed. Ingram Bywater (Oxford: Clarendon Press, 1963), X.7.1177a12–18.

63. Thomas Aquinas, *Sententia libri Ethicorum* (hereafter, *SLE*), Editio Leonina, vol. 47, ed. René-Antoine Gauthier (Rome: Commissio Leonina, 1969), I, lect. 2, lin. 199–202; *ScG* III, c. 44 [2216].

64. On Thomas's construal of this twofold happiness, see, for example, *Scriptum* IV, d. 48, q. 1, a. 2, q.la 1, co.; *ST* I-II, q. 3, a. 6, co.; I-II, q. 4, a. 5, co.; I-II, q. 62, a. 1, co.; II-II, q. 186, a. 3, ad 4. On the twofold end, *Scriptum* II, d. 41, q. 1, a. 1, co.; Thomas Aquinas, *Quaestiones disputatae de veritate* (hereafter, *De veritate*), Editio Leonina, vol. 22, ed. Antoine Dondaine (Rome: Editori di San Tommaso, 1970), q. 14, a. 2, co.; *ST* I, q. 23, a. 1, co. On his distinction between a twofold good, see, for example, *ST* II-II, q. 11, a. 4, co.; II-II, q. 26, a. 3, co.; *De veritate* q. 24, a. 14, co.

65. Aristotle, *Politica* III, 4, 1276b29–34.

fied. The acquired moral virtues are suited to life in political society and the happiness attainable in this life. The just, on the other hand, are fellow citizens of the saints and members of God's household (Eph 2:19). In this life, therefore, the just possess infused moral virtues. These empower them to behave as good citizens of God's kingdom, just as the acquired moral virtues dispose us to behave as good citizens of a state.[66]

Aquinas specifies that the imperfect happiness attainable by acting in accord with reason is the proximate rather than the ultimate end of human life.[67] He thereby throws into relief a first function of natural law: its status as the ethico-political standard. Considered as right practical reason, natural law directs us toward our proximate end, the happiness attainable in this life, within political society. This degree of happiness consists in the acquired virtues.[68] Accordingly, the content of natural law is worked out, therefore, through virtue-ethical inquiry.

However, natural law performs a further function within Aquinas's theological anthropology. This is because, as a rule, the moral precepts of Scripture enjoin infused moral virtue.

In Aquinas's view, the moral precepts of Scripture are mainly directed toward instructing us on how to put grace into action through the works of the virtues. In this case, they exhort and command the practice of those moral virtues that are proper to the graced: the infused ones.[69] How, though, can Aquinas still claim that they belong to natural law?

A solution to this antinomy can be gleaned from his account of how an infused moral virtue differs in kind from its acquired counterpart.

As already noted, each kind of moral virtue is directed to a different end. As a result, the object of each is also formally distinct. Each is the counterpart of the other because the two have the same "matter" or object: a specific kind of good. Each moral virtue makes us desire that good, amid varying circumstances, according to a measure (*modus*) that

66. *ST* I-II, q. 63, a. 4, co.; Thomas Aquinas, *Quaestio disputata de virtutibus in communi*, in *Quaestiones disputatae*, ed. Egidio Odetto, 2 vols., 10th ed. (Turin: Marietti, 1965), 707–51, a. 9, co. Both passages cite Aristotle, *Politica*, ed. William David Ross (Oxford: Clarendon Press, 1957), III, 4, 1276b29–34: the former to distinguish between the two kinds of polity; the latter, to recall that the virtue of a good citizen is not identical to that of the good person. Both passages also cite Eph 2:19.

67. Aquinas describes the life according to reason (*bonum rationis*) as the proximate end of human life. *Scriptum* III, d. 33, q. 2, a. 3, co. See also *ST* II-II, q. 23, a. 7, co.

68. *SLE* X, lect. 12, lin. 1–16; *Quaestio disputata de virtutibus in communi* a. 9, ad 6.

69. *ST* I-II, q. 100, a. 12, co.

is right from reason's standpoint. For example, the moral virtue called "temperance" prompts our sensitive appetency (*concupiscentia*) to respond in the right and reasonable measure when it comes to the pleasures of touch. Now, when we act reasonably, according to our own lights, acquired temperance will result. For example, we will eat with moderation to be healthy and behave rationally. In this case, we take our own reason, and so natural law, as the rule of our action. However, should we, in exercising practical reason, take divine law as our rule, we are acting with infused temperance. We will start eating moderately, maybe even fasting, to grow in grace. What is worth noting here is that an infused moral virtue has an acquired counterpart which regards the same matter. At the same time, each has a formally distinct object. How so? In each case, a different rule of action (reason or God, natural law or divine law) is regulating our desire of that matter and does so for the sake of a different overall end (natural or supernatural happiness).[70]

So, while a moral precept of the Bible is mainly a commandment to practice some infused moral virtue, it still belongs to natural law. It belongs to it materially. It is directed toward some matter or action which the infused virtue, whose practice it commands, shares with its acquired counterpart. It thereby supposes and implicitly enjoins the correlative natural law precept on the corresponding acquired moral virtue. This is what Aquinas means, I propose, when he claims that it belongs to natural law, is comprehensible to reason, and is derived from the principles of practical reason.[71] The moral teaching of Scripture does not supplant but supposes natural reason's understanding of the moral virtues, while broadening its horizon.

This point can be better understood by comparing it to Aquinas's position on beatitude. In his view, it can be shown philosophically both that beatitude is our ultimate end and that it cannot be attained by acting according to mere reason.[72] Beatitude is a reality that is comprehensible

70. *ST* I-II, q. 63, a. 4, co.

71. *ST* I-II, q. 100, a. 1.

72. In *ST* I-II, q. 3, a. 8, Aquinas argues that beatitude consists in beholding God as God really is. This theological argument is articulated in philosophical terms. He thereby commits himself to the view that the nature of beatitude is comprehensible to natural reason. However, by providing another argument, also articulated in philosophical terms, on how we cannot attain beatitude through our own natural exertions, he is also committed to the view that it is unattainable to natural reason (*ST* I-II, q. 5, a. 5).

to reason yet outside the range of what one can achieve by merely acting in according with reason. Moreover, it is comprehensible because it constitutes a specific conception of happiness, a broader notion that finds application in ungraced human life. Now Scripture's moral teaching is also comprehensible from the standpoint of ungraced reason. Unlike the domain of the acquired moral virtues, it is not immediately comprehensible to ungraced reason. It is nonetheless comprehensible because it builds upon and broadens our understanding of acquired moral virtue. It thereby belongs to natural law. At the same time, it enjoins that which is unattainable through action that accords with reason alone. Instead, it enjoins the infused moral virtues.

The preceding point can be expressed as follows.

> If it is virtuous to Φ_1 for the sake of E_1, our proximate, naturally attainable end, then, should God empower us to attain E_2, our ultimate though supernatural end, it would be virtuous to Φ_2 for the sake of E_2.

In this proposition, Φ_1 stands for the kind of act proper to some acquired moral virtue; Φ_2, for the kind of act proper to its infused counterpart; Φ, for their common matter or object. This proposition illustrates how divine law's commands to practice the infused moral virtues (Φ_2) are comprehensible to reason, and so belong to natural law, even when they make moral demands that go beyond what one can achieve by acting according to natural reason and natural law.

Aquinas attributes, then, not only an ethico-political function to natural law but a religious one too. He thereby makes an important contribution to medieval debates on natural law. Each function corresponds to a different role that virtue-ethical reflection plays and how working out natural law is really a matter of working out which kinds of act are virtuous.

On the one hand, virtue-ethical reflection constitutes the grounds on which moral and political debates can be conducted. It also constitutes the grounds on which members of other religious traditions have reason to accept or challenge Aquinas's account of natural law. Of course, there is a conceptual difference between natural law and virtue ethics, even though they are coextensive with one another. Natural law, as Aquinas presents it, is virtue ethics viewed through the lens of the metaphysics of creation. To put it another way, it amounts to a theonomous account of practical reason and virtue.

Virtue-ethical reflection or natural law also has a religious function. It is the basis of our understanding of revealed moral teaching. An action or disposition is morally good if and only if it is in accord with reason. Consequently, any revealed moral commandments must belong to natural law. This does not mean that divine law can be reduced to natural law. The former does not consist of moral teaching alone but also contains legislation on worship and community life. Moreover, it expands upon natural law in that its moral precepts enjoin acts of infused moral virtue. Its moral commandments nonetheless belong to natural law since they also enjoin the correlative acquired moral virtues, the object of the precepts of natural law. Indeed, it is only by doing so that they are only intelligible. By stressing the religious function of natural law, therefore, Aquinas articulates an argument against fideism about morality, on the one hand, and a moderate ethical rationalism, on the other. Not only does he argue that we rely on divine law, in practice though not in principle, to know natural law but he also explains how any revealed moral teaching must belong to natural law and be comprehensible to reason—even if it directs us to an end and virtues that we cannot attain through our own exertions, but only through God's loving grace.

Part II ∽ Scholastic Theories of Natural Law

5 ∞ *Lex naturae*, *lex naturalis*, and *ius naturale* in Saint Bonaventure

The terms "law of nature," "natural laws," and "natural right" figure in the works of Bonaventure.[1] To understand how he uses these terms, a

My thanks to Carlo Fantappiè and Antonia Fiori, for their indications on medieval canon law, and to Matteo Valdarchi, who helped draft the text.

1. Odon Lottin's monumental work remains an indispensable reference point on the subject. See Odon Lottin, *Psychologie et morale aux XIIᵉ et XIIIᵉ siècles*, 5 vols. (Louvain: Abbaye de Mont César, 1942–59). Lottin addresses various aspects of Bonaventure's thought and their historical background: free will (1:174–82); *ignorantia iuris* (3:86–88); synderesis and the distinction between it and conscience (2:101–349), along with Bonaventure's thought on the matter (2:203–10). The work offers an effective and wide survey of natural law theory in general. At one point, though, it provides a succinct overview (2:9–100). Significantly, it locates the birth of the treatise on natural law in the Franciscan milieu (2:52–58) and broaches the Franciscan school of Paris and Bonaventure (2:86–90). For a recent historiographical study that offers a panoramic view of medieval thought on natural law, see Élisabeth Dufourcq, *L'invention de la loi naturelle. Des itinéraires grecs, latins, juifs, chrétiens et musulmans* (Montrouge: Bayard, 2012). For the section on Bonaventure, see Dufourcq, 372–401. Although this work has the merit of offering a synoptic view on the connection between the three great medieval traditions and their Greek roots, it is very generic and, when it comes to the subject of Bonaventure, superficial and inaccurate. See also Antonio Di Salvatore, "La legge naturale in S. Bonaventura da Bagnoregio" (Doctoral Dissertation Pontificia Universitas Lateranensis, 2000). This doctoral dissertation offers a succinct overview (pp. 34–36) of the few studies on Bonaventure's thought on natural law that have been published since Lottin's work. It studies four properties that Bonaventure attributes to natural law: immutability, universality, innateness, and knowability (pp. 113–40). However, it treats "natural law" and "natural right" as synonymous (p. 39) and does not adopt a lexicographical approach.

See also Gianfranco Maglio, "Il diritto e la legge naturale in Bonaventura da Bagnoregio," in *L'uomo nel pensiero di Bonaventura da Bagnoregio*, ed. Irene Zavattero (Rome: Aracne, 2019), 233–69. There, Maglio delves into the theological foundation of conscience and synderesis. As for the Franciscan School of Paris, see Riccardo Saccenti, "'Impressio legis aeternae.' La legge naturale nel trattato *De legibus* di Giovanni de La Rochelle," in *Rappresentazioni della natura*

preliminary clarification of the concept of nature is in order.[2] This can be done by drawing up a judicious inventory of the various uses and senses that "nature" has in Bonaventure's writings, and then going on to reconstruct the meaning of the syntagmata *lex naturae, lex naturalis* (in relation to *lex aeterna*), and *ius naturale*.[3] Only then will it be possible to appreciate Bonaventure's highly original, relevant, yet underrated conception of the circular process by which positive norms are produced from natural right and traced back to it.

NATURA

In Bonaventure's writings, the term "nature" (*natura*) has the following meanings. In the most general sense, also applicable to the divine, it indicates that which is communicable, namely, that which is either common or can be made so, as opposed to that which is one's own (*proprium*).[4]

---

nel Medioevo, ed. Giovanni Catapano and Onorato Grassi (Florence: SISMEL, 2019); and Lydia Schumacher, *Early Franciscan Theology: Between Authority and Innovation* (Cambridge: Cambridge University Press, 2019).

2. See Andrea Di Maio, *Il vocabolario bonaventuriano per la natura* (Roma: Edizioni Miscellanea Francescana, 1988), 301–56; Andrea Di Maio, *La dottrina bonaventuriana sulla natura* (Roma: Miscellanea francescana, 1989), 335–92; Andrea Di Maio, *La concezione Bonaventuriana della Natura quale potenziale oggetto di comunicazione* (Roma: Miscellanea francescana, 1990), 61–116.

3. All Latin texts are taken from the electronic database *Library of Latin Texts, Series A e B*, offered by Brepols (last consulted in March 2019). The works of Bonaventure surveyed there are taken from Bonaventure, *Opera omnia*, 11 vols. (Florence: Ex Typographia Collegii S. Bonaventurae, 1882–1902), with the exception of: Bonaventure, *Collationes in Hexaëmeron et Bonaventuriana quaedam selecta*, ed. Ferdinand M. Delorme, Bibliotheca Franciscana scholastica medii aevi, vol. 8 (Florence: Ex Typographia Collegii S. Bonaventurae, 1934); Bonaventure, *Sermones dominicales*, ed. Jacques Guy Bougerol, Bibliotheca Franciscana scholastica medii aevi, vol. 27 (Grottaferrata: Collegio S. Bonaventura Padri Editori di Quaracchi, 1977); Bonaventure, *Sermons "de diversis,"* 2 vols., ed. Jacques-Guy Bougerol (Paris: Éd. franciscaines, 1993). The intermediate punctuation, missing in the electronic edition, is that of the printed editions. The lemmata under consideration have been italicized. In these cases, the italics are mine.

The following abbreviations will be used for Bonaventure's works: *Brev* (*Breviloquium*); *Don* (*De donis*); *Hex* (*In Hexaëmeron*, ed. Quaracchi); *HexD* (*In Hexaëmeron*, ed. Delorme); *Itin* (*Itinerarium mentis in Deum*); *LegMa* (*Legenda maior sancti Francisci*); *MyTrin* (*Quaestiones disputatae Mysterio Trinitatis*); *PerfEv* (*Quaestiones disputatae de perfectione evangelica*); *Red* (*De reductione artium ad theologiam*); *ScienChr* (*Quaestiones disputatae de scientia Christi*); *Sent* (*In Sententiarum libros*); *SermDi* (*Sermones de diuersis*); *SermDo* (*Sermones Dominicales*); *SermTe* (*Sermones de tempore*); *TriQ* (*De tribus quaestionibus*).

4. Richard of St Victor also construes "nature" in this way. In his view, nature is communicable whereas a person is not. The first and most general meaning of "nature," therefore, is that

1. In a determinate sense ("*haec* natura" as opposed to "*illa natura*"), it indicates the kind of thing that something is (*sic esse*), according to the three fundamental levels of being: the *natura divina* (*supra*), the *natura spiritualis* (*intra*), and the *natura corporea* (*extra*). The last of these is further distinguished into various species, whereas *natura humana* is a fusion of spiritual and bodily natures. There are also natures which are "natured" (*naturatae*), namely, finite. In this case, "nature" is used in a constitutive (essence), concretive (individuals in general), or collective (genera and species) sense.[5]

2. In a broad global sense, it indicates whatever God produces: the created world (collective sense) or simply any creature (constitutive or concrete sense). In a narrower global sense, it refers solely to the sensible world or macrocosm.

3. In a modal sense, where "natural" (*naturalis*) is the contrary of "voluntary" (*voluntarius*), and "in the manner of nature" (*ad modum naturae*) the contrary of "in the manner of the will" (*ad modum voluntatis*), it indicates communication by duplication in opposition to communication by way of unification. Generation, which duplicates the begetter's nature in the begotten, is a case of the former; friendship, which unifies wills, an example of the latter.

4. In the context of salvation history (here *naturalis* and *innatus* are opposed to *acquisitus, infusus,* and *supernaturalis*), it indicates that which is innate as opposed to an acquired result, the reception of a gift, or the empowerment, consequent upon grace, to act at a level higher than that of one's own nature.

5. In a temporal sense, it designates man's original condition, as opposed to the successive states of guilt (*culpa*) and toil (*industria*), grace (*gratia*) and glory (*gloria*).[6]

---

which is *ontologically communicable*. As such, "nature" is opposed to "a thing" (*res*), an ontologically unrepeatable individual, and, in particular, to "a person" (*persona*).

5. As with many abstract lemmata in "-itat-" (e.g. *humanitas*), the lemma "natura" signifies: a thing's constitutive identity (in an intentional sense and as a quasi-synonym of *essentia*, *Sent* III, d. 5, a. 2, q. 2, ad s.c. 4; *Hex* 8, 9); a concrete reality, taken in a general sense (not this or that); a collective group (in an extensional sense and as a synonym of genus or species).

6. Sometimes *natura* is used to indicate creation in its entirety, namely, nature in a global sense, whether it be all creatures or only physical ones. At other times, it is a synonym of *mundus* (Hex 10, 7). Bodily nature, taken globally, coincides with the microcosm, which is sometimes simply called natura.

Normally, we represent things linguistically with a *stare pro aliquo* locution. Drawing on certain remarks of Bonaventure, we can make the following generalization: the concept of "nature" designates that to which common names refer.[7] The concept of "individual" or "person" designates that to which proper names refer.

However, if nature is the concept to which a common name refers, the term "nature" indicates a second-order reflection on nature.

LEX NATURAE

Bonaventure associates the compound noun "law of nature" (*lex naturae*) with two others, "the law of Scripture" (*lex Scripturae*) and "the law of grace" (*lex gratiae*), to designate three periods of history. The first period extends from Adam to Moses; the second, from Moses to Jesus; the third, from Jesus to the end of the world.

The main source for this threefold classification of laws is Romans 1–2. There, Paul teaches that what the Mosaic Law requires of Jews is also required of the Gentiles, albeit analogously and through an inner law, namely, through reason and conscience. Nevertheless, neither Jew nor Gentile is justified by observing these respective laws. It is only through grace that they are *justified*.

Now, like "lecture," *lex* originally signifies a teaching rather than a rule. In this vein, Bonaventure plays on the words of Psalm 119 [118]:105–6 and speaks of the law as a light (*lex lux*). Each of the three fundamental divine laws corresponds, therefore, to one of the three stages in which God progressively manifests himself to humankind. First, there is the original manifestation of the Creator in the world. Then, there is the initial revelation of the one true God in the Old Testament. Finally, there is the full revelation of the Holy Trinity in the New Testament.

As a manifestation of God, each of these laws is also a manifestation of what we humans can and should become. Each one expresses both ontological and ethical normativity.

Furthermore, grace does not suppress nature but perfects it. Consequently, the law of grace does not suppress either the law of nature or

7. The name *Deus* takes on a different sense in each of the following two propositions: "Deus est Trinitas"; "Deus generat." Bonaventure specifies that: in the former, it designates the divine nature; in the latter, a divine person. See *Sent* I, d. 29, a. 1, q. 2, co.

the written law. Rather, it clarifies the law of nature and renders it more explicit. It also brings the written law to completion and only abrogates those contingent precepts that were meant for the preceding stage of salvation history.

Hence, on various occasions, Bonaventure uses the Exodus of Israel as a metaphor to indicate that, just as the chosen people was forbidden from returning to Egypt, so too there is a sequential progression from one law to the next. An intermediate law may not be unqualifiedly good. Rather, it is only good if, by following it, one advances toward its true end; bad, if, in following it, one moves away from its true end. Bigamy, for instance, is permitted during the age of the patriarchs, but forbidden from Moses on.

Each law—the natural, the written, and that of the New Testament— is a law in the proper and yet most general sense. Within each we find many single laws, whether moral or positive. Nevertheless, the "law of nature" has a special place in the distinction that Bonaventure draws between the three successive addressees of divine Revelation: philosophers, Jews, and Christians.

Under the "law of nature," namely, the order of creation, the philosophers seek wisdom. Like the patriarchs and the prophets, they perceive the truths that the created order contains. Nevertheless, they do not have access to the uncreated Word. In fact, despite recognizing the divine essence as the principle, the mean, and the end of all things, the philosopher "does not know this as the Father, Son, and Holy Spirit." The magi, on the other hand, are guided by the light of the uncreated Word and come to adore the Incarnate Word.[8] The law of nature, therefore, prepares the gentiles for the advent of the "law of grace or law of the New Testament" in a manner analogous to how the "written or Old Testament law" prepares the Jews.

In Bonaventure, "law" (*lex*) also has the same generic meaning as "religion," in the modern sense of the term. For example, he refers to Islam as the *lex Mahumeti*.[9] For this reason, the "philosophy" of the gentiles living in antiquity and the Exodus of Israel are both quests for a divine

---

8. Cf *Hex* 4, 1; 1, 14; 3, 4; 1, 12–13. On the Magi, *De modo inveniendi Christum* 3.

9. *LegMa* 9, 8. Francis asked the Sultan to submit him to trial by fire to convince him "to renounce the law of Mohammed on account of faith in Christ" (*propter fidem Christi legem Mahumeti dimittere*).

law and wisdom. The Christians bring these searches to completion. In his view, they therefore are both the true philosophers, insofar as they are "lovers of wisdom" (*amatores sapientiae*), and the true Israelites.[10]

LEX NATURALIS/LEGES NATURALES

From the lex naturae, through the dictamen naturae, to the lex naturalis

Through creation, the eternal law is grafted naturally (*naturaliter inserta*) onto the human heart. It is thereby innate.[11] Any human can know it as a natural law (*lex naturalis*) through a natural dictate (*dictamen naturale*).[12] We access it through conscience and synderesis.[13] To use an appropriation (*appropriate*), synderesis, conscience, and natural law differ from one another as do a power or faculty, its *habitus*, and its object, respectively.[14]

Indeed, natural law is understood in two ways. On the one hand, it is a *habitus* of the soul. As such, it has both an intellective and an affective component. The former consists in understanding right, wrong, and how they differ; the latter prompts one to pursue the good and avoid evil. In second place, "natural law" designates an object. "Natural law is called the collection of precepts of natural right and as such names the object of synderesis and conscience: that of the former, insofar as it dictates it; that of the latter, insofar as it inclines one towards it."[15]

In calling natural law a *collectio* of precepts, Bonaventure does not mean that it is a recompilation of precepts, made after the fact. Rather, as will become clear, he is indicating that the one natural law is articulated

---

10. Cf *Itin* 1, 9.

11. *HexD* 1, 2, 18.

12. *Brev* 6, 4.

13. The ups and downs of the term "synderesis" are well known: see Lottin, *Psychologie et Morale*, 2:101–249. The concept results from a clumsy transliteration of the Greek term *syneidesis* and was passed on in the texts alongside its Latin translation, *conscientia*. The scholastics were puzzled by this and dedicated themselves to explaining how one term should be distinguished from the other. This shows how an error of transmission can stimulate the development of a doctrine.

14. *Sent* II, d. 39, a. 2, q. 1, co. Under a different appropriation: synderesis regards good and bad in general; conscience, good and bad in particular; both, the moral law.

15. "*Lex naturalis* vocatur collectio praeceptorum *iuris naturalis*; et sic nominat obiectum synderesis et conscientiae, unius sicut dictantis, et alterius sicut inclinantis." *Sent* II, d. 39, a. 2, q. 1, co.

into an ordered series of precepts. For this reason, ignorance of the law (*ignorantia iuris*) is only blameless whenever one is afflicted by invincible ignorance or one's reason is impeded through no prior fault (infants and the non compos mentis). The right is rooted in reason. Similarly, only those who have acted with due diligence are not to blame for their ignorance of a relevant fact (*ignorantia facti*).[16]

All morality, therefore, insofar as it is dictated by reason, is rooted in the natural law. However, the moral laws that are stated explicitly in Scripture, namely, in the written law and the evangelical law, are designated globally with the syntagma "divine right" (*ius divinum*). The fundamental role of divine right is to subordinate every affect to God.[17] It branches out into the two tables of the Decalogue.[18] The first is dedicated to love of God; the second, to love of neighbor. Both are brought together, though, in Christ, "who is our God and our neighbor."[19]

Nevertheless, is the evangelical law merely a restatement of natural law? Bonaventure does not think so. It is rooted in natural law, but also perfects it and accomplishes a reparation for sin. In this sense, even though the evangelical counsels of humility, poverty, chastity, and obedience are rooted in the law of nature, they take on a fuller, Christological import within the life of Christian perfection.[20]

Natural right, then, comes from God but does not fully express or account for divine right. For example, whereas natural right requires mercy, divine right demands piety (*pietas*). Mercy, understood as compassion, is an attitude that is suited to our nature and is founded upon the bond that we share with fellow members of our species. Piety, on the other, is an attitude that is founded upon our relation to God and, insofar as they are creatures made in his image, to our fellow humans.[21]

---

16. Bonaventure argues that an *ignorantia iuris* and an *ignorantia facti* attenuates the responsibility of Adam and Eve for their sin in paradise; that of Lot for his sin of incest. However, it does not eliminate it altogether. See Lottin, *Psychologie et Morale*, 3:86–88; *Sent* II, d. 22, a. 2, q. 1, ad 1–2; *Sent* II, d. 22, a. 2, q. 3 co.

17. "Dictat enim ius divinum, quod omnis appetitus debet esse Deo subiectus." *Sent* III, d. 17, a. 2, q. 3, co. "Ille enim recte vivit qui dirigitur secundum regulas iuris divini." *Red* 24.

18. *Brev* 5, 9.

19. *Itin* 4, 5.

20. *PerfEv* q. 4, a. 1, co.

21. "Differt etiam, quia misericordia conformatur dictamini iuris naturalis et secundum regulam prudentiae; pietas vero conformatur suasioni iuris divini, et hoc secundum regulam doni scientiae." *Sent* III, d. 35, a. un., q. 6, co.

From the lex naturalis to leges aeternae and leges naturales

While there is just one divine law, there are various "precepts of the law." These manifest divine law, depending on which of the three kinds of law they belong to: that of nature, the written, or the evangelical.[22] The law of nature, however, governs not only the patriarchs and the ancient philosophers. It continues to constitute the foundation of what is normally considered *natural law*, which is studied in turn by philosophy and the theology of creation. It also constitutes the foundation of the various *laws of nature*, which can be taken in an ontological, epistemological, or moral sense. God "inserts" these laws of nature into any nature that he creates (*leges naturae inditae*). Furthermore, in working our redemption and sanctification, God perfects but does not suppress them.[23] As Bonaventure notes, "The eternal law commands that the natural order be observed, not disturbed."[24] Finally, all positive laws flow from natural law, in the moral sense of the term. They do so as its outgrowth (*pullulatio*).[25]

Anticipating Kant, Bonaventure stresses that any law is eternal in character. In his view, a law is that which does not pass. It is for this very reason that the five books of Moses and the four Gospels of Christ are called a *lex*.[26]

How, then, is the eternal law related to natural law?

Bonaventure illustrates how they are related in his explanation of the dynamism of human knowledge. On the one hand, there are empirically known facts. These are only valid within time. We also know certain truths that are eternal and supra-temporal, such as the laws of the nature that science studies. This makes recourse to "higher reason" (*ratio superior*) necessary. Higher reason uses that which inheres naturally in the soul to lead empirical knowledge back to the eternal laws.[27]

---

22. *Brev* 5, 9; *Brev* prologus 2; *Itin* 4, 6.

23. "Rursus quoniam deus sic reformat quod *leges naturae inditas* non infirmat, ideo sic hanc gratiam tribuit libero arbitrio ut tamen ipsum non cogat sed eius consensus liber maneat." *Brev* 5, 3.

24. "*Lex aeterna* ordinem *naturalem* observari iubet, non perturbari." *SermDi* II, 51.3. Preaching on the assumption of Mary, Bonaventure asks rhetorically whether it is *contra iura* that a child venerate its mother. He concludes that it is not.

25. *HexD* 1, 2, 18.

26. "Scriptura [...] describit aeterna, quae sunt leges et Evangelia; in Psalmo: Praeceptum posuit Dominus, quod non praeteribit." *Hex* 13, 17.

27. "Ratio superior dicitur in quantum conuertitur ad *leges aeternas* per prius et *naturaliter*

Hence, this higher part of human reason judges according to a three-fold light: the higher one of the eternal laws, its own, and that which comes from lower realities.[28]

Bonaventure clarifies the Augustinian distinction between higher and lower reason by applying to it the Aristotelian notions of power, disposition, and weakness (*debilitas*) of will. He specifies that the higher and the inferior parts of reason are not powers but two different uses of reason, each with its own role and disposition. At times, reason bears on realities higher than itself, as when it contemplates the eternal laws, the immutability of both divine virtue and God's equity. It is thereby strengthened in the good. However, when it bears on realities lower than itself, it is dragged down and weakened to some extent.[29]

On the other hand, the condition of possibility for our defectible free choice is the gap which exists between our perception of the eternal law (or eternal laws) and the aeviternal or temporal dimension of the subject. Angels and humans are aeviternal subjects. Consequently, it is possible for an angel to make an irreversible decision, whereas the moral situation of humans is set irreversibly at their death. We humans, on the other hand, are also temporal. For this reason, it is always possible for us to reverse our decisions during this life. The moral order is founded, so to speak, on the axiological or ontological order: wherever there is free choice, it must mirror the ontological order exactly.[30]

---

inest animae cognitio aeternalium quam temporalium ergo impossibile est quod aliquid ab ipsa cognoscatur certitudinaliter nisi ab illis aeternis rationibus adiuuetur." *ScienChr* q. 4, arg. 27.

Although it is only an *argumentum* of the dispute, Bonaventure agrees with this step: "ratio superior dicitur, in quantum legibus aeternis intendit." *Sent* II, d. 24, pars 2, a. 1, q. 1, arg. 4.

28. "Ratio superior non solum habet iudicare secundum *leges aeternas*, sed etiam habet iudicare secundum *lumen proprium*, et secundum *lumen sibi ab inferiori acquisitum*." *Sent* II, d. 24, pars 2, a. 1, q. 1, co.

Here, Bonaventure denies that the *ratio superior* coincides *simpliciter* with synderesis. If it did, it would be flawless. When it comes to the relation between the higher portion of reason and synderesis, some hold that they are one and the same and so that former is, in and of itself, always right and strong, unless it weakens and buckles under the lower portion. Bonaventure, however, objects that synderesis designates a natural power that is always inclined toward the good, whereas our higher reason also contains free choice. Second, he claims that it is both against reason and contrary to experience (*contra experimentum*) to claim that sin is born in our lower reason alone. This is because "higher reason judges not only according to eternal laws, but also according to its own light, and the light it acquires for itself from lower reason" (*Sent* II, d. 24, pars 2, a. 1, q. 1, co.).

29. *Sent* II, d. 24, pars 1, a. 2, q. 2, co.

30. *Brev* 3, 8.

Following Anselm, Bonaventure argues that recourse to the eternal laws allows us to understand truth and goodness better in terms of rightness. The intellect is right whenever it is aligned with the eternal laws and mirrors them. Truth and goodness differ from cognitive and moral error in the same way as a straight line does from a slanted one.[31]

In fact, since the soul perceives eternal laws, we can say that a sinner punishes himself. However, he does so with God-given authority and so it can be said that God punishes him.[32]

This account of the relation between natural law and the eternal law is founded upon exemplarism: the thesis that the archetype of all creatures is found in God.

God is the "cause of causes" in various ways. As creator, he is art. As provident governor, he is our leader. As teacher, he is our light. As judge, he is the right (*ius*).[33] All these functions belong to him insofar as he is the exemplar of all things: of the natural sphere first, then the rational, and finally the moral. Moreover, for Bonaventure, God is *ius per se iudicans*. He is the book of judgment in which all the eternal laws are written. This book, however, has been copied onto one's own conscience so that it too becomes a book in which all the eternal laws are written (*In illo libro scribuntur omnes leges aeternae*).[34] This explains, then, how the laws of being, of a thing's operations, of intention, and moral action are immutable and derived from the divine exemplar. To put it in modern terms, Bonaventure develops a variety of exemplarism that harmonises both transcendental autonomy and transcendent heteronomy in an archeonomy.

We are now in a position to further clarfiy the notion of "right" (*ius*).

31. *Sent* III, d. 33, a. un., q. 3, co.

32. *Sent* IV, d. 14, pars 2, ad dub. 6.

33. "Deus est rerum conditor, gubernator actuum, doctor intellectuum, iudex meritorum, quod intelligitur quia est causa causarum, est ars praestantissime originans, dux providentissime gubernans, lux luculentissime declarans vel repraesentans, ius rectissime remunerans." *HexD* 2, 5, 7.

34. In a suggestive commentary on Revelation 20:12, Bonaventure interprets John's vision of two books being opened in the final judgment. For Bonaventure, one is the Book of Life; the other, the Book of One's Own Conscience. The judgment will be salvific if the two agree; damning, should they disagree. Appealing to Psalm 139:16 (Vulgate 138:16, "will be written in your book," *et in libro tuo omnes scribentur*), he notes that this is a matter not of writing something out anew, but of manifesting what was already written there.

IUS, IUS NATURALE, IURA POSITIVA

Ius, iustum, iudicium

Although *ius* is normally translated as "a right," it does not have the same connotations that this last term has taken on in modernity. It is not the correlate of a duty. Rather, it indicates the power that A has over B insofar as B has some duty toward A according to justice. It is to this sense of *ius* that the classical definition justice refers: "giving to each person his or her right."[35]

Hence, having a right on someone (*habere ius in aliquo*) is to have a power over that person. It is also possible to have a right to a thing (*habere ius in aliqua re*), such as an inheritance. The modern notion or "rights," on the other hand, is rendered by *habere ius* followed by a genitive of action.[36]

Consequently, in rendering Bonaventure's conception of *ius*, it is more accurate to speak of precepts (*praecepta*) of natural right (*ius naturale*) and positive right (*disciplinae*) rather than rights.[37] A similar view can be found in the thought of Simone Weil.[38] She maintains that rights are abstract so long as nobody has the duty to guarantee them.[39]

Furthermore, as Bonaventure notes, the term for taking an oath (*iurare, iuramentum*)—the act of invoking God as one's witness in a judgement—is connected etymologically to *ius*.[40]

The notion of *ius* is also connected to that of judgment (*iudicium*) as

35. "[Iustitia] ad quam spectat unicuique tribuere iura sua." *Sent* III, d. 33, a. un., q. 4, co.

36. On the linguistic construction *habere ius in* + accusative of person or an accusative of the thing over which one has power, and *habere ius* + genitive of the act that is in one's power, see *Sent* III, d. 10, ad dub. 2; *Sent* III, d. 19, ad dub. 3; *Sent* III, d. 20, a. un., q. 3, co.; *Sent* III, d. 39, a. 3, q. 2, co.; *Sent* IV, d. 9, a. 2, q. 4, co.; *Sent* IV, d. 19, ad dub. 6; *Sent* IV, d. 28, a. un., q. 6, co.; *Sent* IV, d. 32, a. 2, q. 2, co.; *Sent* IV, d. 32, ad dub. 4.

Interestingly, the soul has power only when the devil does not have any rights over it: *Hex* 22, 36.

37. *Sent* IV, d. 26, a. 1, q. 3. Generally, the term *disciplina* indicates the communication of knowledge from the standpoint of the recipient, just as *doctrina* indicates it from the standpoint of the one imparting it. Here, however, it indicates the conditions, including the external ones, to which the disciple must submit and so those which a community must accept for it to be ordered.

38. Cf Matteo Papini, *Il diritto è estraneo al bene. Lo scandaloso pensiero di Simone Weil* (Assisi: Cittadella, 2009), 60–69.

39. "*Scientia iuris* quae sub morali reponitur, [...] ad hoc instituta [...] <est>, ut mores componat et docere debeat honeste vivere, alterum non laedere, ius suum unicuique tribuere." *HexD* 1, 2, 21.

40. *Sent* III, d. 39, ad dub. 3.

opposed to an arbitrary decision (*arbitrium*). Bonaventure distinguishes, therefore, two kinds of decision that we can make by exercising free choice (*liberum arbitrium*). A judgment is a decision made according to rules of truth or a higher law. A decision is called arbitrary, on the other hand, when it is made at the will's command. "Hence, the one who has the remit of bringing a lawsuit to an end according to what is just, is called a judge. However, the one who brings a lawsuit to an end in accord with his own command of will is called an arbiter."[41]

Finally, it is only against the backdrop of the dialectic between the just (*iustum*) and orders (*iussum*) that the notion of *ius* can be understood. Bonaventure, for example, provides an interesting discussion of the propositions, "It is just because it has been ordered (*iustum quia iussum*)," and, "It has been ordered because it is just (*iussum quia iustum*)." He thereby anticipates *ante litteram* the modern debate between legal positivists and proponents of natural right. Indeed, he adopts an interesting position in defense of the latter. In his view, divine right contains commandments that render certain requirements of our rational and physical nature explicit and determine them. Occasionally, these requirements are so implicit that they cannot be known without the Word of God. For example, there is a biological basis for monogamy. This does not provide sufficient grounds, though, for a determinate precept on monogamy. The same is true of the precept to rest on the Sabbath or Sunday. In these cases, we obey the divine precept because it has been commanded (*quia iussum*), but, upon further reflection, we understand that it has been commanded because it is just (*iussum quia iustum*). Hence, Bonaventure is not as concerned as fourteenth-century Franciscan theologians are about divine voluntarism. This is not because he believes that God's will is constrained by necessity. Rather, his theological outlook fosters respect for the mystery of God and follows the rule of "thinking about God in the most elevated and pious way" (*altissime et piissime cogitare de Deo*).[42]

Ius naturale

Semantically, the term "natural right" is connected to "natural law" but has quite a different origin and import.[43]

---

41. "Unde ille dicitur iudex, cuius est secundum iura causam terminare; ille autem dicitur arbiter, qui ad proprium voluntatis nutum causam terminare habet." *Sent* II, d. 25, ad dub. 1.

42. *MyTrin* q. 1, a. 2.

43. *Sent* IV, d. 33, a. 1, qq. 1–2.

Furthermore, we need to be careful not to read modern conceptions into medieval thought unwarrantedly. It is important to note in this regard that *ius* does not refer to the same thing as modern talk of rights. Strikingly, for example, *ius* is used only in the singular because it designates the whole juridical sphere rather than single human or civil rights.

The term, *ius naturale*, is the Latin translation of a Stoic concept, adopted in Justinian's *Digest*, a crucial juncture in the development of civil and canon law.

Under the influence of the first Franciscan theologians working in Paris, Bonaventure notes how Isidore distinguishes three senses of "natural right." In a general sense, it designates that which is contained in the Mosaic Law and the Gospel: the right that is directly revealed by God in the Scriptures. More specifically, it designates that which is common to every nation: that which is dictated by true human reason, which in turn is created by God. In a very specific sense, it designates that which nature has taught every animal. In this last sense, moral good is, when all is said and done, naturally good as well. In other words, that which is morally good is, ultimately, suited to the whole species from a biological standpoint, though not to every individual. In a certain regard, therefore, even nature tends toward moral goodness.[44]

Hence, the moral order commanded expressly by Scripture, makes explicit the universally binding and rational moral order, which, to some extent, is rooted implicitly in the biological order. Though we may become aware of some *ius* through Scripture's explicit precepts (*iustum quia iussum*), that *ius* is ultimately grounded in what is intrinsically just rather than a mere command (*iussum quia iustum*).[45]

From ius naturale to positiva iura

As already noted, natural law, in the objective sense, is the *collectio* of the precepts of natural right.[46] Ancient philosophers and jurists also referred to natural right, insofar as it is universal, as the "law of nations" (*ius gentium*), an expression that Bonaventure uses on just one occasion.[47]

The concept of natural right is important for theologians too. It pro-

---

44. On polygamy, see *Sent* IV, d. 33, a. 1, q. 1. On the sabbath rest, see also *Sent* III, d. 37, ad dub. 3.

45. *Sent* IV, d. 33, a. 1, qq. 1–3.

46. *Sent* II, d. 39, a. 2, q. 1 co.

47. *PerfEv* q. 4, a. 1, co.

vides the theologian with an explanation of how the various kinds of *ius* converge.[48] It also enables the theologian to explain the juridical and moral evolution of some *ius* within salvation history.[49]

Bonaventura notes, for example, that there is a difference between the way in which canon law and civil law, namely, the *decretista* and the *legista*, calculate the degrees of consanguinity. This difference arises because the former is concerned with *iura canonica*; the latter, *iura civilia*.[50]

Furthermore, natural right needs to be completed with positive right, even if divine right can dispense from the latter. Some things are only implicit in natural right. Positive right is needed to render explicit that which is only implicit in natural law.[51] This is why, as noted above, one is not blameless for ignorance of the law.

The plural form, *iura*, on the other hand, indicates a set of positive norms that, as Bonaventure is well aware, are of a different kind and have undergone a historical evolution. He draws a contrast, therefore, between the new laws (*nova iura*) and the ancient or earlier laws (*antiqua/ priora iura*) of canon law.[52]

He refers to these sets of norms with expressions such as "in accord with the law" (*secundum iura* or *sicut iura dicunt*) and "against the laws" (*contra iura*).[53] Moreover, the terminology used helps us appreciate that there is a gap between the eternal law and these norms. Unlike eternal law, the latter regard and govern events that happen for the most part: "a set of norms judges and institutes that which occurs frequently, not that which is always the case" (*iura iudicant et instituunt non ea quae semper, sed ea quae fiunt frequenter*).[54]

Iurisdictio canonica *and* civilis *(and the* praelatio religiosa*)*

Jurisdiction (*iurisdictio*) is the operation exercised habitually by an authority that determines what is right (*dictat ius*). In other words, it estab-

---

48. *Sent* IV, d. 36, a. 1, q. 3, co.

49. For example, concubinage and polygamy were allowed at the time of the patriarchs because God could dispense from the precepts of the *ius naturae* whereby we are directed toward our neighbor. See *Sent* IV, d. 33, a. 1, qq. 1–3.

50. *Sent* IV, d. 40, praenotata.

51. For example, Mary's intention to live in virginity did not render her marriage to Joseph null because she did not withhold her consent but accepted God's plan. See *Sent* IV, d. 42, a. 2, q. 2, ad 1; IV, d. 28, a. 1, q. 6, ad 4.

52. *Sent* IV, d. 18, pars 2, a. 1, q. 3; IV, d. 34, a. 2, q. 1; IV, d. 40, a. un., q. 1.

53. Such expressions are scattered throughout the *Commentary on the Sentences*.

54. *Sent* IV, d. 36, a. 2, q. 1.

lishes a law and enforces it. For Bonaventure, this power finds expression in the correct, natural worship of God. By contrast, in modern thought it is associated with the meta-juridical foundation of the values proper to life in society. Bonaventure also claims that it has three different functions. Whereas we speak of the legislative, executive, and judiciary branches or functions, he distinguishes between: determining a form of social life; the exercise of government or the norm of presiding; and the censure of judging.[55]

Drawing on Pseudo-Dionysius's distinction between substance, power, and operation, Bonaventure defines jurisdiction as sending an emissary or delegating authority: "The one sent receives from the one sending either existence, power, or an operation. He is also separate in substance from the one sending. Plural subjects do not partake of the very same substance. It is necessary, therefore, that the one sent receive another power from the one who sends and a separate, inferior jurisdiction."[56]

In other words, whoever has authority has jurisdiction. This jurisdiction includes the power to produce an *ius* and then apply it, whether in governing or in sentencing.

As the operation of one who has authority, jurisdiction differs from a negotiation. Unlike jurisdiction, the latter takes place between equals. Both, however, are dialectical procedures. As such, they are persuasive rather than demonstrative.[57] This means that jurisdiction has a further field of application: the judiciary forum, namely, the power to resolve disputes and to issue penal sentences.[58]

This leads to the issue of dispensations. A penal norm is applied automatically: in equity and strictness of the law (*de aequitate iuris et rigore*). Its removal is a release (*de iuris relaxatione*).[59] Bonaventure cites the following definition of a dispensation: "A dispensation is a relaxation of a law, made, with knowledge of the cause, by the one who has the power

---

55. *Hex* 5, 15–20.

56. *Sent* I, d. 15, a. un., q. 1, co. It is dealing with the missions of the Son and the Spirit, distinguishing these from the way in which a creature is sent, namely, by delegating authority. With such a delegation of authority, the one sent is subordinate to the one sending and is meant to act at a distance from the latter.

57. *HexD* 1, 1, 22. This passage is on the science of rhetoric, which falls within rational philosophy.

58. *Sent* IV, d. 18, pars 2, a. 1, q. 3, co.

59. *Sent* IV, d. 19, ad dub. 6.

to dispense."[60] In canon law, a dispensation is given at last instance by the Pope, whose task it is to clarify the law (*ius dilucidare*).[61] However, it is not possible to dispense someone from God's precepts (*ius divinum*).[62] For this reason, they are called commandments (*mandata*).[63]

This raises the question, though, of how to resolve conflicts between these bodies of norms. For Bonaventure, that which holds under positive right (*de iure positivo*) cannot act as a constraint for that which holds under natural right (*de iure naturali*).[64] What if there is a conflict between two sets of positive laws, though? In discussing the free or servile condition of children, Bonaventure notes that there is a difference between the imperial law (*leges civiles* in Justinian's sense) and the customary law then in vigor in some regions of France. The former stipulates that the child always shares the same legal status as the mother; the latter, that the child will be a servant if either of the parents is. Bonaventure maintains that the constitution (*constitutio legalis*) is much more noble and reasonable than this custom (*consuetudo*). When all is said and done, this way of resolving a conflict between norms resembles what we would call a *hermeneutical* approach. As Bonaventure puts it, "This is what civil law dictates, canon law approves, the divine law confirms, and the natural law recommends" (*hoc dictat ius civile, et ius canonicum approbat, et divinum confirmat, et naturale commendat*).[65]

The scientia iuris and politica

Bonaventure is aware of the complex relation that exists between ethics (*scientia moralis*) and law (*scientia iuris*), by which he means the science that interprets and applies positive laws. Moreover, he believes that the

60. "Dispensatio est iuris relaxatio, facta cum causae cognitione ab eo qui habet ius dispensandi." *Sent* IV, d. 19, ad dub. 6. This definition is common among the decretists, such as Rufinus.

61. *Sent* IV, d. 38, a. 2, q. 3, co.

62. *Sent* IV, d. 24, pars 1, a. 1, q. 4.

63. "Illud igitur mandatum sive praeceptum [scilicet dilectionis] adeo Dominus de novo firmavit ut ratione suae firmae obligationis cum nullo dispensetur." *SermDo* 22, n. 4. On the question of dispensation, Bernard is cited. He states that "necessity and the common advantage are the reason required for a dispensation from one of the commandments" (*ratio dispensationis in praeceptis est exigenda necessitas vel communis utilitas*).

64. *Sent* IV, d. 36, a. 1, q. 1, s.c. 3 et co. To bring itself into line with the natural right, the *ius novum*, reformulation of canon law by jurist Popes of the preceding century, does not treat servitude as an impediment to marriage.

65. *Sent* IV, d. 36, a. 1, q. 3, co.

latter is "put back" (*reponitur*) under the former, namely, that law should safeguard morality and restore it whenever it is disregarded. Unfortunately, lust for profit or vain curiosity sometimes sets the law down the contrary path.[66]

Drawing on an earlier study, I propose to highlight the role played by legislation within Bonaventure's innovative political thought.[67]

In his *Collationes in Hexaëmeron* (1273), Bonaventure discusses the new philosophical sciences. In a brief but significant passage, he introduces political philosophy (*politica*) with a series of rather surprising statements (*Hex* 5, 14; *HexD* 1, 2, 14). Said science is the third offshoot of moral philosophy, which, for its part, is the third outgrowth of the light of natural truth. Political philosophy is directed toward the achievement of "moral justices" and consists in understanding the right dictate of political laws from a philosophical rather than a theological or canonical standpoint. It is a science, though, that has not received an exhaustive treatment at the hands of earlier philosophers. Consequently, it is only by working out a new synthesis of the various contributions of the preceding heritage that political life can be grounded philosophically in four "functions," with one consequent upon the other. These functions are: monotheistic worship; the derivation of political (positive) laws from natural law; the limitation of the exercise of government power; the establishment of measures for judicial activity.

By comparing the two transcripts of the speech, it emerges that Bonaventure's intention is to downplay the novelty of this striking claim.[68] According to the first version, philosophy has lacked an adequate understanding of the four functions, even if some of its contributions outline them in part. According to the Delorme edition, no philosopher has set it out in full (*plene*).

Which philosophers does Bonaventure have in mind? He is undoubtedly thinking of pagan philosophers, but not only. In the preceding dis-

---

66. *HexD* 1, 2, 21.

67. Andrea Di Maio, "'*Secundum dictamen legum politicarum…, sicut philosophus loquendo*'. Ermeneutica dei testi e del lessico di Bonaventura di Bagnoregio sulla comprensione della dimensione politica fra eredità classica, innovazione cristiana e peculiarità francescana," in *I francescani e la politica atti del convegno di studio, Palermo, 3–7 dicembre 2002*, ed. Alessandro Musco (Palermo: Officina di studi medievali, 2007), 307–42.

68. "Haec comprehensio est circa quatuor. Nullus autem philosophorum dedit hanc, sed si fuerit collecta ex multis, aliquid proveniet." *Hex* 5, 14. "Hanc nullus philosophorum plene tradidit, quia haec consideratio ex pluribus considerationibus provenit." *HexD* 1, 2, 14.

cussion of the other eight philosophical sciences, he has no qualms about also citing Christian authors, such as Augustine and Boethius.

Which political texts from the philosophical tradition had Bonaventure read, then? According to Bougerol's analysis of his sources, he never cites Aristotle's *Politics*.[69] At most, he cites Cicero and his *De officiis* here and there. This might lead us to think that Bonaventure makes his claim about the nonexistence of an organic political philosophy simply because he is not acquainted with any works that articulate one. This is not the reason, though. It is equally surprising that he does not even mention his beloved Augustine in this context. Augustine's *De civitate Dei* inspires, after all, the idea of the medieval *respublica Christiana*.[70]

What Bonaventure's peremptory remark is getting at, therefore, is that the politics that he has in mind has yet to be provided with an adequate foundation.

Political life needs to be rethought in light of the four abovementioned functions.[71] With the exception of the "norm of presiding" (*norma praesidendi*), which is added on this occasion, the other three terms of the quadrinomial constitute a trinomial that Bonaventure is familiar with and cites elsewhere. It comprises the syntagmata: "the rite of worship" (*ritus colendi*); "the form/norm of life in common" (*forma/norma vivendi/convivendi*); and "the censure of judgment" (*censura iudicandi*).[72]

What do the four political functions that Bonaventure lists consist of?

There are four spheres of life in political society: that of conscience and its values; that of the laws (which entails the legislative function); that of government; that of the judiciary. However, unlike the framework that we trace back to Montesquieu, these are not separate powers, but functions that are connected, somewhat in the manner of a flow chart.

With regard to the first function, that of conscience and its values, Bonaventure cites the "true philosophers."[73] He also mentions *pietas*.[74] It

69. Jacques Guy Bougerol, *Introduzione generale*, Opere di san Bonaventura, 9 vols., vol. 1 (Rome: Città Nuova, 1990), 39.

70. With regard to Augustine, in *TriQ* 12, Bonaventure says that "the masters have not taught anything that cannot be already found in his works."

71. "Attenditur autem quantum ad ritum colendi, quantum ad formam convivendi, quantum ad normam praesidendi, quantum ad censuram iudicandi. Ad censuram iudicandi non pervenitur nisi per norma praesidendi; nec ad normam praesidendi nisi per formam convivendi; nec ad istam nisi per primam." *Hex* 5, 14.

72. *Don* 4, 12; *Hex* 16, 14–20.

73. *Hex* 5, 15.

74. "Cultus Dei pietas est fidei. Unde dicit Tullius, quod pietas consistit in cultu deorum.

consists in treating God with a filial attitude.[75] It also leads one to treat others with innocence (*innocentia*), the disposition to do no harm to them, and benevolence (*benevolentia*), the disposition to do them good in accord with the order of justice.[76] This dimension grounds a shared ethos.

The second function is the legislative one: the "form of life in common."[77] It is the *regula aurea* (or "natural law") out of which positive laws "pullulate." The form of life in common may be not only that of civil society but also that of the Church; the norms which spring forth from natural law, not just those of civil law, but ecclesial canons too.[78]

The third function is the norm of presiding.[79] This consists in the way in which government is structured and its power exercised. It thereby binds those governing and those governed. However, placing it after the rite of worship and the shared form of life in the "flow chart" of political functions, has far reaching consequences. It amounts to a germinal statement of the principle of the delimitation of sovereignty. Power descends from upon high, "from the first truth," namely, God. However, it does not proceed from him directly to the sovereign (except perhaps, through the mediation of the Pope) but by way of exemplar causality (*manat exemplariter a primo Praesidente* [*HexD* 1, 2, 19]). In other words, it proceeds from God through the fundamental ethical values and the form of life in common.

The judiciary function, namely the "censure of judgment," is the final one.[80] Its judgments regard persons, material goods (*res*), procedures, and actions. Given its connections with the preceding dimension of political life, this power derives from the norm of presiding (in fact, judges were appointed by those governing) and the form of life in common. Nevertheless, there is a germinal assertion of the judiciary power's independence from the others. Bonaventure states that it, like the other

---

Non placet, quod dicit deorum. Scriptura nunquam vocat Angelos deos, ne venerentur sicut dii, sed homines dicuntur dii. [...] Cultus autem Dei consistit in laude et sacrificio." *Hex* 5, 15.

75. *Don* 3.

76. *Praec* 5 and 7.8.

77. "Secundum modus est forma convivendi, ut 'Quod tibi non vis fieri, ne facias alteri.' Hoc in corde scriptum est per legem aeternam. Ex hac naturali lege emanant leges et canones, pullulationes pulcrae." *Hex* 5, 18.

78. *Hex* 5, 18; *HexD* 1, 2, 18.

79. *Hex* 5, 19.

80. "Ultimum est censura iudicandi, ut homo sciat quid de quacumque re sit iudicandun, quod spectat ad personas, ad res, ad modum agendi. Haec omnia manant a veritate prima." *Hex* 5, 20.

powers, emanates from the first truth, namely, God. This means that the judge is beholden to truth alone.

Given the subject of this study, it is important to focus on the second function, the legislative, and the manner in which positive norms are derived from natural right, as well as the way in which positive norms should be discussed, interpreted, and traced back to natural right. In dealing with this matter, Bonaventure uses two procedures. On the one hand, he recurs to that of derivation (*derivatio*) or issuance (*emanatio*) (which in the case of juridical output is also described as a *pullulatio*). On the other hand, he employs that of tracing something back to its source (*reductio*). These procedures constitute the so-called intelligible circle.[81]

THE "INTELLIGIBLE CIRCLE" OF THE LAW

The pullulatio of Positive Norms as an emanatio from Natural Right

> "From this natural law flow laws and canons,
>   its beautiful offshoots."[82]

Positive laws, both canonical and civil, grow out of natural law. In the *reportatio* published by Delorme, this outgrowth is described even more explicitly. All laws and canons, the statutes of each, which inform and safeguard human life in common, flow from natural law. The positive law does not have, therefore, an essentially ethical or religious end but a specifically political one: to safeguard human life in society.

What, though, does Bonaventure mean by "statutes"?[83] A first possible reading is to see them as the genus (positive law in general) under which both civil law and ecclesiastical canons fall. However, he may be referring to a third species of norms: those that, in both civil and ecclesial law, were devised over the course of the preceding two centuries. The statutes of the city states or the statutes and constitutions of religious

---

81. *Brev* 2, 4; 5, 1.

82. "Ex hac naturali lege emanant leges et canones, pullulationes pulcrae." *Hex* 5, 18.

The *reportatio* edited by Delorme further specifies this point. "Ex hac lege naturali manant omnes leges et canones et statuta utriusque iuris, pullulationes mirandae et pulcherrimae, humanum convictum etiam ex Salomonis doctrina et libris tutissime informantes; ita quod ius canonicum in duobus voluminibus principaliter traditur, scilicet compilatione nova *decretalium*." *HexD* 1, 2, 18.

83. See Francesco Calasso, *Medio Evo del Diritto*, 2nd ed. (Milan: Giuffrè, 2005), 419.

orders are a case in point. Furthermore, these statutory norms did not have the same coercive and universal value of civil and canon law. Rather they applied these laws to a certain context. Once the Franciscan Rule was inserted into the papal bull of Innocent III, for example, it acquired the force of canon law. The subsequent general chapters, up to that of Narbonne, attached *constitutiones* to it. Nevertheless, in general the laws, canons, and statutes all draw on the teaching or books of Solomon, who, according to the Bible, is the model of good governance. Significantly, the Mosaic Law is ignored and considered as a preparation for the law of the Gospel. There are generic references, though, to the books and teaching of Solomon. According to a literary fiction and tradition, the books in question are *Wisdom, Proverbs, Ecclesiastes*, and the *Song of Songs*. We can leave out the last one, which Bonaventure, following a long interpretive tradition, considered to be about the mystical life. Surprisingly, however, the other books do not deal with actual legislation, but with prudence. This supports the principle according to which positive laws should germinate, by way of sapiential reflection, from natural law.

At this stage, the second *reportator* slavishly lists the sources of the law. Significantly, canon law is not considered a theological discipline but is listed among philosophical ones. It regards the Church but deals with its institutional and human side. The two collections of decretals are singled out: the first, called the *antiqua* (divided into five parts), and the more recent *corpus decretorum*. Civil law is handed on extensively in the old and the new Digest, the Code of Justinian, the books entitled *Infortiatum* and *Authenticum*, and the Institutes, which are flanked by the *summulae* of contemporary jurists.[84]

However, why is natural law's relation to this mass of positive norms described as a "pullulation"? To answer this question, it is necessary to study how this term is used metaphorically in medieval Latin.

The term *pullulatio* comes from *pullus*, which originally means "small," and comes to mean "pup" and "scion." In general, *pullulatio* is

---

84. At least, this is how the *reportator* breaks it down. The two sources of canon law that are cited actually correspond to the *compilatio nova*, in five books, of Gregory IX (1234), whereas the *Corpus decretorum* corresponds to Gratian's *Decretum*, which comprises 101 distinctions, 33 cases, and the treatise *de consecratione*.

The sources of civil law are the *Digest* (divided into the *vetus, Infortiatum*, and *novum*), the *Code*, the *Novellae Constitutiones* (Authenticum) and Justinian's *Institutes*. In addition to these sources, there were the books and numerous *summae* on each law.

the act of pullulating: the biological act of generating. The meaning of the term is extended to the natural world (for example, the Italian word *polla*, which means a water source). The term is rarely used to refer to the realm of culture rather than nature. Only Bonaventure uses it in a juridical sense. In the 2018 edition of the *Library of Latin Texts*, the lemma *pullulatio* only appears in 74 contexts in writings of twelfth- and thirteenth-century authors (notably Bernard of Clairvaux, Alexander of Hales, the *Summa Halensis*, Pseudo-Dionysius's commentator Thomas Gallus, Thomas Aquinas, and Bonaventure). In Bonaventure's writings alone, it appears in thirty-seven contexts and, significantly, always in works from his mature period: from his time as minister general and never from his stint as a *baccalaureus*. This indicates that the use of the term may be inspired by an ulterior, original insight.

Trinitarian theology—the eternal and temporal processions of the divine persons—is the first area to which he applies the term.[85] In second place, the term is applied to the theories and meanings of Sacred Scripture.[86] Scripture is compared to a "forest of forests," in which the meanings and interpretations of the text "pullulate." Indeed, Scripture is the subject of a further metaphor, especially in Bonaventure's work *Lignum vitae*: Christ as the tree of life that bears foliage and fruits.[87]

In a celebrated reply to an unnamed master, Bonaventure explains that the works of Christ do not decrease but grow. This indicates that the term "pullulation" is understood in a diachronic and not only in a synchronic sense. Similarly, a body of norms undergoes an evolution. The criterion to be followed in deriving positive norms from natural right, is that the former should be a development of the latter and not in contradiction with them. According to Alexander of Hales's lapidary definition, natural right is that from which earthly authorities cannot dispense.[88] Bonaventure, however, explains that, when it comes to variable aspects, such as the matter promised by a vow, some dispensations are

85. See *MyTrin* q. 1, a. 2, ad 12.

86. See *HexD* 3, 2, 3; 3, 2, 6; 3, 5, 4; 3, 5, 8.

87. "Quia ergo Verbum increatum est origo omnium pullulationum naturalium, Verbum incarnatum omnium pullulationum gratuitarum, ideo dicitur in Apocalypsi quod ex utraque parte fluminis erat lignum vitae afferens duodecim fructus per singulos menses." *SermDi* vol. 2, sermo 34 (de s. Andrea apostolo), redactio longa, collatio, n. 5.

88. "Ius naturale non recipit dispensationem." Alexander of Hales, *Glossa in quattuor libros sententiarum Petri Lombardi*, 4 vols. (Florence: Typographia Collegii S. Bonaventurae, 1951–57), l. 4, d. 33, n. 2, § a, p. 518.

possible, whereas God can dispense from it in exceptional cases, for the sake of a higher right.

The Interpretation of Positive Norms as a reductio to Natural Right

The process of generating positive laws from natural right, and the latter from the eternal laws, is one of emanation and pullulation. Within the Neoplatonic framework of Bonaventure's thought, this process is one of division and derivation. This in turn leads Bonaventure to distinguish a higher juridical science, which deals with the principles, and a lower one, which deals with their application. Inversely, there is a process of interpreting and assessing the laws, which consists in tracing them back (*reductio*) to their underlying principles.[89]

Within this procedure, the notions of *ius naturale* and *ignoratia iuris* are fundamental instruments when it comes to framing metajuridical and metaethical discussions that are particularly relevant for theology. In this regard, it is worth considering two issues that Bonaventure discusses in his *Commentary on the Sentences*: the sabbath rest and, second, polygamy and concubinage (where he also offers some observations on incest). He argues that in each case there is a clear variation in the norm.

The issue of polygamy has far-reaching implications. There are many cases of it in the Old Testament. During the age of the patriarchs, it appears to be permitted under an explicit divine concession. Furthermore, Islamic law allowed for polygamy, whereas concubinage was practiced in the French and Italian countryside. The issue of polygamy and concubinage merited, therefore, an in-depth discussion. Bonaventure addresses the issue by applying three meanings of natural right (*ius naturale*). These three senses of *ius naturale* are propagated by Isidore of Seville, but originally set out in the *Code of Justinian* and taken up by Gratian's *Decretum*, the two foundational texts of civil and canon law. In a broad sense, natural right is that which is inherent to nature, necessary, and not amenable to dispensation. It is the law announced in the Pentateuch and the Gospels. In a stricter sense, insofar as it is not written but inscribed in right reason and human nature, it is the moral law that is common to all peoples. In the strictest sense, it is that which is inscribed in animal na-

---

89. *Sent* IV, d. 25, a. 2, q. 4, co.

ture and grounded in natural science.[90] Polygamy is clearly against natural law in the first sense. The Gospels condemn it explicitly, with an eye on the sacrament of marriage; the Pentateuch, implicitly. There are also grounds to deem it contrary to natural right, in the second sense. As to the third sense of natural law, it suffices to show that monogamy not only goes against nature but is also present in nature: insofar as it is a feature of the form of life of some species (such as turtle doves). In this sense, while the divine prohibition may be more explicit than the nature of a life form warrants, it nonetheless shows monogamy is apt for certain life forms.[91]

In replying to certain objections, Bonaventure states an important theological principle: in ancient times and in exceptional circumstances, God can suspend a precept of natural right that regards one's neighbor, but not those which regard himself and so are always unqualifiedly binding. "With regard to the objection that God does not act against natural right, it must be said that it is true that he does not act against the natural right that orders others to him, but he can act against the natural right that orders others with regard to their neighbor. However, he does not work against it, but above it."[92]

In the Old Testament, then, God suspended the duty to live in monogamy for some, such as Abraham. In other cases, as explained earlier, the *ignorantia iuris* could excuse one, such as Lot, but only partially. A general tenet of this account is that there is a growing awareness of natural right and of the relation between divine norms and human nature. Initially, the norm is perceived as arbitrary. Only after carful reflection does one understand that it is in accord with nature. Then, in the light of an exemplarist foundation of natural right, one comes to see that nature itself has been created in accord with the divine norm.

The second metajuridical and metaethical problem regards the shift of the obligation to rest from the seventh to the eight day of the week.[93]

---

90. *Sent* IV, d. 33, a. 1, q. 1, co.

91. In the 2018 edition of the *Library of Latin Texts*, the phrase "prohibitum, quia malum" only occurs in the *Summa Halensis* and in Bonaventure.

92. "Ad illud quod obicitur, quod Deus non facit contra ius naturae, dicendum quod verum est contra ius naturale quod ordinat in ipsum; sed contra ius naturae quod ordinat in proximum potest; non tamen facit contra, sed supra." *Sent* IV, d. 33, a. 1, q. 1, ad 1.

This is an instance *ante litteram* of the "teleological suspension of the ethical" that is proposed by Søren Kierkegaard, under the pseudonym of Johannes de Silentio, in the first problem of *Fear and Trembling*.

93. See *Sent* III, d. 37, ad dub. 3.

This is the problem of the Christian reinterpretation of the third commandment. In this case, Bonaventure does not use the syntagmata "natural right" (*ius naturale*) or "positive right" (*ius positivum*). Rather, like other Latin theologians from the patristic period and the Middle Ages, he uses the analogical categories of *moral precept* and *ceremonial precept*. The former is invariable, but the latter can change because, as the figure of something that has already been accomplished, it must cease once its antitype is accomplished.

SOME PRACTICAL IMPLICATIONS

Equally significant is his theory of the evolution of obedience. In the state of created nature (*natura condita*), namely, Eden, the natural law commands filial obedience unqualifiedly (*simpliciter*). In that state, the natural law suffices to ground all social relations. The natural law also commands filial obedience unqualifiedly in the state of fallen nature (*natura lapsa*). Moreover, there it commands "servile obedience, but not unqualifiedly." In other words, it commands servile obedience as a punishment for sin rather than an intrinsic good, and as a dictate of the law of nations (*ius gentium*), which flows from reason and nature but is not identical to them. Finally, it commands jurisdictional obedience as long as we are wayfarers (*in statu viae*): in the state of nature that can be repaired or already has been.[94] Hence, there is a passage from natural right (*ius naturale*) to the *ius gentium*. The latter proposes the former anew and in accord with our fallen nature. It involves, therefore, a dynamic mediation between reason and history. The right of jurisdiction, on the other hand, is meant to help us overcome the fall and will cease *in patria*.

Bonaventure describes the juridical process that exists in this path (*via*) or transition from the fall to restoration as both a restriction and a relaxation (through dispensations) for the sake of that which is more advantageous (*utilius*) in a concrete case. A dispensation needs to be both legitimate and advantageous. Otherwise, it would constitute a dissipation (*dissipatio*) rather than a dispensation.[95]

---

94. *PerfEv* q. 4, a. 1, co.

95. "In *relaxatione* autem ad hoc, ut fiat, consideranda est in eo qui facit, potentia, ut sit talis, qui supra *ius* possit et non sit illi iuri subiectus; et in eo cui fit, sit causa idonea, scilicet *necessitas, vel utilitas*; alioquin non *dispensatio*, sed *dissipatio* debet dici." *Sent* IV, d. 19, ad dub. 6.

For this reason, a legal order needs to have a supreme authority (*summum simpliciter*), such as the Pope in the case of the Church, whose competency it is to clarify what is right (*ius*) and to grant dispensations from norms. Should a dispensation become commonplace and be most advantageous, it tends to become a new law (*lex*) that modifies the preceding one.[96]

More necessary though is that the juridical order be grounded in a core that is hidden but known to the believer. In a celebrated discussion of the Christ-centeredness of all the sciences, Bonaventure presents Christ, in the moment of the universal judgment, as the center of justice who gives full meaning to science and to the action of the jurist and the politician. Christ in his ascension is the center of ethics, which deals with the good and the better. Ethics is founded upon a mean of modesty (*medium modestiae*), which does not consist in a static equilibrium, but in a continual growth in virtue.[97] Law, on the other hand, deals with the ugly, the beautiful, and the more beautiful, according to the mean of justice (*medium iustitiae*). This mean is the standard used by the jurist and the politician. Through it, they render ugly actions beautiful, and beautiful action even more beautiful, until they are as beautiful as possible.[98] On this suggestive note, Bonaventure likens legislating, governing, and juridical decision-making to the activity of an artist. Their peculiarity though is that they need to succeed in rendering the ugly beautiful. In art, this occurs, for example, with the gargoyles of the Gothic cathedrals. In this case, we have a work of compensation. However, legislators, judges, and political authorities also need to make things more beautiful. They do so by incentivizing people to become ever better. Bonaventure's point, then, is that good politics consists in preventing or at least reduc-

---

96. See *Sent* IV, d. 38, a. 2, q. 3, co.; IV, d. 49, a. 1, q. 3, co. On the Pope's supreme jurisdiction, see *PerfEv* q. 4, a. 3.

97. "31. Quintum est medium modestiae morali electione praecipuum. Modestia enim virtus est; virtus autem in medio consistit; hoc medium considerat ethicus. 32. Hoc medium fuit Christus in ascensione. [...] Sic Christianus debet ascendere de virtute in virtutem, non statuendo terminum virtutis, quia ex hoc facto desineret esse virtuosus." *Hex* 1, 30.

98. "34. Sextum medium est iustitiae iudiciali recompensatione perpulcrum seu praecelsum. Quod medium erit Christus in iudicio. Hoc considerat iurista sive politicus, ut fiat retributio secundum merita. Hoc totum mundum pulcrificat, quia deformia facit pulcra, pulcra pulcriora et pulcriora pulcherrima. [...] 36. Agant ergo iuristae de iudiciis pecuniarum, nos agamus de iudicio nostro." *Hex* 1, 34. See also the other *reportatio*: "Sequitur de sexto medio quod est medium iustitiae scilicet iudiciali compensatione praecelsum. [...] Istud est medium pulcrificativum mundi et completivum." *HexD* Principium, 1, 34.

ing and compensating social ills, and in promoting the common good in such a way that, in the end, it will turn out to be better overall than one's private good.

This is the way in which Bonaventure understands governance, even his own as superior of his order. It is a "hierarchization": the progressive accomplishment of a "divine order, science and action, as similar as possible to the Deiform."[99] To put it in modern terms, governing is the task of bringing order to society through education and other efforts to bring persons into communion with one another.

Summing up, Bonaventure addresses the notions of law of nature, natural law, natural right, and positive law, whether civil, canonical, or even that of religious orders. He does so not only as a theologian but also as a philosopher, and to some degree with the sensibility of a jurist. In developing his legal thought, he carefully takes into account both the supratemporal and the historical dimension, gives a role to prudence in dealing with contingent matters, and provides insights that continue to be relevant.

99. Here Bonaventure's highly personal reinterpretation of Pseudo-Dionysius's concept of hierarchy comes into play. Moreover, this interpretation is probably influenced by the Franciscan topos of "repairing God's house" from within. See *Hex* 21, 16–18.

Riccardo Saccenti

6 ∞ Natural Law after Aquinas
Peter of Tarentaise and Matthew of Aquasparta

In a famous passage of his *De Vulgari Eloquentia* (I, xviii, 5), Dante discusses the existence of a unified tribunal (*curia*) in Italy and explains that its elements "have been brought together by the gracious light of reason" (*membra huius gratioso lumine rationis unita sunt*).[1] This phrase has been the subject of several discussions among Dante scholars, particularly because of its reference to the "light of reason."[2] Back in 1951, Alessandro Passerin d'Entrèves noted in a celebrated essay that such a lemma has a clear "Thomist" origin. It echoes the idea of the "light of natural reason" (*lumen rationis naturalis*), which is at the basis of Aquinas's doctrine of natural law.[3] Dante certainly had a direct knowledge of the

This paper has been written as part of the research project "Authority and Innovation in Early Franciscan Thought (c. 1220–45)." This project has received funding form the European Research Council under the European Union's Horizon 2020 research and innovation programme under grant agreement 714427.

1. Dante Alighieri, *De vulgari eloquentia*, ed. and trans. Steven Botterill, Cambridge Medieval Classics (Cambridge: Cambridge University Press, 1996), 42–43.

2. Arrigo Solmi, *Il pensiero politico di Dante: studi storici* (Florence: La Voce, 1922); Francesco Ercole, *Il pensiero politico di Dante* (Milan: Alpes, 1927–28); Alessandro Passerin d'Entrèves, *Natural Law: An Introduction to Legal Philosophy* (London: Hutchinson's University Library, 1951).

3. Passerin d'Entrèves, *Natural Law*, 106. For the Thomistic references see Thomas Aquinas, *Scriptum super libros sententiarum magistri Petri Lombardi*, ed. Pierre Mandonnet and Marie-Fabien Moos, 4 vols. (Paris: Lethieilleux, 1929–56), II, d. 42, q. 1, a. 4, ad 3; III, d. 14, q. 1, a. 3, q.^la 1, co.; Aquinas, *De Regno Ad Regem Cypri*, Editio Leonina 42, ed. Hyacinthe-François Dondaine (Rome: Editori di San Tommaso, 1979), I, 1; Aquinas, *Summa theologiae* (hereafter, *ST*), ed. Institut d'Etudes Médiévales d'Ottawa, 5 vols. (Ottawa: Harpell's Press, 1941–45), I-II, q. 19, a. 4, co.; q. 91, a. 2, co.; q. 109, a. 1, co.; II-II, q. 171, a. 5, arg. 3; q. 173, a. 4, arg. 2.

writings of Aquinas and it is possible that the aforementioned passage from the *De Vulgari Eloquentia* is referring to the Dominican master's discussion of natural law in the *Summa theologiae*.[4] Moreover, Dante was probably aware of the doctrinal debate on natural law during the second half of the thirteenth century, a debate in which Aquinas's position was just one of various accounts and was called into question by some important theologians.

After all, in the early 1270s, when Aquinas outlines his idea of natural law, other theologians discuss natural law in their teaching and in their writings, cite the achievements of jurists and of canon lawyers in particular, along with a new reading of the theological and philosophical sources. Moreover, natural law was seen not just as a moral category. The development of interest in physics and metaphysics had brought into play a more complex understanding of the meaning of the terms "nature" and "law."

The purpose of this contribution is to offer a survey of how natural law is understood in the writings of two major theologians from the second half of the thirteenth century, whose work deals directly with the development and the reception of Aquinas's thought. Peter of Tarentaise was regent master in Paris in the late 1260s, when Aquinas started his second Parisian period of teaching, and thus his account of natural law is contemporaneous with Aquinas's composition of the *Prima Secundae* of the *Summa theologiae*.[5] Matthew of Aquasparta, whose academic career dates from the decade after the death of both Aquinas and Peter of Tarentaise, develops his idea of natural law in the early 1280s and mainly in response to Aquinas's doctrine.[6]

Through an examination of Peter of Tarentaise's and Matthew of Aquaspartas's texts, this contribution will consider some specific issues connected with the idea of natural law, namely: the meaning of key terms, such as *natura* and *naturalis*, the relation between natural law and

4. Justin Steinberg, *Dante and the Limits of the Law* (Chicago: University of Chicago Press, 2013), 70–71.

5. Thomas M. Käppeli, *Scriptores Ordinis Praedicatorum Medii Aevi*, 4 vols. (Rome: Typis Polyglottis Vaticanis, 1970–73), 3:261–64.

6. *Matteo d'Acquasparta, francescano, filosofo, politico atti del XXIX convegno storico internazionale, Todi, 11–14 ottobre 1992*, Atti dei convegni del Centro italiano di studi sul basso Medioevo, Accademia tudertina e del Centro di studi sulla spiritualità medievale nuova serie (Spoleto: Centro italiano di studi sull'alto Medioevo, 1993).

rational creatures, and the moral contents of natural law. This allows us: to reconsider theological accounts of natural law from the second half of the thirteenth century; to see how there is a development with the intellectual and doctrinal background of the discussion over natural law; and to build a picture of the plural doctrinal framework of the debate on this issue.

READINGS OF AQUINAS'S DOCTRINE ON NATURAL LAW AND THE TEXT OF PETER OF TARENTAISE AND MATTHEW OF AQUASPARTA

In his recent volume devoted to the idea of permissive natural law, Brian Tierney offers a reconstruction of the doctrinal tradition of one specific understanding of natural law, that ranges from Gratian to Kant.[7] The American scholar suggests that the idea that natural law is not just a prohibition of wrongdoing, but rather a permission "to do good," crosses the centuries and the disciplines. Tierney's volume develops research whose previous stages are set out in relevant studies, such as *The Idea of Natural Rights*, which stresses how twelfth-century legal discourse on natural law forges the lexicon that has been used, since the end of the thirteenth century, by authors such as Henry of Ghent and William of Ockham, later on, in the age of Conciliarism, and by the major sixteenth and seventeenth century philosophers.[8]

In his studies, Tierney questions the role of Thomas Aquinas in the development of the idea of natural law and, in particular, his importance in connecting the notions of *lex naturalis* and *ius naturale*, "law" and "right." According to one line of scholarship, which goes back to George de Lagarde and Michel Villey, Aquinas's analysis of natural law, especially that of the *Prima Secundae* of his *Summa theologiae*, represents the most complete and consistent account of this issue produced by the "scholastic culture."[9] De Lagarde's and Villey's conclusion is based on

---

7. Brian Tierney, *Liberty and Law: The Idea of Permissive Natural Law, 1100–1800*, Studies in Medieval and Early Canon Law, vol. 12 (Washington, D.C.: The Catholic University of America Press, 2014).

8. Cf. Brian Tierney, *The Idea of Natural Rights: Studies on Natural Rights, Natural Law, and Church Law, 1150–1625* (Atlanta: Scholars Press, 1997).

9. Georges de Lagarde, *La naissance de l'esprit laïque au déclin du Moyen Âge*, 6 vols., vol. 6, *L'individualisme ockhamiste (3me fascicule): La morale et le droit* (Saint-Paul-Trois-Châteaux:

a specific idea of the development of medieval thought: that it reaches its zenith in the work of Aquinas, which is presented as a veritable theological and philosophical system. Accordingly, the *Summa theologiae* offers the most complete and detailed presentation of the "Christian philosophy" (*philosophia christiana*) which characterises the whole of medieval thought. More recently, Michel Bastit has reproposed this interpretation of Aquinas's account of natural law, and John Finnis has adopted it in order to suggest that the content of the *Summa theologiae* is still crucial for the development of a philosophical discourse on natural law and natural rights.[10]

Tierney's research, on the other hand, focuses on reconstructing the origins of the lexicon concerning "natural law." He notes how it crosses the disciplinary borders of canon and civil law and of theology. More specifically, his account of the history of the idea of natural law stresses the crucial role of twelfth-century canon lawyers and shows how William of Ockham is crucial in the redefinition of natural law and in the transmission of this idea to the subsequent thinkers and ages. The American scholar argues that the key figures in the development of the idea of natural law, including the twelfth-century canonists and Ockham, develop their doctrinal discourse by addressing specific, contingent problems and circumstances, such as the foundations of canon law and papal authority, or John XXII's abuses of papal power.

Therefore, two different views emerge within research on medieval natural law. While de Lagarde, Villey, and Bastit argue that Aquinas has offered the most complete medieval scholastic account of the issue, Tierney claims that a more accurate historical reconstruction reveals a plurality of ideas and rival doctrinal traditions. Each of these historiographic traditions contributes to shedding light on some aspects of the development of the idea of natural law in the twelfth and thirteenth centuries. On the one hand, it is clear that Aquinas has a crucial place in the debate on natural law, since his own account has specific features that render it original with regard to the theological discourse of the time. On

---

Éditions Béatrice, 1946); Michel Villey, *Leçons d'histoire de la philosophie du droit* (Paris: Librairie Dalloz, 1957).

10. Michel Bastit, *Naissance de la loi moderne la pensée de la loi de saint Thomas à Suarez* (Paris: Presses universitaires de France, 1990); John Finnis, *Natural Law and Natural Rights*, 2nd ed. (Oxford: Oxford University Press, 1980, 2011).

the other hand, the discussion of *lex naturalis* takes place between several disciplines. Consequently, to understand its development, it is necessary to look at history of: both canon and civil law; theology; and the medieval interpretation of philosophical sources.

In developing their discourse on natural law, medieval authors deal with a series of different *auctoritates*, including texts from: Roman civil lawyers, particularly Ulpian and Gaius, handed down in Justinian's collection of laws; the so-called *sancti* (i.e., the Fathers of the Church), especially Augustine and Isidore of Seville; Cicero's philosophical works; and, from the middle of the thirteenth century on, Book V of Aristotle's *Nicomachean Ethics*. These sources give them access to multiple doctrinal issues: the Stoic idea of natural law, the relation between nature and grace, the connection between divine law and human law, and the foundation of a political and ecclesial legal order.

The use and understanding of this varied legal, philosophical, and patristic heritage within a common doctrinal framework rests on the exegesis of a specific passage of scripture.

> For it is not the hearers of the law who are just before God, but the doers of the law that shall be justified. For when the Gentiles, who have not the law, do by nature those things that are of the law; these having not the law are a law to themselves. (Rom 2:14–15)

The *Glossa ordinaria*, which dates back to the middle of the twelfth century, summarizes the approach of medieval thinkers to natural law.

> *For when the Gentiles.* In fact, he [Paul] said that the gentile is damned for doing evil and saved for doing good. But if, as it were, he has no law and no knowledge of good and evil, it would seem that neither should be imputed to him. On the contrary, the Apostle states that the Gentile does have the natural law even though he lacks the written law, for he knows and is aware of good and evil. Thus, we are to believe that his acts are good or evil and that he is saved or damned deservedly. His doing good and being saved occur only thanks to the grace and faith that renew the natural image of God in man, made sluggish by longstanding vice. Without this renewal he would do evil and be damned, accused of his unnatural vices by his own conscience and, in any case, by the grace that heals what opposes nature. True, the desire for worldly things does not destroy God's image in the human soul such that nothing remains of its attributes; the image of God impressed in the human soul at its creation is not completely lost. But this desire is not removed by nature without grace; rather, it means that the action of grace requires nature.

> Furthermore, because the inner man is renewed with this grace, the law of justice is rewritten, wiping out the guilt of sin.[11]

Once we look at the discussion on natural law against this broader and more complex cultural background, we can no longer read Aquinas as if he worked in some sort of doctrinal isolation but need to see his own account as just one of the various positions in the debate on this issue. To do so, we need to evaluate the contribution of several authors. In the decades in which the Dominican master develops his own ideas and doctrines, composing first of all his *Commentary on the Sentences* and then the *Prima Secundae* of his *Summa theologiae*, several theologians dealt with the notion of "law" and its multiple meanings, including natural law. This is the case of Peter of Tarentaise, co-friar of Aquinas and regent master of theology at Paris in 1258–60 and 1267–69, before starting an ecclesiastical career that would lead him to the cardinalate in 1273, and to the pontificate in 1276 under the name of Innocent V.[12]

Peter of Tarentaise's discussion on natural law falls between Aquinas's *Commentary on the Sentences* and the *Summa theologiae*. It thereby acts as a sort of critical spokesman for Aquinas. The Franciscan master and cardinal Matthew of Aquasparta, on the other hand, composes his own *Quaestiones de legibus* in 1283–84.[13] At that time, Matthew had already taught theology in Paris as *magister regens* (1276–79) and in Bologna as *lector* at the local Franciscan *studium* (1281). In 1283 he was aggregated to the *studium sacri palatii*: the *studium* attached to the Papal curia. Matthew develops an interest in natural law in quite a different context with respect to Peter of Tarentaise: Etienne Tempier's condemnation on March 7, 1277, of 219 heterodox propositions, some of which were Thomistic. The condemnation raised questions about the relation between Christian faith and philosophy, particularly Aristotelianism, on key metaphysical and ethical issues.

---

11. *Biblia latina cum glossa ordinaria: Facsimile reprint of the Editio Princeps* (*Adolph Rusch of Strassburg 1480/81*), 4 vols. (Turnhout: Brepols, 1992), 4: f. 1059vb [facsim. 278b].

12. Kaeppeli, *Scriptores Ordinis Praedicatorum*, 264. Peter of Tarentaise's text will be quoted from Vatican City, Biblioteca Apostolica Vaticana, MS lat. Borgh. 139 (hereafter, *V*), fols. 104v-34v.

13. Matthew of Acquasparta, *Quaestiones disputatae de anima separata, de anima beata, de ieiunio et de legibus* (Florence: Typographia Collegii S. Bonaventurae, 1959).

146   Riccardo Saccenti

NATURA AND NATURALIS

The canon lawyers who lectured on Gratian's *Decretum* from the middle of the twelfth century on offered increasingly detailed analyses of the semantic multiplicity of the key word *natura*, which is crucial to highlighting the value and meaning of the lemmata *lex naturalis* and *ius naturale*.[14] Huguccio of Pisa's *Summa in Decretum* offers a significant example of this analytical approach to the terms *natura* and *naturalis* and examines the impact that each meaning of the terms has on one's understanding of natural law. Distinguishing the different values of *natura* became part of the discussion on natural law among the theologians too. They discuss it in their biblical commentaries as well as in a series of disputed questions written between the end of the twelfth and the beginning of the thirteenth century. It is within this theological debate, particularly in the Parisian intellectual milieu, that this approach to natural law became more structured and started to be considered as part of a more general and comprehensive study of the idea of "law" and of the relations between the genres of laws.

The *Summa fratris Alexandri*, composed in the 1240s, combines materials from the first Franciscan masters of theology active at Paris and offers a first, paradigmatic testimony to this new theological perspective on the issue of law. Book III contains a long treatise on the laws (*De legibus*). It examines the different kinds of law, starting from the "eternal law" and moving on to "natural law," the "law of Moses," and the "law of the Gospel."[15] The Franciscan Jean de la Rochelle is the first to elaborate such a scheme for the analysis of the laws in his *Quaestiones de legibus et praeceptis*. Its contents were fully assimilated in the *Summa fratris Alexandri*.[16] Through this first great theological synthesis, all the authors

14. Atria A. Larson, *Master of Penance: Gratian and the Development of Penitential Thought and Law in the Twelfth Century*, Studies in Medieval and Early Modern Canon Law 11 (Washington, D.C.: The Catholic University of America Press, 2014); John C. Wei, *Gratian the Theologian*, Studies in Medieval and Early Modern Canon Law, vol. 13 (Washington, D.C.: The Catholic University of America Press, 2016).

15. Alexander of Hales, *Summa Theologica seu sic ab origine dicta Summa Fratris Alexandris*, 4 vols. (Florence: Typographia Collegii S. Bonaventurae, 1924–48). For a careful analysis of the theological relevance of the *Summa* and of the early Franciscan masters see Lydia A. Schumacher, *Early Franciscan Theology: Between Authority and Innovation* (Cambridge: Cambridge University Press, 2019).

16. François-Maire Henquinet, "Ist der Traktat De legibus et praeceptis in der Summa

of the second half of the thirteenth century distinguish, in the following order, between *lex aeterna, lex naturalis, lex Mosayca,* and *lex Evangelica.* This classification is crucial not only in the text of Aquinas, but also in the *quaestiones disputatae* on law of both Peter of Tarentaise and Matthew of Aquasparta.[17]

According to this scheme, natural law is subordinated to the eternal law and prior to human law. Peter of Tarentaise explains this as follows.

> A rule which is posited and not dropped is infallible, though not in and of itself. Hence, another rule is required: one which is infallible in and of itself, which is neither posited nor dropped, but is eternal. Therefore, one can distinguish a threefold law or rule of how to act: a temporary one, which is posited and dropped, namely, human positive law; a second, perpetual one, which is posited and not dropped, to wit, the natural law co-created with the rational mind; a third, eternal one, which is neither posited nor dropped, and is the divine law.[18]

According to this classification, natural law is a medium between the eternal law and human positive law: it is a means through which human beings are able to shape their positive law on the contents of the eternal law.

Peter of Tarentaise's account of natural law moves from the assumption that this issue pertains properly to the moral field and thus supposes that the words *natura* and *naturalis* refer to human beings as rational

---

Alexander von Hales von Johannes von Rupella?," *Franziskanische Studien* 26, no. 1 (1939): 1–22, 234–58; Victorin Doucet, *Prolegomena in librum III necnon in libros I et II Summae Fratris Alexandri, Summa Theologica seu sic ab origine dicta Summa fratris Alexandris,* 4 vols., vol. 4/1 (Florence: Typographia Collegii S. Bonaventurae, 1948); Jacques Guy Bougerol, "Jean de La Rochelle: les oeuvres et les manuscrits," *Archivum Franciscanum historicum* 87, no. 3–4 (1994): 211; Carla Casagrande and Silvana Vecchio, "La classificazione dei peccati tra settenario dei vizi e decalogo," *Documenti e studi sulla tradizione filosofica medievale* 5 (1994): 331–95. See also Alexander of Hales, *Summa theologica Halensis: De legibus et praeceptis. Lateinischer Text, deutsche Übersetzung und Kommentar,* 3 vols., ed. Michael Basse (Berlin: De Gruyter, 2018).

17. Silvana Vecchio, "La riflessione sulla legge nella prima teologia francescana," in *Etica e politica le teorie dei frati mendicanti nel due e trecento,* 119–51 (Spoleto: Centro italiano di studi sull'alto Medioevo, 1999); Vecchio, "Precetti e consigli nella teologia del XIII secolo," in *Consilium. Teorie e pratiche del consigliare nella cultura medievale,* ed. Carla Casagrande, Chiara Crisciani, and Silvana Vecchio, 33–56 (Florence: SISMEL Edizioni del Galluzzo, 2004).

18. Peter of Tarentaise, *Quaestiones de legibus,* q. 1 (V 105ra): "regula que ponitur et non deponitur quamuis sit infallibilis non tamen per se; ergo preexigitur alia per se infallibilis regula que nec ponitur nec deponitur sed est eterna. Iuxta hec distinguitur triplex agendorum lex siue regula, una temporanea que ponitur et deponitur, scilicet lex humana positiua, altera perpetua que ponitur sed non deponitur ut lex naturalis menti rationali concreata, tertia eterna que nec ponitur deponitur est lex diuina."

creatures. In doing so, the Dominican master agrees with Aquinas that "natural law" is proper to rational beings. Quoting John of Damascus's *De fide orthodoxa*, Peter distinguishes between the different powers of the soul. On the one hand, there are the irrational powers, which do not need any kind of law to accomplish their role since they act deterministically. On the other hand, the rational powers of the soul are free and their action is not determined.[19] This second kind of power requires a sort of guide that shows its proper objective and action. According to Peter of Tarentaise, natural law is such a guide.

Addressing the radical contestation of the idea of nature that follows Tempier's censure, Matthew of Aquasparta carefully discusses the different meanings of *natura* and *naturalis*, and, accordingly, the different values of "natural law."[20] From a general point of view, the Franciscan theologian considers a specific sense of the term "nature": that which belongs to the physical order. With regard to the human soul, "nature," in this sense, indicates something different from reason and will: it refers to the nutritive and sensitive souls. Accordingly, "natural" indicates whatever originates in natural principles. This notion equates natural law with the "physical law" proper to each nature: that is, the rule according to which an infra-rational thing accomplishes deterministically its proper action and objectives. In the case of the nutritive and the sensitive souls, the natural law is the set of natural desires that moves them and that they have to satisfy.

Matthew introduces a second, broader meaning of "nature," one which encompasses both corporeal and spiritual realities, rational and irrational natures.[21] According to this conception, "natural" means that which is added to nature: a quality that falls outside the "definition" of a thing. This entails, the Franciscan master notes, that every rational creature, whether an angel and or a human, needs to have some natu-

19. Peter of Tarentaise, q. 2 (*V* 106va): "Secundum Damascenum, libro II, capitulo XII, duplex est potentia in anima: quedam irrationalis que agit ex necessitate, quedam rationalis que ex libertate. Prima determinata est ad actum, unde non indiget altera inclinatione uel determinante quia non potest deuiare; secunda indeterminata, unde quia facile deuiare potest indiget altero determinante."

20. See Matthew of Aquasparta, *Quaestiones de legibus*, 459–60 [q. 2].

21. Matthew of Aquasparta, 460 [q. 2]: "Accipi potest 'natura' vel 'naturale' magis large, prout quaelibet creatura cuiuscumque gradus natura quaedam est; et dividimus naturam in corporalem et spiritualem, irrationalem et rationalem sive intellectualem, et sic quaerimus hic de lege naturali."

ral law posited or impressed upon it by nature. Such a law is: "the principle, the rule, the norm of the practical intellect that directs the will to its ultimate end and, in accord with what is required to achieve that end, prescribes what one should desire or abstain from, what one should do, avoid, or refuse."[22]

NATURAL LAW AND *CREATURAE RATIONALES*

Both Peter of Tarentaise and Matthew of Aquasparta, each with a different approach, single out the moral sense of "natural law" and identify it with the rule of the practical intellect, where "intellect" designates the rational power of human soul. Their manner of grounding natural law in the rational powers of the soul has its roots in a specific conception of the structure of human intellect. This conception emerges in the first half of the thirteenth century: in the early discussions on the difference between the speculative and the practical intellect and the metaphysical implications of this distinction. Peter of Tarentaise makes specific reference to some of the crucial sources, such as Augustine and Boethius, of the medieval theory of the so-called "transcendentals," that is, the idea that the notions of good, true, one, and being are interchangeable and refer to one and the same reality.[23]

More specifically, the distinction between the true and the good designates two different perspectives, a metaphysical one and a moral one, from which the human intellect considers one and the same object, namely, God. Accordingly, as Peter of Tarentaise explains, the human intellect takes on two forms. On the one hand, there is the speculative intellect that regards the enquiry of truth (*notio veri*). On the other hand, there is the practical intellect that acts by reason of the love of good

22. Matthew of Aquasparta, 460–61 [q. 2]: "quaedam ratio, regula vel dictamen practici intellectus in ultimum finem dirigens voluntatem, et secundum exigentiam finis dictans quid appetendum quidve fugiendum, quid agendum quidve cavendum vel declinandum."

23. Peter of Tarentaise, *Quaestiones de legibus*, q. 2 (*V* 106va-vb): "Dicit Boethius quod naturaliter nobis inserta sunt notio ueri et amor boni propter premium. Dicit Augustinus, libro X De Trinitate, capitulo I, quod nisi breuiter impressam omnem disciplinarum rationem habemus ad nullam earum tanto dicendi studio flageremus. Propter secundum dicit idem, libro De Trinitate VIII, capitulo I, quod nisi haberemus impressam nobis formam iusticie nullus qui non esset iustus appeteret iustus esse. Intellectus duplex est in nobis uel unus dupliciter consideratus qui uterque errare potest, scilicet speculatiuus cuius finis est ueritas et practicus cuius finis est opus."

(*amor boni*). The Dominican master explains that this distinction coincides perfectly with Aristotle's *Nicomachean Ethics*, where the distinction between the speculative and practical fields is presented as specific of the rational soul.[24] Moreover, since the speculative intellect needs a principle that guides it toward the understanding of truth, so too does the practical intellect require a principle which shows it how to act. Natural law is the knowledge that concerns the supreme principles of moral action and belongs to the practical intellect.[25]

Matthew of Aquasparta also assumes that the same distinction between speculative intellect and practical intellect must be made and that the aforementioned description of the difference between speculative knowledge and practical knowledge is consistent. Furthermore, he agrees that we need to look at the practical intellect to gain an appropriate understanding of natural law. Quoting Book III of Averroes's *Commentary on De anima*, the Franciscan theologian notes that, since the speculative intellect acts on the basis of principles that are *per se nota*, the practical intellect also acts according to supreme moral principles that are *per se nota* and summed up in natural law.[26] As Matthew of Aquasparta explains, rational creatures cannot act properly unless their free will is guided by knowledge of the good to desire and the evil to avoid. This knowledge is natural law.[27] Therefore, natural law is the source of

24. Peter of Tarentaise, q. 2 (*V* 106vb): "Secundum Philosophum, idest VII Ethicorum, ideo intellectui speculatiue inserta est notio principiorum speculatiuorum sicut quod totum est maius sua parte intellectui uero practico inserta est notio principiorum operatiuorum ut nemini faciendam esse iniuriam."

25. Peter of Tarentaise, q. 2 (*V* 106vb): "Dico ergo naturalem legem habitum esse impressum naturaliter in anima in parte eius cognitiua non affectiua, etiam intellectu practico non speculatiuo."

26. Matthew of Aquasparta, *Quaestiones de legibus*, 463 [q. 2]: "De huiusmodi principiis, licet dicat Commentator, super III *De anima*, quod nescit unde in mentem venerint, tamen certum nobis est nonnisi ab aeterna lege vel veritate [illa] nobis esse impressa. Quod si non essent talia principia, per se nota, sed omnia probarentur, nec probarentur in scientia propria, quia nulla scientia probat sua principia, esset abire in infinitum in scientiis, immo, ut praedictum est, nulla esset scientia."

27. Matthew of Aquasparta, q. 2, 465: "Rursus, creatura rationalis, hoc ipso quod rationalis, ex parte voluntatis non tantum est mota, immo et movens, alias opera sua non essent meritoria sicut nec instrumenti. Ergo similiter ex parte rationis sive intellectus practici vel operativi non tantum est regulata, immo est regulans, ita quod regulatur ex se ipso in cognoscendo quid agendum quidve cavendum et regulat voluntatem in operando vel appetendo. Illud autem quo intellectus practicus regulatur in cognoscendo et regulat appetitum vel voluntatem, legem dicimus naturalem."

practical knowledge: the practical intellect receives from natural law a knowledge of the basic moral rules and, thanks to this understanding of the moral principles, it is able to establish rules by which we should desire and will.

NOTIO, REGULA, AND LEX

This examination of the theological reflection on natural law during the second half of the thirteenth century has evidenced that there is some agreement on the idea that natural law represents the basic principle of moral knowledge of the practical intellect. Although the proper sense of "nature" and "natural" pertains to physics, there is a more specific sense of these terms that indicates rational creatures and their psychological features, namely, their capacity to know the difference between good and evil, and to act accordingly. Peter of Tarentaise explains that natural law is both the enquiry of the supreme moral principles (*notio principiorum*) and the major rule of human actions (*regula operandorum*), and that it thereby combines both a cognitive aspect (i.e., the knowledge of the good to pursue and the evil to avoid) and an active element (i.e., being the rule according to which the same practical intellect determines the action of the will).[28]

Matthew of Aquasparta notes that natural law is basically a knowledge of the eternal law that allows rational beings to not only guide their moral action but also to orient their will and desire. Such moral knowledge is proper to the highest part of rational soul and this "enquiry" (*notio*) of the contents and prescriptions of eternal law, which provides practical intellect with a rule, is "impressed" at the moment of its creation. Using a passage from Augustine's *De doctrina christiana*, he explains that the "golden rule," taken from Tobit 4:16 and from Matthew 7:12, that is, "You never do to another what you would hate to have done to you, all things therefore whatsoever you would that men should do to you, do you also to them," states the content of natural law and summa-

---

28. Peter of Tarentaise, *Quaestiones de legibus*, q. 2 (*V* 106vb): "Dicit Glossa Hebreorum I: 'super illud qui cum sit splendor quod omni anime indidit Deus seminaria intellectus', scilicet quo ad speculatiua, et sapientie, scilicet quo ad operabile. Hec autem notio principiorum uidetur uiniuersalium cum sit regula operandorum, lex naturalis appellatur. Unde lex naturalis est habitus cognitiuus anime naturaliter impressus."

rizes a multiple series of precepts whose value is immutable and which are indelibly impressed upon the mind of each individual rational creature.[29] Thus, honouring God, living honestly, respecting one's parents, helping one's neighbour, not offending or insulting anyone, are all precepts of natural law that are impressed upon the intellect, are common to all mankind and cannot be deleted by either evil or sin.

This way of understanding natural law, namely, as the highest form of practical knowledge of rational creatures and, more specifically, as an "impressed" intellectual knowledge of the highest moral principle, makes its questionable to define it with regard to the powers of the soul and to reason in particular. "Natural" can designate part of the nature of a creature. According to the aforementioned conception, however, natural law is not "natural" in this sense. It is not part of the very nature of a rational creature. Rather, this *notio* is impressed on the intellect with the creation of each rational being. It does not belong to the specific "definition" of the rational creature, whether angel or human being. Accordingly, Peter of Tarentaise notes the closeness of this notion of natural law to Aristotle's classification of virtues as habits. In the *Categories*, as well as in *Nichomachean Ethics*, Aristotle explains that virtue is neither a power of the soul, an element proper of the nature of the soul, nor a passion, something which is passively received. Rather, virtue, like science, is a habit: a moral or intellectual quality that human beings acquire through exercise, to the point of becoming stable, as a sort of second nature. According to Peter's reasoning, natural law is a habit because rational beings acquire it with the impression of eternal law in their mind and, more specifically, in the cognitive part devoted to moral knowledge, namely, the practical intellect.

> On this, the *Gloss* on Hebrews 1 says, "the one who is the splendor which God impresses upon every soul, namely, seedbeds of understanding for the realm of contemplation, and wisdom for the realm of action." However, this appears

---

29. Matthew of Aquasparta, *Quaestiones de legibus*, q. 2, 461: "Et haec quidem lex naturalis, quamvis unum habeat generale praeceptum, ut 'quod tibi non vis fieri, alii ne feceris, et alii facias quod tibi vis fieri', secundum Augustinum, III libro *De doctrina christiana*, tamen plura continet alia praecepta, quae derivantur ab isto, ut Deum esse colendum, honeste esse vivendum, parentes esse honorandos, proximis esse subveninendum in necessitate, nulli offensam vel iniuriam irrogandam; quae sunt regulae quaedam immutabiles, indelebiliter scriptae in mente cuiuslibet."

to be a knowledge of universal principles since it is the rule of the works that we should perform. It is called natural law. Natural law, therefore, is a naturally impressed cognitive *habitus* of the soul. Two things are required for a complete cognitive *habitus*: the species of a knowable thing and the single reality that is known distinctly through them. These two correspond to the act of understanding just as color and light do to the act of seeing. The species of principles are not, in fact, innate. As Aristotle notes, the soul of the creature is like a blank slate. Rather, it is through its own inborn light that the soul, once it has taken in the species of unconnected terms, sees immediately the truth of the connection of principles. For example, once it has taken in the species of the whole, the part, and the greater, and is then met with the proposition, "Every whole is greater than its part," it assents to it immediately and without any further reflection. This is because intellectual principles of this kind have more truth and intelligibility. As Aristotle notes in *Metaphysics* I, they are the cause of the truth and intelligibility of other propositions that stand to them in the manner of conclusions. Hence, the soul assents to them immediately, due to their greater likeness to its own inborn intelligible light, and not as it would to conclusions. Due to its readiness to understand them, they are not called conclusions but principles that are innate to us.

Hence, Augustine says in *De Trinitate* XII, 6 that by the natural order the mind is joined to whatever is understandable since, just as the eye sees whatever is sensible in a sensible light, it sees what is understandable in a certain incorporeal light that is *sui generis*. This is the light of which the Psalm (4:6) speaks: "the light of your face shines on us, O Lord." Although the light of the agent intellect suffices to generate intelligible species, perhaps there has been impressed upon the mind another, habitual light: one which sees immediately the first principles themselves, just as the eye, in addition to the exterior light by which visible species are generated, has some kind of light within its very nature. I claim, therefore, that this natural light is a *habitus* that is naturally impressed upon the cognitive rather than the affective part of the soul, indeed upon the practical rather than the speculative intellect.[30]

In his *Summa theologiae*, Thomas Aquinas offers a different conception of natural law and its relation to the powers of the soul and to reason in particular. It is well known that Aquinas defines natural law as the rational creature's participation in the eternal law (*participatio legis aeternae in rationali creatura*, I-II, q. 91, a. 2). Using the idea of "participation," the Dominican master suggests that natural law is not something that

---

30. Peter of Tarentaise, *Quaestiones de legibus*, q. 2 (*V* 106vb).

rational creatures receive but, on the contrary, a product of their reason. *Lex naturalis* means the knowledge that rational creatures have of the eternal law. This definition certainly calls attention to the basic cognitive character of natural law, but it also stresses that this moral knowledge is "natural" because it is proper to the practical intellect as a power of the soul. In a specific and strict sense, natural law is a statement of practical intellect, "Do good and avoid evil," which describes what to do and not how to do it. Accordingly, natural law is not a habit but a knowledge that the practical intellect naturally produces. It is not something according to which someone acts (*quo quis agit*) but something that one accomplishes (*quod quis agit*).[31]

According to Aquinas, using Aristotle's threefold classification of things in the rational soul—powers, passions, and habits—is inappropriate when it comes to natural law. In the *Nicomachean Ethics*, such a distinction concerns the status of virtue, but it is not meant to establish a comprehensive classification of all the things present in a rational soul. Aquinas explains that in a soul there are also other things: "For example, certain acts belong to the soul: willing to those willing, and things known to those knowing. And the natural properties of the soul, such as immortality and the like, belong to the soul."[32] Aquinas believes that natural law is fully proper to reason, not as a habit but as a knowledge produced by reason. This seems to establish a clear distinction between metaphysics and ethics. It treats natural law as a matter that pertains to the practical intellect and attributes to reason the innate capacity to gain a certain understanding of the basic moral principles by itself.

Etienne Tempier's 1277 censure evinces a completely different perspective. It attempts to reaffirm that ethics, physics, and metaphysics are part of a comprehensive discourse, according to which natural law cannot be correctly defined without a strong metaphysical basis. This is, in fact, the doctrinal assumption upon which Matthew of Aquasparta grounds his own analysis of natural law and which leads him to contest Aquinas's view that natural law is not a habit. Rather, the Franciscan theologian believes that natural law is a *habitus impressum* or that it is the principle that creates in the soul the habit which supports the activity of the practical intellect. In his view, natural law is not the rational crea-

---

31. Thomas Aquinas, *ST* I-II, q. 94, a. 1, co.
32. Thomas Aquinas, *ST* I-II, q. 94, a. 1, ad 1.

ture's capacity to achieve some understanding of the eternal law by itself, but rather the result of the impression of the eternal law upon the intellect. This impress of eternal law produces in the rational creature a moral habit capable of guiding the will and desire toward the good.[33]

Therefore, in line with Matthew's argument, natural law is something received by rational creatures and which enables them to develop a "conscience" (*conscientia*): the habit that disposes them to draw practical or operative conclusions. The master notes that this is much more evident in the case of non-Christian thinkers who have a conscience and, thus, are able to distinguish what to do and what to avoid.[34] This conscience could not be based on written law, since, according to Romans, the gentiles do not have access to the written law of Moses. Therefore, "It is certain that in such men, conscience is not formed on the basis of the principles of the written law, and thus it is necessary that it is formed on the basis of the principles posited in it by nature, as well as on the basis of the immediate, evident, and necessary conclusions that follow therefrom, such as, 'Do not commit adultery,' which is an act that each religion considers illicit." Quoting John of Damascus's *De fide orthodoxa*, Matthew explains that "conscience is the law of our intellect," noting that here, "conscience" means not the habit but the set of supreme moral principles that enable the conscience to be formed. Natural law, in this sense, includes the principles that the intellect receives from God, according to which the moral conscience is formed and enabled to guide the powers of the soul.

MORAL LIFE, COSMOS, AND HABIT

This survey of the writings of some major figures from the theological debate on natural law during the second half of the thirteenth century shows that there were multiple cultural perspectives and doctrinal posi-

33. Matthew of Aquasparta, *Quaestiones de legibus*, 472 [q. 2, ad 12]: "Puto quod lex naturalis vel habitus et proprie vel habitum facit in anima et per ipsum redditur facilis practicus intellectus, ut dicatur habitus talium principiorum."

34. Matthew of Aquasparta, 463 [q. 2]: "Nulla autem lege scripta existente, sicut in iis qui nulla scripta lege utuntur, ut gentilibus et paganis, conscientia dictat eis hoc faciedum vel non faciendum, et, si fiat vel non fiat, redarguit et remordet. Certum est autem quod non formatur conscientia in illis ex aliquibus principiis legis scriptae; ergo necessarium est quod formetur ex aliquibus principiis naturaliter inditis, sicut sunt quaedam conclusiones quae ex illis principiis immediate, evidenter et necessario consequuntur, ut quod non est adulterandum, quod in omni secta illicitum est."

tions. Even if they base themselves on common sources, texts, and doctrines that were already collected and analyzed in the twelfth and early thirteenth century, Peter of Tarentaise, Thomas Aquinas, and Matthew of Aquasparta develop quite different positions.

It is clear that there is a significant change in the doctrinal debate between the years in which the two Dominican masters dealt with the issue of natural law (the 1260s and 1270s), and the moment in which Matthew of Aquasparta composes his disputed questions on the laws (the early 1280s). Peter of Tarentaise and Thomas Aquinas focus on the problem of the place that natural law has within the psychology of the human being. Within the structure of the intellect, which is determined by the basic distinction between truth and good and by the different kinds of intellectual activities that follow form this duality, natural law is on the side of the practical intellect. It is the highest moral knowledge, by means of which rational creatures can guide their will in moral action. Where the two theologians diverge is over the issue of the status of natural law with respect to the other things present in the rational creatures.

Peter of Tarentaise considers it knowledge "impressed" upon the rational soul in the manner of a habit; Aquinas holds that natural law is not received but produced by reason and is a result of its natural capability to gain a certain understanding of the eternal law by itself.

Matthew of Aquasparta, on the other hand, seems to focus his attention on the search for a more comprehensive metaphysical foundation of moral discourse. Consequently, he tries to reconsider natural law within a more general discussion on "law" as the basic structure of the metaphysical order of creation. He inherits from his confrère, Jean de la Rochelle, a carefully articulated analysis of law that appears in the *Summa fratris Alexandri* and was written in the early 1240s. From this perspective, Aquinas's conception of natural law as a product of created reason is insufficient, since it fails to explain how moral discourse is consistent with the more general idea of law as the standard according to which a thing must act to accomplish its own nature. According to the Franciscan theologian, natural law, in a moral sense, is proper to rational creatures but it is received as a habit rather than knowledge produced by one's own reasoning: natural law is impressed in created rational beings, as a set of supreme moral principles that shapes conscience and thus enables each subject to guide himself, orienting his own will and desire.

Aquinas understands natural law as a practical knowledge that follows from the "natural" capacity of every created reason to understand at least some of the contents of the eternal law. This makes natural law the basis for the construction of a "natural" ethics. Peter of Tarentaise and Matthew of Aquasparta suggest that such a knowledge of the supreme moral principles cannot be an autonomous product of rational creatures but must be "received" from divine grace at the moment of a rational being's creation and through the "impress" of the eternal law in the highest part of the soul: reason.

In developing their respective positions, Aquinas, Peter of Tarentaise, and Matthew of Acquasparta suppose different conceptions of some crucial theological issues: the nature of human beings, created in the image of God; practical intellect's capacity to know the basic moral principles; and, more broadly, the relation between metaphysics and ethics. For Aquinas, ethics has a proper rational foundation in the nature of the rational created beings: the knowledge of the moral principles as well as the ensuing moral actions are the product of the cognitive activity of the practical intellect, namely, of what Dante, in his *De Vulgari Eloquentia* calls the "light of reason" (*lumen rationis*). In contrast, first Peter of Tarentaise and then Matthew of Acquasparta think that the supreme rules that shape moral life are received from without, are impressed by divine grace onto the created reason, and have the eternal law as their model. Aquinas considers reason, with her universal cognitive capability, as the ultimate warrantor of the correct understanding of the rules of moral life, while Peter and Matthew believe that only compliance with the immutable and eternal precepts of the eternal law, known through an "impressed" natural law, gives certainty about the rightness of one's moral life.

Martyna Koszkało

---

7 ∽ John Duns Scotus and Natural Law

> True law is right reason conformable to nature, universal, un-
> changeable, eternal, whose commands urge us to duty, and
> whose prohibitions restrain us from evil. Whether it enjoins or
> forbids, the good respect its injunctions, and the wicked treat
> them with indifference. This law cannot be contradicted by any
> other law, and is not liable either to derogation or abrogation.
> Neither the senate nor the people can give us any dispensation
> for not obeying this universal law of justice. It needs no other
> expositor and interpreter than our own conscience. It is not
> one thing at Rome and another at Athens; one thing to-day and
> another to-morrow; but in all times and nations this universal
> law must for ever reign, eternal and imperishable.[1]

This famous quote from Marcus Tullius Cicero's *De Republica* succinctly represents the foundations of the Stoic doctrine of natural law—a body of immutable, eternal, and universal rules whose unshakable basis is nature itself and such that no legislator has the power to repeal them. The moral rules of conduct based upon this law are universal principles of action, perfectly fitted to human nature and immediately recognizable by natural reason.

This conception of natural law was received in the Christian world and, naturally enough, related to the law expressed in the Decalogue. However, in the context of the doctrine of creation, Christian theists raised some new questions regarding the foundations of the moral law:

---

1. Marcus Tullius Cicero, *On the Commonwealth*, in Marcus Tullius Cicero, *Treatises of Marcus Tullius Cicero*, trans. Charles Duke Yonge (London: H.G. Bohn, 1853), 363 [III, 22].

questions concerning the precise relationship between natural law and the Ten Commandments; the absolute immutability of natural law; the dependence of natural law on God's nature, or, more precisely, on God's intellect or on God's will.

The subject of this paper is John Duns Scotus's conception of the relationship obtaining between natural law and the moral laws as laid down in the Decalogue.[2] Since the Ten Commandments depend on God, the supreme lawgiver, I also take into consideration the question of how moral principles (in general) are related to God's (sovereign) will. However, it seems to me that the key to the correct understanding of Scotus's conception of the essence of the moral law contained in the first and the second tablet is found in his conception of the contingency of the world. Hence, first the pairing necessary/contingent needs to be adequately clarified, and only then that of intellectualism/voluntarism.

In the present article, I analyze the strands of John Duns Scotus's thought that, as they develop, lead him to affirm that the commandments of the second tablet of the Decalogue are not decrees expressing necessary moral laws.[3] I shall argue that Scotus takes the principal reasons for their non-necessity to be: the contingency of the actual world; the nature of dispensations; and the nature of the legislator. I round off this discussion by briefly considering the current debate on the so-called Consonance Problem and by presenting my own proposed solution.

2. The research on which this article is based has been supported by National Science Centre, Poland, grant: The Nature of Will. Freedom and Necessity. The Analysis of John Duns Scotus' Theory in Comparison to St. Augustine, St. Anselm of Canterbury and St. Thomas Aquinas, 2013/09/B/HS1/01985. I am grateful to Dr. Roman Majeran, Dr. Stefan Loska, Prof. Rafał Urbaniak and Prof. Wojciech Zelaniec for their help and important comments.

3. For the *Ordinatio* and the *Lectura Oxoniensis* (or *Lectura in Librum primum Sententiarum*, hereafter *Lectura*) I have used the following volumes of the *Commissio Scotistica Internationalis* edition of Scotus's works (Vatican City: Typis Vaticanis, 1950–). *Ordinatio*: *Liber primus, distinctio prima et secunda* (vol. 2); *Liber primus, a distinctione vigesima sexta ad quadragesimam octavam* (vol. 6); *Liber secundus, a distinctione quarta ad quadragesimam quartam* (vol. 8); *Liber tertius, a distinctione vigesima sexta ad quadragesimam* (vol. 10); *Liber quartus, a distinctione quadragesima tertia ad quadragesimam nonam* (vol. 13); *Lectura in Librum primum Sententiarum, prologus et distinctiones a prima ad septimam* (vol. 16). I have also used John Duns Scotus, *Reportatio I-A = The Examined Report of the Paris Lecture: Latin Text and English Translation*, trans. Allan B. Wolter and Oleg V. Bychkov (St. Bonaventure, N.Y.: Franciscan Institute Publications, 2008); John Duns Scotus, *Reportata Parisiensia* III, in *Opera Omnia II/2 Opera Theologica*, ed. Giovanni Lauriola, *Opera Omnia: Edito Minor* (Alberobello, Ita.: Editrice AGA, 1999).

NATURAL LAW

In Distinction 37, Book III of his *Ordinatio*, Scotus considers the following problem: "Do all the commandments of the Decalogue belong to natural law?"[4] He opens his discussion of this problem by observing that the term "natural law" can be understood in two different ways. The first way is to take this term in the strict sense, which is to designate the law whose very first principles are known to be true solely in virtue of the terms included in its formulation and, by extension, all the conclusions that follow necessarily from these principles.[5] There is also another, broader meaning of the term "natural law." In this broader sense, some commandments belong to natural law because they are highly consonant with that law, even though they do not follow with necessity from the first principles of practical reason. These first principles, qua such, are known to be true solely by grasping the meaning of their constituent terms and thus are necessarily known by every intellect capable of comprehending these terms.[6] Scotus himself adopts the position according to which: (1) the commandments of the second table do not belong to natural law in the strict sense; (2) the first two commandments of the first table belong to natural law, in the strict sense of the term; (3) it is debatable whether the third commandment of the first table belongs to natural law, in the strict sense of the term; (4) all the commandments (including those of the second table) of the Decalogue belong to natural law as taken in the aforementioned broad sense.[7]

From these statements it is clear that the distinguishing mark of natural law in the strict sense, as opposed to the broad, is the evidence of the propositions belonging to the former (either self-evidence, as in the case of the first principles, or apodictic evidence), which is related to the necessity characteristic of all the precepts of natural law. Thus, all the practical judgments that follow necessarily from the first and necessary principles of practical reason share in the feature of necessity and, consequently, form part of natural law, in the strictest sense of the term. In this, Scotus remains faithful to the basic assumption of his metaphysics

4. *Ordinatio* III, d. 37, q. un.
5. *Ordinatio* III, d. 37, q. un., n. 16.
6. *Ordinatio* III, d. 37, q. un., n. 25.
7. *Ordinatio* III, d. 37, q. un., n. 29.

(and the corresponding language), according to which the concepts "natural" and "necessary" are correlates, indeed, equivalent. Any judgment belonging to natural law in the strict sense must, ultimately, be reducible to a judgment, whose truth is immediately recognized once the terms forming that judgment have been correctly comprehended. According to Scotus's characteristic usage, Antonie Vos remarks, a judgment is "naturally" (*naturaliter*) true, if truth is included in the inherent nature of that judgment. This has a bearing on how we should understand the terms "nature" and "natural" in relation to natural law. These terms ought to be construed in an analytical-logical way, and not as referring to nature in the cosmological sense (the essence of the existing physical world). Scotus may be viewed here as departing from the classical concept of natural law.[8]

Yet natural law, understood as strictly necessary, can only be related to an object that is absolutely necessary. For this reason, Scotus affirms that the laws of the first table have a different status from those of the second one. The former regard God, the only necessary being, while the latter regard creation, a contingent being.[9]

Scotus affirms that the first two commandments—"You shall not have other gods before me," and, "You shall not take the Lord's name in vain,"—are equivalent to the injunction "You shall not act irreverently toward God," and that both belong to natural law conceived in the strictest sense. This is a conditional that is necessarily true: "If there is a God, God is the only one that should be loved as God," whence, "No other (thing or person) should be revered as God, and God should not be treated with irreverence," follows.[10] So, the first two commandments of the Decalogue follow directly from a judgment that is self-evident, and the truth of that judgment reposes on the correct comprehension of its subject term, "God." In the prologue to his *Lectura,* Scotus quotes St. Anselm's famous definition of God, "God is that than which no greater can be thought," and concludes that such a being is the most deserving of loved. This leads to the conclusion that God ought to be loved above all things and more than anything else.[11] In a like way, he develops this

---

8. Antonie Vos, "The Scotian Notion of Natural Law," *Vivarium* 38, no. 2 (2000): 213.

9. *Ordinatio* III, d. 37, q. un., n. 19.

10. *Ordinatio* III, d. 37, q. un., n. 20.

11. *Lectura*, Prologus, pars 4, q. 2, n. 172.

argument in Distinction 27 of *Ordinatio* III. "Loving God above all other things" is represented as an act consonant with right natural reason, which prescribes the love of that which is good in the highest degree. Consequently, the act of loving God above all things is an act that is right and appropriate in itself. The goodness of that act is self-evident: the good that is the highest good should be loved in the highest degree just as the highest truth is the truth for which the intellect ought to strive the most. Since all moral precepts belong to natural law, the precept, "You shall love God, your Lord," is part of natural law and is naturally recognized as right and appropriate.[12]

In a response to some objections, Scotus introduces an important specification to this claim that the affirmative precept, "You shall love God," is not unconditionally a law of nature, but only its negative content constitutes an absolute precept. "You must not hate God," is the precept that unconditionally binds every creature. According to the Subtle Doctor, the positive formulation of the commandment of love of God would lead to difficulties like those related to the problem of the unconditional binding force of the third commandment.[13]

The norms formulated in the first two precepts of the first tablet of the Decalogue are, as we see, unconditional. They are absolutely binding and are recognized by right human reason as self-evident. They are negative consequences of the principle, "One ought to love God to the highest degree possible," which is but the conclusion of the following syllogism.

Major	The highest good should be loved to the highest degree.
Minor	God is the highest good.
Conclusion	God should be loved to the highest degree.

The unconditional status of the first two commandments of the Decalogue means that even God himself, in his absolute power, cannot conditionally suspend their binding force: command actions that are contrary to what they prescribe. Even God cannot order anyone to hate God.[14] Thus, the commandments of the Decalogue that regard God immediately meet the condition specified by Gratian (in his *Decretum*) for natural law: natural law never undergoes any alteration in time but al-

---

12. *Ordinatio* III, d. 27, q. un., n. 14, w.

13. *Ordinatio* III, d. 37, q. un., n. 32. In this article I omit discussion of Scotus's treatment of the third commandment, whose necessity he regards as debatable.

14. *Ordinatio* III, d. 37, q. un., n. 21.

ways remains immutable.[15] Even God himself, the supreme lawgiver, cannot abrogate or make exemptions from the laws that constitute natural law. They admit of no limitation whatever and they cannot be other than they are, for they are true statements in virtue of the terms constituting them. They are necessary statements: either immediately, in virtue of the meaning of their constitutive terms; or mediately, as being derivable by necessary inferences from such immediate necessary truths. Scotus emphasizes the fact, that the truth of these precepts of natural law is prior to any act of willing whatsoever. In other words, they are true irrespective of any willing: they do not depend on anyone's will, not even on any act of God's will.[16] God does not institute by his own will the rules concerning himself. Thus, these rules are placed by Scotus safely beyond the context of any voluntarist justification whatsoever. This feature of Scotus's theory of the foundations of ethics shows clearly that his ethical theory as a whole cannot be interpreted in terms of a strong divine command ethics, whether one that takes God's will to be a sufficient condition of moral obligation, or one that makes God's will a necessary condition thereof. Rather, for Scotus, there are moral principles that bind any will regardless of (any act of) God's will.

Things are different if we consider the commandments of the second table of the Decalogue. These precepts concern relations between human beings. Hence, they are relative to creation, which is contingent. For this reason, Scotus affirms that, as far as the essential content (*ratio*) of acts prescribed or prohibited in the second table is concerned, no practical principles can be formulated that would be absolutely (*simpliciter*) binding. In this domain, there are neither first principles, whose truth is unconditional, nor absolutely necessary conclusions following from such principles.[17]

From what has been said, it is clear that the modal character of the moral laws related to God and those related to creatures are different from each other. Only the former are necessary, while the latter are not. The absence of the character of necessity in the laws of the second tablet is directly linked to contingency, which is the essential characteristic of creatures, to which these laws relate. Moreover, Scotus cites further rea-

---

15. *Ordinatio* III, d. 37, q. un., n. 17.
16. *Ordinatio* III, d. 37, q. un., n. 14.
17. *Ordinatio* III, d. 37, q. un., n. 18.

sons for why the moral laws concerning creatures should be unnecessary rather than necessary. Most importantly, fulfilling the requirements set by these laws is not indispensable for achieving the ultimate goal of created reasonable beings. As Scotus puts it, among the things prescribed by the laws of the second table, there is no good that is necessary for achieving the ultimate end of human beings, and, among the things that these laws forbid, there is no evil that makes the achievement of that goal impossible. The ultimate end of man could in principle be achieved and loved even if these particular goods were not prescribed and these partial evils were not forbidden.[18] What is more, there were moments in human history when dispensation from some specific moral laws was granted by God to particular human beings.

DISPENSATION FROM NATURAL LAW

Duns Scotus critiques the conception of natural law that the editors of the Vatican Edition of his complete works ascribed to Thomas Aquinas and Richard of Middleton. In Scotus's view, this conception represents natural law as a body of prescriptions deriving from the first principles of practical knowledge that are apprehended immediately, in virtue of a correct comprehension of the terms constituting these principles. The first principles of practical reason are the first seeds of truth to which the intellect is naturally inclined once it understands the terms of these principles, whereas the will has a natural inclination to appropriate these principles by virtue of their apprehension by intellect. According to this conception, all the commandments included in the Decalogue follow immediately or mediately from these principles.[19] Scotus construes natural law, as represented in this conception, as a body of normative statements linked to one another by relations of logical inference. Hence, it follows that if the laws of the first table are necessary, so too are the laws of the second table. Moreover, according to the Subtle Doctor, the conception under discussion holds that all actions prescribed in the Decalogue possess formal goodness owing to which they are by themselves related to the ultimate end of man, whereas all actions forbidden possess formal evil, which necessarily separates the perpetrator from an

18. *Ordinatio* III, d. 37, q. un., n. 18.
19. *Ordinatio* III, d. 37, q. un., n. 9.

achievement of his ultimate goal. In this way, it is not the case that the prescribed actions are good only by reason of being prescribed. Rather the reverse holds true: "because they are good, they are prescribed." Similarly, the things forbidden by natural law are not bad because forbidden. It is the other way round: "they are forbidden because they are bad."[20]

In opposition to this conception, Scotus objects that if all commandments possessed the feature of necessity, there could be no real dispensation from natural law at all. If all of them possessed the character of necessary laws connected to one another by necessary relations, no one of them could be conditionally suspended, as such a suspension would imply contradiction (within the whole system of divine injunctions). Thus, a revocation, albeit temporary and conditional, of these commandments would be impossible, even to the absolute power of God. Contradiction constitutes the limit to the sphere of possible divine action. Nevertheless, in salvation history there are instances in which God dispenses someone from a commandment of the second tablet. The Israelites are allowed to despoil the Egyptians (Exodus 12:36). Abraham is ordered to offer his son Isaac as a sacrifice (Genesis 22). The prophet Hosea is told to take a promiscuous woman for his wife (Hosea 1).[21] These instances clearly indicate that God has the power to grant such a dispensation. Apparently, the only way to account for this fact, short of admitting the possibility that God can issue contradictory dispositions, is to attribute to the commandments of the second tablet a weaker binding force: one that is not

20. *Ordinatio* III, d. 37, q. un., n. 9.

21. It is worth noting that only two of the above-mentioned commands, which are clearly in contravention of laws of the second table of the Decalogue, were carried out, while the third one, the sacrifice of Isaac, was not. Scotus does not address this problem when discussing possible exemptions or dispensations from natural law. However, he returns to the sacrifice of Isaac elsewhere, while discussing whether God acts consistently with regard to this injunction. There, he distinguishes two kinds of will in God and notes that they do not always agree with each other: the *voluntas signi* (God's will as indicated in signs imparted to someone) and the *voluntas beneplaciti* (God's will insofar as it takes pleasure in something or simply God's will as it is in itself). The latter is that which God really wants. The former, which is also the sign itself, is the way in which God usually indicates his will to creatures: injunctions, prohibitions, dispensations, advice, and actions. Scotus expressly affirms that "there are many things that God wills by his *voluntas beneplaciti,* which he apparently forbids in his injunctions given through signs, and, inversely, many things that he does not really want to happen, which he, however, apparently enjoins, as, for instance, he did not really want Isaac to be sacrificed, which he nevertheless ordered to happen." *Ordinatio* II, d. 34–37, n. 167.

This clearly shows that, in the case of the sacrifice of Isaac, God's *voluntas beneplaciti* did not in fact go against the fifth commandment and that God only intends to test Abraham's faith.

an absolute, strictly unconditional necessity. According to Scotus's previous assumptions, unconditional norms are not subject to any decisions of any will whatsoever. What is entirely wrong and therefore illicit by its own nature cannot be made permissible by any will, no matter to whom that will belongs.[22]

The problem posed by the apparent contradiction between the possibility of dispensation from the commandments of the second tablet and their necessity, as parts of the system of necessary natural law, was noticed by proponents of the conception of natural law whom Scotus criticizes. Richard of Middleton tried to steer clear of the difficulty by claiming that, even if dispensation from a norm prohibiting a certain kind of action was admissible for a singular case, a general dispensation from a prohibition that is contrary to the intention of the lawgiver would never be admissible.[23] In fact, according to that position, it is never possible to exempt one from the essence of a prohibition contained in natural law.

Aquinas offers a different explanation. In the case of laws instituted by human lawgivers, exemptions are granted in singular cases, namely, in circumstances in which strict adherence to the letter of the law would in fact be contrary to the intention of the legislator. There is no legitimate dispensation from general principles, say, from the principles of justice. Admissible exemptions are only possible in the case of derived rules, which specify particular ways in which these general principles are to be implemented, and which might be altered according to changing, particular circumstances. As for the laws of the second table of the Decalogue, God promulgated them as a way of preserving justice and, as such, they are beyond dispensation. The Old Testament cases of a seemingly authorized departure from some of these laws are not departures at all. The despoliation of Egyptians by Israelites was no theft. The injunction to offer Isaac as a sacrifice was no demand for murder and Hosea's relationship with the promiscuous woman was not adultery.[24] Thus, Thomas's opinion is that there are no cases of divinely authorized exemption from, or suspension of, any second table law and that God never issued any command contradicting his own established decrees.

---

22. *Ordinatio* III, d. 37, q. un., n. 10.

23. *Ordinatio* III, d. 37, q. un., n. 11.

24. Thomas Aquinas, *Summa theologiae*, 5 vols. (Ottawa: Harpell's Press, 1941–45), I-II, q. 100, a. 8, ad. 3.

Aquinas's remarks suggest that he takes the dispensation from a law to be simply an exemption from that law granted to a particular subject under particular circumstances, while the law itself remains intact and in force. This is not Scotus's view. For the Subtle Doctor, dispensation from a norm is equivalent to the introduction of a new norm. He affirms that "granting a dispensation from a commandment" is not merely suspending it for one particular case and allowing a subject to act otherwise than prescribed by that commandment. For Scotus, to grant a dispensation from a law means either to revoke or to elucidate that law. He distinguishes two kinds of dispensation: the revocation of a law or its declaration (elucidation).[25] In either case, the old law undergoes suspension and a new law comes into force. For that reason, Scotus assumes that when God orders actions different from those prescribed by the commandments of the Decalogue, the laws of the second tablet were in fact changed.[26] This clearly shows that these laws belong to a so-called "contingent ethics," to use Antonie Vos's terminology, and not to a "necessary ethics," since the principles of the latter are never subject to any possible dispensation.[27] If the laws of the second tablet were absolute and thus necessary, God would not be able to render acts prohibited in these laws permissible under certain conditions. God would not be able to permit killing, which is forbidden under the law of the fifth commandment. However, he does, as with the sacrifice of Isaac, to name one case among many.[28] In this sense, Scotus's argument follows *modus tollendo tollens*. If a law is necessary, then God cannot possibly change it. However, God has changed that law. Therefore, it is not necessary. Aquinas's and Scotus's different treatments of the laws of the second table derive from their different conceptions of dispensation. Aquinas can assume that the law

25. *Ordinatio* III, d. 37, q. un., n. 13.

26. Scotus's understanding of the term "dispensation," according to which a dispensation from a law is not an exemption from a law which continues in force, but rather the institution of a new law, has been pointed out and clarified by Hannes Möhle, "Scotus's Theory of Natural Law," in *The Cambridge Companion to Duns Scotus*, ed. Thomas Williams (New York: Cambridge University Press, 2003), 312–21. The novelty of that conception has not been evident to all historians of Scotus's thought. For example, Frederick Copleston claims that Scotus explains the changes of the second table commands as an introduction of exceptions, usually justified by specific circumstances: Frederick Copleston, *A History of Philosophy*, 11 vols. (New York: Image Books, 1993), 2:549–50.

27. Antonie Vos, *The Philosophy of John Duns Scotus* (Edinburgh: Edinburgh University Press, 2006), 439.

28. *Ordinatio* III, d. 37, q. un., n. 13.

of the second table possesses all the necessary features of natural law: immutability, eternity, and irrevocability. This is because he construes a dispensation from a commandment as an exemption from a law that nevertheless remains in force and valid. For Scotus, on the other hand, God, by granting a dispensation, introduces new rules and effectively changes the laws of the second table.[29] Scotus is thereby constrained to draw the inevitable conclusion: that the law of the second table of the Decalogue is not natural law, in the strict sense of the term.

THE CONDITIONS OF POSSIBILITY FOR A CHANGE IN MORAL NORMS

In attempting to identify the conditions under which it is possible to alter a law of the second table, one is well-advised to look at conditions on the part of the object—namely, its contingency—and on the part of the subject: the nature of the lawgiver and the nature of God's will.

As noted above, necessary moral laws regard objects that are necessary and have a relation of necessity to their objects. For this reason, all norms regarding God directly, must possess the attribute of necessity and they admit of no dispensation or exemption. Even God cannot institute norms that would be contrary to them.

By contrast, legal or moral norms regarding creation and contingent created realities do not have a necessary relation to their objects. If they did, God would not be able to change these norms. This reveals the objective conditions of the contingent nature of the laws of the second table: the contingent nature of their objects.

According to Scotus, a state of affairs is contingent if a contrary state can exist at any moment of its duration. In other words, any contingent fact is by its nature such that a contrary state remains an actual possibility (as long as this contingent fact endures in existence).[30] The legal norms regarding contingent realities are by nature contingent too. They do not obtain in a necessary way. This means that other, contrary norms could always in principle obtain instead. It appears that, for Scotus, these

---

29. It is fair to point out that in the case of the despoliation of Egyptians by Israelites, Scotus admits the explanation (also accepted, as indicated above, by Aquinas) that far from robbing the Egyptians, the Israelites simply took from them what was due to them as a reward for their slave labour. See *Ordinatio* III, d. 37, q. un., n. 43.

30. *Ordinatio* I, d. 2, pars 1, qq. 1–2, n. 86.

contingent moral principles are not unlike empirical laws of physics. They are a kind of synthetic judgment. They are judgments whose negation does not imply a contradiction.

Besides the objective conditions of changes in moral norms, Scotus identifies and discusses subjective ones too. These regard the concept of the legislator or lawgiver. This leads Scotus to examine the essence of the lawgiver. In distinction 44 of Book I of the *Ordinatio*, he states that the power to change the established norms belongs to the nature of the lawgiver. The power to comply with, or contravene, the established law is a characteristic feature of every intelligent subject capable of acting freely. Regardless of what is right or wrong, one can distinguish in God, indeed in every subject capable of acting according to what is right, the ordained power (*potentia ordinata*) of action and the absolute power (*potentia absoluta*). In legal parlance, Scotus remarks, we say that someone can do something *de facto*, that is by his absolute power, or *de iure*, that is according to the law or by his ordained power.[31] Insofar as God is a sovereign and free agent, he has power outside the constraints of the law that he himself has instituted. In principle, he could always govern the universe differently than how he does. He could institute a new and different law which would be just as consistent and binding as the existing one, and his ordained power would then conform to this new law.

Before embarking on a discussion of God's status as supreme legislator, Scotus considers how a free and rational agent acts when confronted by an established law, over which he has no efficient or legislative power. The absolute power of action of such an agent cannot exceed his ordained power regarding any object of action. If it does, the action becomes inordinate. If such an agent is bound by a law and contravenes it, his action is wrong and inordinate. This is the condition of all agents subject to a divinely instituted law. They are free to comply or not, yet they cannot change it. For such agents, failure to act in compliance with this law involves a violation of order and is itself an inordinate action.[32]

The situation is very different, however, when the agent is the legislator and so has power over the law itself and its binding force. In this case, the absolute power of action does not exceed the ordained power absolutely, for any exercise of the absolute power involves the laying down of

31. *Ordinatio* I, d. 44, q. un., n. 3.
32. *Ordinatio* I, d. 44, q. un., n. 4.

a law and so will be in accord with a law, whether the existing one or the newly established one. Consequently, the absolute power of a legislator will always be an ordained power. However, if the lawgiver acts contrary to or regardless of the established law, then his absolute power exceeds his ordained power in regard to that law. In the human world, the way in which a sovereign and absolute ruler governs subjects through law best illustrates this sort of situation.[33]

Hence, legislative power entails the power to institute new laws, different from and even contrary to the laws previously instituted. This power is embodied in the life of political bodies and societies. Changes in legislation may involve corrections and specifications of already existing laws, but they may also be more substantial. This holds true of God especially. He institutes the moral law of the second table of the Decalogue. Just as the legislator generally preserves his sovereignty *vis-à-vis* the law he institutes, so God, the supreme legislator, remains sovereign with respect to the contingent order he has established and thus preserves the power to introduce changes into that order without falling into disorder or inconsistency.

Another strand of Scotus's discussion of the institution of contingent moral norms concerns the relationship between God's will and his intellect. Undoubtedly, it is God's will, and not the divine intellect, that is ultimately responsible for instituting norms. The intellect, of course, has a role to play. The divine will makes its choice on the basis of conceptions presented to it by the divine intellect.

A normative judgment becomes law and acquires normative force when it pleases a free will, in this case, the will of God, the supreme lawgiver. Scotus invites us to consider the principle "whoever is to be glorified, must first be given grace."[34] This principle is no necessary proposition. Consequently, its recognition as a law by God is an entirely free decision. There is no objective reason compelling such a recognition. God's will, like any free will, acts as it will, without any external agency necessitating its acts. Additionally, with regard to creatures, God's will is free to choose whatever action it wants, for there is nothing in contingent objects to compel a necessary recognition on the part of God's will. God's will tends contingently toward whatever is not God him-

---

33. *Ordinatio* I, d. 44, q. un., n. 5.
34. *Ordinatio* I, d. 44, q. un., n. 6.

self.[35] If we were to assume that the commandments of the second tablet of the Decalogue are a set of necessary propositions, as is the case with the commandments of the first tablet, then we would have to acknowledge that any intellect grasping these conceptual structures, regardless of any wishes and inclinations of the will, would grasp them as necessary normative propositions. This is true above all of God's intellect. It would comprehend these norms as true by themselves and then God's will would necessarily agree with, and follow, that recognition, or else it would be a perverse will itself.[36]

In other words, the will would have to yield to the force of the necessary relations between concepts forming these normative statements and, consequently, acknowledge the unconditional validity of the commandments of the second tablet. However, this would be to affirm that God's will is necessarily determined in its willing by objects other than the divine essence, and this is something Scotus cannot accept.[37]

On the other hand, Scotus shows that moral normativity is not the same as logical normativity. He lays considerable emphasis on the fact that practical principles, laws, and general practical judgments have been established by God's wisdom. However, it is even more appropriate to say that they have been established by God's will. How so? The reason is that in practical laws and normative propositions there is no necessary relation between the constituent terms.

To illustrate this point, the Subtle Doctor considers the following practical law: "Every just person must be saved, while every evil person must be damned." He compares this with a proposition that he takes to be self-evident: "Every whole is greater than any of its proper parts." The latter proposition is necessary because, to use Scotus's way of speaking, its subject-term is the cause of its predicate-term. This, however, is not the case with the former proposition, which states a practical law. No just person is the cause of his own salvation. God's will could, in principle, accept either a just person or an evil or unjust one. There is nothing in the terms of this proposition to determine his decision either way. It is ultimately down to God's will that the aforementioned proposition becomes a law or practical principle.[38]

35. *Ordinatio* III, d. 37, q. un., n. 14.
36. *Ordinatio* III, d. 37, q. un., n. 14.
37. *Ordinatio* III, d. 37, q. un., n. 14.
38. *Reportatio* I-A, d. 44, q. 1. n. 9.

Since there is no necessary relation between the subject-term and the predicate-term, no contradiction will follow from the denial of that statement. Hence, Scotus feels authorized to affirm that God is free to follow many different courses of action and that only the principle of (non)contradiction constrains him. In principle, he could act otherwise than what is required by his ordained power under the present disposition.[39] He could, Scotus concludes, lay down the following norm: "Every rational soul should be saved."[40]

Clearly, these examples of normative statements are chosen to show that laws of this kind are set down by both God's intellect and will but depend more on the latter. This is because the lack of any necessity included in the very terms of the formulation of these laws results in an indeterminacy which leaves God's will free of any constraint and at liberty to decree these norms rather than others.

Scotus thus assumes that no contingent being has the power to make God choose one principle determining the morally obligatory actions of a being rather than another principle. It appears that the foundation of this impotence is precisely the contingency of that being. In a contingent being there are not necessary connections between its nature and the norms determining duties concerning them. God himself is free to do anything that does not involve contradiction and he is free to choose between diverse actions.[41] Just as God can in principle act otherwise than he actually does, so could he set down different laws than those he has actually established. An establishment of new and different laws is possible, and these new laws would be just as right and binding as those actually in existence, for they would enjoy the same sanction and authority that comes from God's acceptance of them.[42] Ultimately, it is the acceptance by God's will that is the foundation and source of the binding force of all established laws.

Given these considerations, Scotus feels authorized to affirm that, since all things other than God are contingent in nature, God could, in principle, create other possible worlds, where moral agents other than and different from human beings would exist, who would be given other

---

39. *Reportatio* I-A, d. 44, q. 1. n. 9.
40. *Reportatio* I-A, d. 44, q. 1. n. 10.
41. *Ordinatio* I, d. 44, q. un., n. 7.
42. *Ordinatio* I, d. 44, q. un., n. 8.

moral laws than those humans actually possess. God could also improve the existing universe by introducing new laws, such as morally more restrictive ones. He could also disregard his own established principles of justice. For example, out of magnanimity, he could offer salvation to the ultimate reprobate. It would not be contradictory for him to save Judas by virtue of his absolute power of action (*potentia absoluta*).[43]

The aforementioned potential, arbitrary courses of divine action contain nothing contrary to our moral intuitions. However, Scotus goes further and claims that God could give a commandment contrary to the principle, "You shall not kill," without any change of the circumstances determining human existence: without introducing additional conditions that would somehow justify in our eyes such an arbitrary act of God. All the circumstances of any act of "killing a human being" are exactly the same, except one: its "being forbidden or not." God could decide that in one instance it is forbidden and illicit; in another, permitted and licit.[44] This is a strong statement indeed. It appears to justify an extremely voluntarist interpretation of Scotus's moral philosophy. Promulgation of a new (contingent) principle does not imply contradiction on the part of the legislator, it concerns a merely contingent object and lies in the legislator's absolute power, thus it fulfils the conditions of a legitimate dispensation, which, in Scotus's terminology, is the same as the power to introduce a law that is contradictory with respect to the one in force.

Naturally, this gives rise to various questions. The strong emphasis laid on the contingency of creatures and the consequent contingency of natural laws leads unavoidably to the question as to whether, in Scotus's moral philosophy, there is any intrinsic relationship between a creature's nature and normativity (or the power to ground or justify norms). This aspect of Scotus's moral philosophy has stirred up much controversy, and still does, and has prompted a number of interpretations, most of them ranging from strong to moderate voluntarism.

THE NATURE OF THINGS AND NORMATIVITY

Scotus leaves no room for doubt that the laws of the second table of the Decalogue, even though contingent, have a certain relation to the laws of

43. *Ordinatio* I, d. 44, q. un., n. 11.
44. *Ordinatio* III, d. 37, q. un., n. 13.

the first table. This relation is not that of necessary inference. That would imply that the inferred norms were necessary. Rather, Scotus specifies the connection in the following way. The laws of the second tablet can legitimately be described as natural law, as their rightness (*rectitudo*) is highly consonant (*valde consonat*) with the first practical principles. This means that moral laws concerning relations between human beings fit in, and coexist harmoniously, with the first principle of practical life, which is known in a necessary way and enjoins humans to love God.[45]

There are many interpretations about how Scotus understands this "consonance" (*consonantia*). The term leaves no room for much linguistic interpretation. It refers to the world of sounds and it connotes a combination of sounds without dissonance. Metaphorically, it signifies agreement, harmony, mutual fitting, suitability, appropriateness. In his excellent study, Jeff Steele presents three interpretations of the notion of consonance in Scotus's theory of natural law: teleological, reductionist, and aesthetic.[46]

The aesthetic interpretation claims that God does not have any moral reasons to prefer one possible moral order to another. However, he has aesthetic reasons to do so.[47] In making a case against this interpretation, Steele points to the fact that the term *consonantia* does not always have an aesthetic meaning in Scotus's writings.[48] More importantly, however, on such an interpretation, God is represented as bound by principles standing over and above his own goodness, and this appears to contradict Scotus's well attested position. This interpretation also runs counter to Scotus's claim that the only restriction on God's otherwise unbounded freedom of will is the requirement of noncontradiction.[49]

The teleological interpretation of Scotus's conception of consonance is characterized by Steele as follows. The proponents of this conception

---

45. *Ordinatio* III, d. 37, q. un., n. 26.

46. Jeff Steele, "Duns Scotus, the Natural Law, and the Irrelevance of Aesthetic Explanation," *Oxford Studies in Medieval Philosophy* 4, no. 1 (2016): 79.

47. See Steele, "Duns Scotus, the Natural Law," 82. Steele discusses the views of two proponents of this interpretation: Richard Cross, "Natural Law, Moral Constructivism, and Duns Scotus's Metaethics: The Centrality of Aesthetic Explanation," in *Reason, Religion, and Natural Law: From Plato to Spinoza*, ed. Jonathan A. Jacobs (New York: Oxford University Press, 2012), 175–97; Oleg Bychkov, "'In Harmony with Reason': John Duns Scotus's Theo-Aesth/Ethics," *Open Theology* 1, no. 1 (2014): 45–55.

48. Steele, "Duns Scotus, the Natural Law," 85–86.

49. Steele, 92.

hold that the laws of the second table not only agree with the first principle of practical reason but also suit, perfectly albeit indirectly, human nature as such and the purposes it is destined to fulfil within the universe. In Steele's view, this position is crypto-Aristotelian teleologism. He mentions Allan B. Wolter and Mary Beth Ingham as its foremost proponents.[50] In a passage quoted by Steele, Wolter affirms that there are indeed certain aspects of the laws of the second table that can be suspended in accordance with right reason. This is the case when strict adherence to these laws would bring more harm than good. On the whole, however, Wolter concludes, God could not institute a total dispensation from all the commandments of the second table, for this would entail a complete change of the way man has been created and a total reorientation of human activity. This would be contrary to that which God "owes to human nature in view of his own magnanimity."[51] Wolter also points out that when God issues commandments, the laws these commandments embody, in particular the laws of the second tablet, lose their impersonal character.[52] They begin to serve as the ground for interpersonal relations between human beings and their creator. The establishing of such relations appears to be the true objective of the Decalogue.

Can Wolter's interpretation be brought into agreement with Scotus's claim that God can render an act that, in exactly the same circumstances, is forbidden and reprehensible at one point in time, permissible and acceptable at another?[53] True, Scotus gives the example of only one commandment being suspended by God. Nevertheless, it appears that he is indicating a general principle about God's absolute sovereignty over contingent moral law: one that applies to the whole second table. Wolter's thesis—"God could not possibly suspend all the commandments of the second tablet simultaneously"—has come under criticism from Richard Cross.[54]

Wolter's interpretation of the law of the second table raises some other questions. What kind of connection obtains between God's com-

50. Allan B. Wolter, *Duns Scotus on the Will and Morality* (Washington, D.C.: The Catholic University of America Press, 1986), 24; Mary Beth Ingham, "Letting Scotus Speak for Himself," *Medieval Philosophy and Theology* 10, no. 2 (2001): 173–216.

51. Wolter, *Duns Scotus on the Will and Morality*, 24.

52. Wolter, 25.

53. Wolter, 25, footnote 42.

54. Richard Cross, "Duns Scotus on Goodness, Justice, and What God Can Do," *The Journal of Theological Studies* 48, no. 1 (1997): 75.

mandments and human nature? Above all, is this connection decisive for God's choice of contingent laws and commandments? It seems that, on the strength of Scotus's own statements, no factor whatsoever determines God's decision. Instead, he is always free to act otherwise and the only thing binding his will is his own goodness. Given this assumption, even if there existed some close connection between human nature and the divinely decreed, contingent moral law, God would in no wise be bound to respect this connection. This would render any such connection completely devoid of significance for his ultimate decision concerning the contingent moral law.

In the reductionist interpretation, the Scotist conception of consonance is equated with fulfilment of the commandments of the first table. Steele attributes this solution to Thomas Williams.[55] According to this conception, the commandments of the second table do not have any positive content. Their value lies in the opportunity they offer man to express love for God.[56] The term *consonantia* does not refer to the content of the commandments of the second tablet, for these could be altogether different. It refers instead to the possibility they give us to become obedient to the divine decrees through our actions. By following the injunctions contained in these commandments, we fulfil the very first commandment governing our practical life: God ought to be loved (or, God ought not to be treated irreverently). In consequence, the fulfilment of the commandment, "You shall not kill," does not fit human nature in any particular way, but is an expression of human love for God, who issued this commandment as a decree of his will. If God had issued a contrary decree, its fulfilment would be as consonant with the first practical principle as is, at present, compliance with the injunction, "You shall not kill."

Each of these three interpretations of the consonance that obtains between the first and the second tablet of the Decalogue leads to different theoretical consequences for an understanding of Scotus's philosophy. The first two minimize the voluntarist import of his thought. Instead, they make God dependent in some way on extrinsic factors when it comes to establishing the moral norms of the second table. The third in-

---

55. See Thomas Williams, "Reason, Morality, and Voluntarism in Duns Scotus: A Pseudo-Problem Dissolved," *The Modern Schoolman* 74, no. 2 (1997): 73–94.

56. Steele, "Duns Scotus, the Natural Law," 79, note 4.

terpretation safeguards God's absolute independence. However, it makes the content of the moral norms of the second table seem wholly accidental. In the context of this interpretation, Scotus's thesis—"God wills in the most orderly way"—takes on an extremely voluntarist meaning.[57] It means that God does whatever he likes. If we accept this reductionist interpretation, we seem to commit ourselves to the holding that it does not matter at all which moral decrees God issues. What really matters is compliance with his commandments. Any act of obedience to his decrees, regardless of their content, will satisfy the principle of consonance equally well. Another upshot of this assumption is that, given the totally arbitrary character of God's legislative activity, we would never know why he had issued these decrees rather than others.

These divergent interpretations point to the fact that Scotus's views on the matter of contingency of the second table are not sufficiently clear. Difficulties of interpretation also arise from the fact that the following elements of his moral philosophy are not easily brought into agreement with one another: a libertarian conception of divine freedom, omnipotence and absolute independence; a very particular conception of dispensations; a firm belief that God creates a rationally ordered universe.

I shall now propose a possible solution to the problem of consonance. Whereas the first part of my argument is firmly rooted in Scotus's own explicit statements, this second part attempts to reconstruct Scotus's views. Nevertheless, in my opinion, this reconstruction does not contradict any of Scotus's statements on ethics and the philosophy of religion and so can seriously be considered as representing his intended meaning.

> 1. Scotus holds that the laws of the second table of the Decalogue can undoubtedly be called natural laws since their "rightness is highly consonant with the first practical principles," that is, with the principle, "God is to be loved."[58]

To specify further Scotus's position, it is worth considering how he uses the Latin term *valde* in relation to *consonantia*.

Does the term matter at all in the phrase *valde consonat*? After all, the contingent nature of the world means that God is not obliged to in-

---

57. "Deus est ordinatissime volens." *Reportata Pariensia* III, d. 7, q. 4, n. 66.

58. "Praecepta—etiam secundae tabulae—esse de lege naturae, quia eorum rectitudo valde consonat primis principiis practicis." *Ordinatio* III, d. 37, q. un., n. 26.

troduce any specific laws. Nevertheless, since all the laws that God could possibly decree are equally contingent, the question arises as to whether they are all highly (*valde*) consonant with the first practical principle, and equally so. In other words, the question is whether the rightness or correctness of law is a gradable quality. In moderate voluntarist accounts of Scotus's thought, the appropriateness of different contingent laws would appear to vary in degrees: some systems of commandments would be more in agreement with the first practical principle than others. On these grounds, it is legitimate to believe that a hypothetically possible system of norms that contradicts the commandments of the second table is less consonant with the first practical principle than they are. Its relationship with the absolute principle of practical wisdom might be so slight that God would never have adopted it as the moral law governing the created universe, even though it is one of the possibilities available to his absolute power. In extreme voluntarist accounts of the Subtle Doctor's thought, all the possible contingent systems of moral laws are equally right and equally consonant with the first practical principle since the divine decree remains the only criterion for preferring one system over all the others. It seems, however, that if this were Scotus's position, he would never use the phrase *valde consonat* but simply *consonat*. If instead *valde* is crucial, one system of commandments is more in accord with the first practical principle than another. In this case, we can no longer accept the reductionist account. It is too strong and lacks textual support. It ignores the content of the possible contingent laws, even though this content is essential for determining their degree of consonance with the necessary principle.

Hence, I take consonance to be a gradable quality and, consequently, the content of the commandments of the second tablet to be either favorable and acceptable or censurable and rejectable to God's will. That Scotus treats consonance as a gradable attribute finds further support in one of the formulas that he uses: "it is more consonant with reason that this be done in secret than in public."[59]

> 2. The nature of the commandments of the second table is such that, by understanding them, we gain some understanding of God's nature and, by observing them, we imitate God's love.

---

59. "Et magis consonum est rationi quod in secreto quam quod in publico." *Ordinatio* IV, d. 17, q. un., n. 26.

True, there is another context in which Scotus discusses law as such and in which he quotes approvingly a teaching of St. Paul: "he who loves his neighbor has fulfilled the law" (Rom 13:8).[60] God is, of course, a lawgiver. However, he is a charitable one who, in legislating, is motivated by love alone. What, though, is the essence of God's love? We know that the act of divine love is by its very nature directed first and foremost to the ultimate object of his love, God himself, and secondarily, to anyone who is meant to share in his love. Consequently, he wants created persons to have the gift of grace and the various other goods that are necessary for their destiny, such as the world of the senses.[61] This intrinsic ordering of God's all-embracing act of will manifests the perfect rational structure of that act. By performing finite acts of love, created persons introduce an analogous ordering into them and thereby imitate this supreme act of love. We too ought to direct our acts to the supreme good, our ultimate end, and subordinate our concern for all other objects to this overarching concern.

At the same time, God is revealed to us as the one who freely creates the world. Creation consists in imparting a share of divine being to creatures. It thereby constitutes a sort of descent of God to the secondary reality of the world. Even if this descent is ultimately for his sake, it still constitutes the model that creatures are meant to follow in their own action and reveals what God is really like.

According to Scotus, God intends his own goodness as the ultimate end of creation, and creatures as a subordinate end. Precisely because he wants to reveal and impart his own goodness and beatitude, he calls into being a multitude of individuals within each single species of intelligent beings. As is well known, Scotus is convinced that God intends to create the individual person as such rather than the species.[62] He thereby views God as the supreme goodness and benevolence, who freely, and without any compulsion or ulterior motive, imparts some of his reality to the creatures who are capable of appreciating and enjoying it. Love is the only adequate response to this supreme goodness, and what makes us love God is not merely his infinite goodness. As Scotus is keen to emphasize, it is the fact that the supreme goodness is the first to love me

60. *Ordinatio*, Prologus, pars 5, q .1, n. 222.
61. *Ordinatio* III, d. 32, q. un., n. 21.
62. *Ordinatio* II, d. 3, pars 1, q. 7, n. 251.

and has generously imparted some of its own riches.[63] In his view, an essential feature of divine goodness is not only its intrinsic value but also its self-communication through love. Indeed, it is because it loves that it deserves to be loved in return. In short, we love God because he loves us first.[64]

For this reason, not every possible set of second table norms is equally consonant with the first two commandments. Not every such set enables finite moral subjects to imitate his love and gain a comprehension of who he really is. The goodness of God's activity *ad extra* is the model for all the moral norms contained in the second tablet.

If we assume that the main feature of the activity of his perfect goodness is love, then it is easy to see how observing a second table precept makes us resemble God and our activity similar to his. After all, each of these commandments prohibits some inordinate desire. Fulfilling them, therefore, is highly consonant with love of God insofar as it is construed as becoming like him rather than simply obeying him or achieving the full potentiality of human nature. The weaker binding force of the second table accounts for how these laws do not necessarily determine God's will.

However, in terms of their content, not all conceivable bodies of commandments are equally consonant with love of God. If Scotus underscores the universal validity of the laws of the second table, it is probably because they exhibit the highest degree of consonance with this absolute principle of practical life. In his view, they were binding in paradise, retain their force in the present life, and will continue to do so in heaven. This universal validity, however, is not equivalent to necessity.[65]

According to this approach, God's will would be well-pleased in issuing some commandments just for his own sake. Hence, God could issue codes of norms regulating interhuman behavior that are wholly contradictory to those that hold within our world. He could, in principle, impose these different codes and make them binding laws. Due to the nature of his love, however, such legislation, even if free of internal con-

---

63. *Ordinatio* III, d. 27, q. un., n. 31.

64. *Ordinatio* III, d. 27, q. un., n. 31.

65. *Ordinatio* III, d. 37, q. un., n. 42. Here, Scotus considers two possible ways in which those living before the fall (*in statu innocentiae*) came to know the Ten Commandments: either from within (what we might call *nativism*) or from without. They would have been learned from within if they were inscribed within each one's heart and discovered by each one through introspection. Otherwise, they would have been discovered from without. Originally, they were taught by God and then handed on from one generation to the next.

tradition, would only be minimally consonant with the first practical principle or not at all. A possible code of human behavior that resulted from such alternative legislation would be possible in itself and compossible with the rest of creation, yet it would not be representative of God's nature and designs. In particular, it would not enable finite moral subjects to imitate and follow the pattern of God's own activity. Neither would it allow moral subjects to gain an insight into God's nature. On the other hand, we can also envisage a code of norms that would be even more consonant with the first practical principle than the Decalogue: one enjoining heroic actions or prohibiting acts that we currently regard as morally neutral. This more demanding code might allow moral subjects to imitate God and his actions in a more perfect manner.

To some extent, we can regard the New Law (in the New Testament) as the promulgation of a new code, whose prescriptions are more consonant with the first practical principle than the law of the Old Testament and allow for a more perfect imitation of God. It is also a more perfect revelation of God and the essence of his love. Scotus asks though whether the New Law is more demanding and harder to comply with than the Old Law. He points to two seemingly contradictory answers to this question. As to the moral demands it imposes on the faithful, the New Law is more exacting. The call to give one's tunic to one's neighbor makes a greater demand than the mere prohibition of stealing. Likewise, it is far more of a moral challenge to love one's enemies than one's friends.[66] Scotus affirms that the New Law comprehends all the moral commandments of the Old Law and, over and above that, imposes new precepts, or at least gives a new interpretation to certain regulations of the old dispensation.[67]

Moreover, Scotus argues that the New Law is actually light and easy. This is not because of its content and the demands it imposes but on account of the powerful assistance the faithful receive from the sacraments, whose efficacy flows from Christ's sacrifice.[68] The channels of help and grace are more numerous and more powerful in the new dispensation than in the old. It is in this sense that the New Law is lighter and easier than the old one.

66. *Ordinatio* III, d. 40, q. un., n. 9–10.
67. *Ordinatio* III, d. 40, q. un., n. 23.
68. *Ordinatio* III, d. 40, q. un., n. 18.

Summing up: the New Law appears to be more consonant with the first practical principle than the Old Law and it affords us a far better insight into who God really is. Hence, putting its precepts into practice makes us more similar to God than any other set.

What has been discussed opens a way to clarifying Scotus's conception of consonance. Although the proposed interpretation is not borne out by any explicit statement from Scotus's writings, it does provide a way of resolving apparently incompatible theses within the Subtle Doctor's moral philosophy. It: (1) preserves Scotus's claims about God's absolute freedom, which is constrained only by the law of noncontradiction; (2) steers clear of the paradoxical implication of the voluntarist reading, which reduces consonance to mere obedience, makes the moral content of the commandments of the second table completely irrelevant, and renders God's legislative activity purely arbitrary.

At the same time, the proposed interpretation allows us to preserve the valuable insights of the other three interpretations of Scotus's moral doctrine. In particular, it preserves the libertarian conception of God's will and freedom while giving importance to the moral content of the commandments of the second table. On this interpretation, God is supremely free, constrained only by the law of noncontradiction, whereas not every conceivable code of laws is equally pleasing to his will. Rather, he gives his creatures those laws that allow the finite subject to somehow become similar to him and understand that his love involves his going out toward others, descending to us, and renouncing himself for our sake. They also allow us to understand that, like him, we should transcend our own selves and lovingly embrace our neighbors. Hence, living the second table is not primarily a matter of obeying God's commands or of working to attain the fulfilment proper to human nature but of loving God, which consists in imitating and following his love.

Although the proposed interpretation is not directly backed up by Scotus's writings, it is worth noting that the other interpretations—the teleological, reductionist, and aesthetical—also have limited, direct textual support. The key reason for this seems to be that Scotus fails to provide a clear and explicit definition of *consonantia* and its bearing on these issues.

Moral obligation as such is a result of God's creative act. One could say that God extends his creative act by complementing the metaphysically contingent world with moral normativity. There are some necessary connections that result from the very nature of being. Human nature, for instance, cannot exist without rationality. Scotus affirms, therefore, that creating a *homo irrationalis* is even impossible for God, in his absolute power. Moral normativity in the realm of mutual human relations (second table), is of another kind. It needs to be instituted by a legislative act of God's will since, for Scotus, morality is not merely a matter of fulfilling human nature. As Copleston observes, here Scotus departs from Aristotelian ethics and moves toward a Christian ethics, which situates fulfilment in our relationship with God. That is why, for Scotus (and for a Christian), any transgression of a norm of the moral law is not merely unreasonable but also sinful.[69]

Summing up, Scotus holds that in principle it must be metaphysically possible for God the creator to act differently from how he has, even when establishing certain normative aspects of this world. If the second table of the Decalogue could consist of a different set of commandments, its norms are contingent. That does mean that they are arbitrary. They may be contingent, but they still retain their universal validity. Contingency is not synonymous with arbitrariness.

Moreover, if the commandments of the second table can have varying degrees of consonance (*consonatia*) with the principles of natural law, then their content is relevant for what it means to accept or reject the commandments that God wills and gives us.

Nevertheless, Scotus is not an extreme voluntarist. He insists that the norms that regard God himself are inviolable and absolute. They are binding on all wills, even God's. Scotus, therefore, is a moderate theological voluntarist. Indeed, it is mainly his understanding of dispensations, an essential element of his metaethics, that leads him to defend an ethics in which most norms are contingent. For Scotus, a dispensation is not an exception to the existing law, an exemption from it, or its temporary suspension, but a change in it through the introduction of a new law.

69. Frederick C. Copleston, *History of Philosophy*, 2:547.

Alessandro Mulieri

8 ∽ Marsilius of Padua's Political Theory of Natural Law

Marsilius of Padua is usually considered one of the first thinkers in the history of political thought who rejects natural law or, as Gewirth argues, who "does not have a theory of natural law."[1] In his famous study, *Natural Right and History*, Leo Strauss unequivocally subscribes to this same view, arguing that Marsilius does not believe natural law to be in any way natural but rather founded entirely on human conventions.[2] Let me be clear that, in this chapter, I am not going to try and challenge this widely accepted view on Marsilius's original position. However, I wish to develop further some insights that can be found in two relatively recent contributions devoted to this topic. In their analyses of this problem, both Annabel Brett and Holly Hamilton-Bleakley suggest that the

1. Alan Gewirth, *Marsilius of Padua: The Defender of Peace*, vol. 1, *Marsilius of Padua and Medieval Political Philosophy* (New York: Columbia University Press, 1951), 148–49. See Joseph Canning, "Law, Sovereignty and Corporation Theory, 1300–1450," in *The Cambridge History of Medieval Political Thought c. 350–c. 1450*, ed. J. H. Burns (Cambridge: Cambridge University Press, 1988), 454–76 at 461; Roberto Lambertini, "Marsilius and the Poverty Controversy in Dictio II," in *A Companion to Marsilius of Padua*, ed. Gerson Moreno-Riaño and Cary J. Nederman (Leiden: Brill, 2012), 229–64 at 244–45. On Marsilius's specific conception of rights, see the classic study, Ewart Lewis, "The 'Positivism' of Marsiglio of Padua," *Speculum* 38, no. 4 (1963): 541–82. More recent treatments are Brian Tierney, *Liberty and Law: The Idea of Permissive Natural Law, 1100–1800*, Studies in Medieval and Early Canon Law, vol. 12 (Washington, D.C.: The Catholic University of America Press, 2014), 136–41; Alexander Lee, "Roman Law and Human Liberty: Marsilius of Padua on Property Rights," *Journal of the History of Ideas* 70, no. 1 (2009): 23–44.

2. Leo Strauss, *Natural Right and History* (Chicago: University of Chicago Press, 1953), 157–64.

relationship between Marsilius's view and the traditional Thomistic position on natural law might be more complicated than it is usually assumed to be.[3] Brett claims that Marsilius derives the justification of his theory of rights exclusively from the political sphere.[4] However, she also argues that Marsilius's position does still attest to an extra-political dimension of right that, despite not being legally binding, retains some traditional elements of the canonical definition of natural law as observed in the Middle Ages. Hamilton-Bleakley's analysis of natural law in Marsilius aims to underline some important analogies between the Paduan's ideas on the origin of natural law and Aquinas's treatment of the relationship between primary and secondary precepts of natural law. Eventually, even if Hamilton-Bleakley specifies that she does not intend to oppose Gewirth's position, she does claim that the Paduan has an important story to tell for the natural law tradition.[5]

Building on these suggestions, in this chapter I wish to show that Marsilius's position is better explained as a testament to the political irrelevance of natural law rather than a simple rejection of natural law *tout court*. As I will try to show, Marsilius provides two definitions of natural law in II, 12, the only passage of the *Defender* in which he discusses the subject in greater depth. While he explicitly rejects the first definition of natural law, as he considers it to be a synonym of a ubiquitous convention, his attitude toward the second definition of natural law as the "dictate of right reason" is more ambiguous. Marsilius appears to place his second definition of natural law under divine law, thereby suggesting some kind of overlap between natural and divine law. Moreover, he does not deny there being something called divine law, which establishes what is *licitum* and *illicitum* in "absolute" terms (*simpliciter*). He explains, however, that if, and when, there is a mismatch between that which is prescribed by human law and that which is prescribed by divine law, we should consider the criterion for what is *licitum* and *illicitum* according to divine law, or that which includes the meaning of natural law

---

3. Annabel Brett, "Political Right(s) and Human Freedom in Marsilius of Padua," in *Transformations in Medieval and Early-Modern Rights Discourse*, ed. Virpi Mäkinen and Petter Korkman (Dordrecht: Springer, 2006), 95–116; Holly Hamilton-Bleakley, "Marsilius of Padua's Conception of Natural Law Revisited," in *The World of Marsilius of Padua*, ed. Gerson Moreno-Riaño (Turnhout: Brepols, 2006), 125–41.

4. Brett, "Political Right(s) and Human Freedom."

5. Hamilton-Bleakley, "Marsilius of Padua's Conception of Natural Law."

as the "dictate of right reason." Furthermore, as Brett rightly emphasizes, for Marsilius, there is an extrapolitical dimension of right that can help to establish normative absolute standards regarding right or wrong. However, this extrapolitical dimension does not have any legal force or political validity in this world. This certainly amounts to a dismissal of the traditional medieval belief that natural law should constitute an extralegal standard for assessing the quality and function of human laws in the political community. However, I shall demonstrate that this position does not represent a dismissal of natural law as a source of moral action, something that throughout his *Defensor*, the Paduan hardly doubts.

DEFINITIONS OF LAW, RIGHT, AND *LICITUM/ILLICITUM*

Marsilius discusses natural law in chapter 12 of the second *dictio* of the *Defender*. Here, Marsilius presents his thoughts on one of the most important and controversial issues of his time, namely, the question of evangelical poverty. In a nutshell, the Paduan's ideas fit together very well with his anticlerical stance as he defends the Franciscan doctrine of evangelical poverty that had been condemned by Pope John XXII.[6] The poverty controversy provided an intellectual training ground upon which the idea of natural law came to play an important role in the defense of the mendicant position on poverty.[7] However, as Lambertini shows, Marsilius presents an original view that selects arguments from both sides of the secular-mendicant controversy and, despite his open support for the mendicant position, he defends "the *simplex usus facti* without drawing on the Franciscan interpretation of natural law."[8]

At the beginning of II, 12, Marsilius clarifies several key terms that are usually involved in this dispute—*ius, lex, licitum, iustum, dominium, usus,* etc.—and that are essential for understanding his specific ideas on

6. Tierney, *Liberty and Law*, 123, 136–41. For a reconstruction of the poverty controversy in all its complexity see Virpi Mäkinen, *Property Rights in the Late Medieval Discussion on Franciscan Poverty* (Leuven: Peeters, 2001).

7. There is vast literature on this. See Brian Tierney, "Natural Law and Natural Rights: Old Problems and Recent Approaches," *The Review of Politics* 64, no. 3 (2002): 389–406; Tierney, "Marsilius on Rights," *Journal of the History of Ideas* 52, no. 1 (1991): 3–17; and his classic study, *Liberty and Law*. A detailed analysis of Marsilius's position in the poverty controversy can be found in Lambertini, "Marsilius and the Poverty Controversy," 245–63, esp. 262.

8. Lambertini, "Marsilius and the Poverty Controversy," 262.

natural law. There are three terms in particular that are central to our present analysis: they are "law" (*lex*), "right" (*ius*), and "licit/illicit" (*licitum/illicum*).

Let us start with the term "law," the meaning of which Marsilius clarifies in chapter 10 of *dictio* I. Here, Marsilius distinguishes between four different notions of *lex*.[9] While the first two definitions of *lex* refer, respectively, to a disposition of the soul and the rules governing a work of art, the third notion of *lex* is used as a synonym for *secta*, a term that can be translated as religion. Marsilius presents Mosaic Law as an example of this kind of law. Moreover, he argues that, under this meaning, law indicates a "rule containing admonitions for those human acts that result from an imperative, insofar as they are ordered toward glory or punishment in the world to come."[10] Here Marsilius presents an argument that he later develops in greater depth particularly in the second part of the *Defender*. He argues that, even if religious laws include rules and precepts, these are only aimed at salvation in heavenly, and not in the present, life. These rules and precepts must not be binding for any legislator during our earthly life because Christ, in the afterlife, is their only proper coercive judge.

According to the fourth use of the term, *lex* means "a science or doctrine or universal judgment of matters of civil justice and benefit, and of their opposites."[11] This fourth definition of *lex* can mean two different things. It can refer to "a science or doctrine of right" and be conceived in terms of its content, or it can be thought of as a norm that should be effectively enforced.[12] However, this idea—that the law couples justice with coercion—should not lead one to think that any law is just by virtue of its simply being coercive. Marsilius mentions the case of a murderer who is absolved from civil penalty "if he offers some price in goods for this offence" as an example of laws that are unjust and yet still have coer-

---

9. For the English translation, I rely on Marsilius of Padua, *The Defender of The Peace*, trans. Annabel Brett (Cambridge: Cambridge University Press, 2005). Henceforth, *The Defender of Peace* followed by page number. For the analysis of law see *The Defender of Peace*, 51–54. If necessary, I shall cite Richard Scholz's edition of the Latin text: Marsilius of Padua, *Defensor pacis*, ed. Richard Scholz, Monumenta Germaniae Historica, Fontes iuris germanici antiqui in usum scholarum separatim editi (Hannover: Hahnsche Buchhanldung, 1933).

10. *The Defender of Peace*, 52.

11. *The Defender of Peace*, 52.

12. *Defensor pacis*, 49–50: "iuris sciencia vel doctrina."

cive power.[13] Therefore, he argues that in order for a norm to be considered a *lex*, it should be perfect. In Marsilius's view, a perfect *lex* couples justice with coercive power. Interestingly, to refer to the concept of justice here, Marsilius uses *iustum* rather than *licitum*, which, as we will see, has a much broader scope.[14] As I shall show, he believes that the perfect law (*lex perfecta*) is created by the people or the whole body of citizens acting as legislators, and that this law that must withstand the passage of time in order to guarantee the stability of the *politia*.

In II, 12, Marsilius defines the concepts of "right" (*ius*), "licit" (*licitum*), and illicit (*illicitum*). He attributes to "right" (*ius*) two primary meanings. The first, which is quite canonical in the works of many medieval thinkers, identifies "right" with the third and fourth meanings of "law," as explored above.[15] Under this meaning, "right" and "law" are synonyms. The second definition of "right" (*ius*) identifies it with every "human act, power or acquired disposition that issues from an imperative of the human mind."[16] Tierney and Brett characterize this second definition of "right" as a subjective sense of "right," which is included but, at the same time, specifically distinct from the "law."[17] Indeed, according to this second meaning, "right" means a capacity or power to act rather than a "law" that sets binding rules for human conduct.

As for the couple *licitum*/*illicitum*, Marsilius ascribes to it a very general definition based upon the concept of "law." He argues that "everything that has been done according to a command or permission of the law, or omitted according to a prohibition or permission of the law, has been licitly done or omitted, and can be called licit," thereby defining "its contrary or opposite 'illicit.'"[18] Here, Marsilius offers two simple ideas about his definitions of "licit" and "illicit." First, he claims that "licit" refers to that which is done as the law (or "right" in its first meaning) prescribes or omits, while "illicit" refers to its contrary. However, and this is

---

13. *The Defender of Peace*, 54.

14. *Defensor pacis*, 49–50 [I, 10]: "Et sic accepta lex dupliciter considerari potest: uno modo secundum se, ut per ipsam solum ostenditur quid iustum aut iniustum."

15. *The Defender of Peace*, 250: "Thus, 'right' in one of its significations is predicated of law so called in the third and the final signification of law, as discussed in chapter 10 of the first discourse."

16. *The Defender of Peace*, 250.

17. Brett, "Political Right(s) and Human Freedom," 101, which also draws on Tierney, "Marsilius on Rights," 2. On this point, see also Tierney, *Liberty and Law*.

18. *The Defender of Peace*, 252.

an important elaboration upon Marsilius's first idea, he uses "law" in a general way and does not at all specify whether he is referring to divine or human law. Lacking any further specification, we can safely assume that Marsilius defines "licit" and "illicit" to refer to both human and divine laws taken together.

MARSILIUS'S TWO DEFINITIONS OF NATURAL LAW

We said that the definition of these key phrases is essential for understanding Marsilius's view of natural law. He discusses the latter in chapter 12 of the second *dictio* of the *Defender of Peace*. Here, he says that human law can be divided into two subspecies, natural and civil. He then distinguishes between two different meanings of natural law (*ius naturale*). It is worth citing Marsilius's entire passage here as his argument is quite intricate:

> There exists another division of "right"—and properly of human right—into natural and civil right. And according to Aristotle in *Ethics* IV, the treatise on justice, "natural right" is said to be that statute of a legislator upon which almost all agree as something honest that should be observed, for example that God should be worshipped, parents honored, human offspring brought up by their parents until they come of age, that no one should be wronged, that injustices should be repulsed in a way that is licit, and others similar. Although they depend on human enactment, they are called "natural rights" by transposition because they are believed to be licit and their opposites illicit in the same way in all lands: just as the actions of natural entities, which lack purpose, are produced in the same way everywhere, like "fire" which "burns here" in the same way as it does "among the Persians."
>
> There are those, however, who call "natural right" the dictate of right reason in respect of things that can be done, and place it under "divine right": in that everything that is done in accordance with divine law and in accordance with the counsel of right reason is licit, without qualification; but not so everything done in accordance with human laws, since in some things these laws are deficient in right reason. But in truth, the term "natural" is used equivocally here and above. For there are many things which accord with the dictate of right reason but which are not granted to be honest by all nations, viz. those which are not self-evident to all and in consequence not admitted by all either. So too there are certain commands, prohibitions and permissions according to divine law which are not in agreement with human law in this respect; but because this is familiar in many cases, I have omitted to

bring in examples in order to keep the discussion short. And hence it also arises that there are some things that are licit according to human law that are not licit according to divine law, and so too the other way round. But in those commands, prohibitions or permissions in which they are at odds, what is licit and illicit in absolute terms should be understood according to divine law rather than human.[19]

To understand Marsilius's position, we have to divide this passage into several parts and make sense of each one, one at a time.

At the beginning, Marsilius draws on Aristotle and restates his thoughts about natural law in the *Nicomachean Ethics*. Marsilius explains that, according to the first meaning, natural law can be taken as a synonym of the concept of *honestum*, upon which all people must agree. This definition encompasses, for instance, the worship of God and the duty of parents to take care of their children. Few medieval thinkers would deny that such activities are examples of natural law. However, Marsilius only partially subscribes to this view. He reports a view that lists the aforementioned acts under the Aristotelian definition of natural law as natural phenomena, comparing them, for instance, to the fire that burns everywhere on earth. Since it is valid among all people and throughout all lands, natural law would seem to have the same universal value as those laws of nature that explain the structure of the sublunar world. The idea here would be for Marsilius to show that, as fire burns here and among the Persians, so a parent has a natural duty to take care of his children not only here, but among the Persians as well.

However, for Marsilius, since these acts depend on human action and commonly accepted convention, they are only natural laws "by transposition." This would also explain why, in other parts of the *Defender* where Marsilius uses the language of natural law to refer to these acts, he uses the phrase "quasi-natural law." Indeed, in I, 3, 4 he argues that in early human communities it was necessary for the elder to "dispense what was just and advantageous by some reasonable ordinance or quasi-natural law."[20] Similarly, in I, 19, 13, he follows Cicero in claiming that "by a law that is quasi-natural" any man owes to any other man the debt of human friendship and society.[21] In these passages, as in II, 12, the "quasi-" refers

19. *The Defender of Peace*, 253–54.
20. *The Defender of Peace*, 16.
21. *The Defender of Peace*, 136.

to the fact that the legitimacy of these acts does not depend on them being natural law but on them being conventions among all people.[22]

Aristotle was the first to undermine the comparison between the laws that govern the natural world and natural law as an extrajuridical criterion of justice. In chapter 7 of Book V of the *Nicomachean Ethics*, on the concept of justice (the passage is quoted in Marsilius), Aristotle provides a short discussion of the problem of natural law. As Strauss rightly notes in *Natural Law and History*, Aristotle's position on natural law is "singularly elusive" and leaves considerable room for different interpretations.[23] In brief, Aristotle distinguishes natural from conventional or legal law. However, he assumes that both laws are similarly changeable. In fact, Aristotle dissolved the contraposition between conventional and natural law in terms of their universality.[24] He thereby rejects *de facto* the Platonic, and later Stoic, position according to which natural law is considered universal, innate, and unchangeable.[25] Aristotle then explains that, even if this comparison between the "naturalness" of natural law and that of natural phenomena were to suggest some sort of analogy between the two, it does not affect the changeability of natural law as such.

In Marsilius's time, there were two opposing interpretations of Aristotle's approach to natural law, among others: that of Thomas Aquinas and that of Averroes's *Commentaries*.[26] The first treated Aristotle's idea of natural law as compatible with Christian theology and therefore closer to another common medieval conception of natural law, which Tierney has named Platonic-Stoic.[27] The second pushed the Aristotelian claim

22. It is noteworthy that the term "quasi-natural law" (*ius quasi naturale*) is also present in the Latin translation of Ibn Rushd's commentary on the *Nicomachiean Ethics*. See Aristotle, *Aristotelis Opera cum Averrois Commentariis*, 11 vols., vol. 3 (Venice: apud Iunctas, 1562), 73.

23. Strauss, *Natural Right and History*, 156.

24. "It is obvious, in the case of contingent things, which sort are by nature, and which are not, but are legal and conventional, assuming that both are similarly changeable. And the same distinction will hold in other cases: by nature, the right hand is superior, but it is still possible for everyone to become ambidextrous." Aristotle, *Nicomachean Ethics*, trans. Roger Crisp (Cambridge: Cambridge University Press, 2004), 93–94.

25. See Strauss, *Natural Right and History*, esp. 146–64.

26. Both Brett and Strauss claim that there is an Averroist position on natural law that tends to push Aristotle's view of the changeability of natural law to its extreme; see Brett, "Political Right(s) and Human Freedom," 101. For Strauss, see his *Natural Right and History*, 158, in which he contraposes this position to the Thomistic position on natural law.

27. See Tierney, *Liberty and Law*, esp. 1–15.

about the changeability of natural right to its extreme, denying any such thing as natural law altogether.

As Brett notes, Averroes pushes Aristotle's skepticism about natural law to its extreme and claims that, just as some people become left-handed, despite the natural tendency to be right-handed, there must be a similar variability in "naturally just things" and customs. Even if she is cautious about applying the label of "Averroism" to Marsilius, Brett argues that the Paduan pushes Averroes's position to its limits.[28] Leo Strauss has no doubt about ascribing to Marsilius an Averroist position on natural law, defining this position as the idea that natural law always "depends on human institution or convention; but it is distinguished from merely positive right by the fact that it is based on ubiquitous convention."[29] In the end, in the first definition that he provides in II, 12, Marsilius rejects natural law or considers it to be "quasi" natural, claiming, as Averroes did, that natural law is founded on human convention and not on a universal standard of justice. But does this mean that Marsilius presents a completely relativistic position on the matter of right and wrong for human communities? The Averroist position opens the path to a radical relativism because it treats right and wrong as founded exclusively on human convention. However, Marsilius's position on natural law appears to be somewhat more complex.

Indeed, there are traces of the Thomistic position in Marsilius's account of natural law. This is evident in the Paduan's second definition of natural law, which differs from the first and for which natural law is taken as a synonym of "dictate of right reason," thereby placing it under the category of "divine law." This definition of natural law echoes Thomas Aquinas's definition of human law as such as a "dictate of practical

28. See Brett, "Political Right(s) and Human Freedom," 101, note 18. Given the usual polemical "verve" associated with Marsilius's Averroism, Brett is understandably cautious and states that, if Averroes's interpretation of Aristotle's natural law emphasizes the conventional aspect of natural law even more than the Stagirite, Marsilius also subscribes to an extreme version of this interpretation.

29. Strauss, *Natural Right and History*, 158ff. There, Strauss claims that there is a unique Averroist position that starts among the Jewish and Islamic Averroists and carries on through what he defines as the Latin Averroists. To reconstruct the polarized debate on the Averroist credentials of Marsilius's thought, see Alessandro Mulieri, "Against Classical Republicanism: The Averroist Foundations of Marsilius of Padua's Political Thought," *History of Political Thought* 40, no. 2 (2019): 218–45.

reason."[30] Although Thomas's *Summa* does not refer to natural law specifically with the phrase a "dictate of right reason," he believes that any law, including natural law, is a "dictate of practical reason." Moreover, in his *De decem preceptis*, he refers to natural law, and only to this, with a phrase that entails the same idea of obligation that is implicit in the word "dictamen." He says that natural law is "the light of human intellect, instilled in us by God and according to which we can know what is to be done and what is to be avoided."[31]

For Aquinas, natural law does not require human convention to ground its legitimization. In the *Summa Theologiae*, Aquinas places natural law in direct relation with eternal law, this being his original reading of Aristotle's position. For him, God's governance of the world also takes the shape of a law.[32] As he explains, since "the whole community of the universe is governed by Divine Reason" we have to assume that "the very Idea of the government of things in God the Ruler of the universe, has the nature of a law."[33] For Aquinas, "since the Divine Reason's conception of things is not subject to time but is eternal [...] therefore it is that this kind of law must be called eternal."[34] According to Aquinas's view, then, eternal law is the providential plan by which God governs the world.

Aquinas argues that the reference to eternal law can explain the epistemological roots of natural law. For him, the rational creature clearly "is subject to Divine providence in the most excellent way, in so far as it par-

---

30. Thomas Aquinas, *Summa Theologiae* (henceforth, *ST*) I-II, q. 91, a. 3, co.; trans. *Summa Theologica* (henceforth, Benziger Edition), trans. by Fathers of the English Dominican Province, 3 vols. (New York: Benziger Brothers, 1948), 1:1335.

31. "[Lex naturae] nihil aliud est quam lumen intellectus insitum nobis a Deo, per quod cognoscimus quid agendum et quid uitandum." Jean-Pierre Torrell, "Les 'Collationes in decem praeceptis' de saint Thomas d'Aquin. Édition critique avec introduction et notes," *Revue des sciences philosophiques et théologiques* 69, no. 1 and 2 (1985): 24, lin. 5–7. Quoted in Iacopo Costa, "Reflets théologiques et psychologiques sur l'élaboration du concept de droit (XIIIe-XIVe siècle)," in *Frontières des savoirs en Italie à l'époque des premières universités XIIIe-XVe siècle*, ed. Joël Chandelier and Aurélien Robert, Collection de l'École française de Rome (Rome: École française de Rome, 2015), 190, note 39.

32. "At any rate, the ultimate consequence of the Thomistic view of natural law is that natural law is practically inseparable not only from natural theology—i.e., from a natural theology which is, in fact, based on belief in biblical revelation—but even from revealed theology." Strauss, *Natural Right and History*, 164.

33. *ST* I-II, q. 91, a. 1, co.; Benziger Edition, 1:1333.

34. *ST* I-II, q. 91, a. 1, co.; Benziger Edition, 1:1333.

takes of a share of providence."[35] This means that the rational creature participates in a share of eternal reason "whereby it has a natural inclination to its proper act and end." This participation of the rational creature in the eternal law is called natural law. In Aquinas's own words, "It is therefore evident that the natural law is nothing else than the rational creature's participation of the eternal law."[36]

That natural law is defined as a form of participation in divine law bears tremendous significance for Aquinas. To begin with, for him, natural law is innate to all men and consists of precepts that are self-evident, general, and indemonstrable. Insofar as one can ascribe content to natural law, this is to be found in the notion of the good, which is the first principle of practical reason. From the notion of the good, which, based on Aristotle's ethics, can be more aptly summarized in the principle, "Good is that which all things seek after,"[37] Aquinas draws the first precept of the law, which is that, "Good is to be done and pursued, and evil is to be avoided."[38] Moreover, since he also claims that all other precepts of natural law are based upon this, he distinguishes between first and secondary precepts of natural law, an aspect of his theory over which scholars have disagreed considerably.[39] Secondary precepts specify how primary principles function in human civil societies. How compatible is Thomas Aquinas's position with that of Marsilius?

We saw that Marsilius's second definition of natural law echoes Aquinas's and, a few sentences later, the Paduan clearly states that, according to this definition, natural law is placed under divine law.[40] Since Marsilius defines natural law as a "dictate of right reason" placed under divine law, acts against natural law are also against divine law. Marsilius's phrasing is ambiguous because it suggests that divine and natural law are not fully identical but that divine law is broader than natural law and just includes the latter as a subspecies. However, since Marsilius stops using the phrase "natural law" in the subsequent parts of the texts and only talks about

---

35. *ST* I-II, q. 91, a. 1, ad. 3; Benziger Edition, 1:1334.

36. *ST* I-II, q. 91, a. 1, ad. 3; Benziger Edition, 1:1334.

37. *ST* I-II, q. 94, a. 2, co.; Benziger Edition, 1:1351.

38. *ST* I-II, q. 94, a. 2, co.; Benziger Edition, 1:1351.

39. A good overview of the interpretative debate on Thomas Aquinas's position is Hamilton-Bleakley, "Marsilius of Padua's Conception of Natural Law," 131–33.

40. "There are those, however, who call 'natural right' the dictate of right reason in respect of things that can be done, and place it under 'divine right.'" *The Defender of Peace*, 254.

the relationship between human and divine law, we can assume that, in this passage, natural law overlaps, if not completely, at least to a large extent, with divine law.[41] The advantage of this definition vis-à-vis the first definition is that it does not rely on human will or human convention but rather derives its legitimacy from divine law. Marsilius also stresses that there are many commands or prohibitions according to divine law that are not in agreement with human law and, vice versa, there are many things in agreement with human law that are "illicit" according to divine law. Here, to keep the discussion short, he refuses to provide examples. Elsewhere in the *Defender*, however, he provides some clear examples of mismatches between human and divine law.

In II, 10, 7, he says that no one who sins against the divine law can be punished by a human legislator.[42] In II, 10, 3 he provides an extreme example of a mismatch between divine and human law. He says that, if it is not forbidden by human law to get drunk or for a heretic to cohabitate with faithful believers, nobody would ever forbid these kinds of behaviour.[43] For Marsilius, nobody could legitimately punish these kinds of behaviour or the people who behave in these ways. This amounts to saying that the only kinds of behaviour that can be forbidden are those that are regulated by a human secular legislator. He clarifies that while many things, like getting drunk and fornicating, are contrary to divine law, they can still be permitted under human law. For the Paduan, one can get drunk and adopt all kinds of unethical behaviour and this, if judged against the normative conduct of Christian religion, certainly does not lead to salvation in heavenly life. However, if these kinds of behaviour are not forbidden by human law, they can still be permitted, despite being prohibited by divine law.[44]

41. For a definition of divine law in Marsilius, see *The Defender of Peace*, 148. Here, Marsilius says that the teaching and learning of commands and counsels in accordance with divine law are "sacraments of the church and their effects, all divine grace, all the theological virtues, and all the gifts of the holy spirit that order us towards eternal life."

42. "For a person is not punished by the prince just because he sins against divine law." *The Defender of Peace*, 237.

43. *The Defender of Peace*, 234–35.

44. This, I claim below, is a clearly anti-Thomistic position in Marsilius. Aquinas also seems to assert that fornication or drunkenness are sins left unpunished by human laws. See *ST* II-II, q. 69, a. 2, ad. 1; Benziger Edition, 2:1988: "Human laws leave many things unpunished, which according to the Divine judgment are sins, as, for example, simple fornication; because human law does not exact perfect virtue from man, for such virtue belongs to few and cannot be found in so great a number of people as human law has to direct." However, as we

If we take Marsilius's second definition of natural law as a standard for assessing the licitness or illicitness of human acts, clearly the latter are unethical and go against natural law. Toward the end of the passage in II, 12, Marsilius emphasizes this very point. He clearly states that "in those commands, prohibitions or permissions"[45] in which human and divine law (here used as a synonym of natural law) are at odds, there is a way of distinguishing the "licit" from the "illicit" "in absolute terms" (*simpliciter*).[46] It consists of sticking to what is prescribed according to divine law. This statement is unequivocal. For Marsilius, whenever there is a mismatch between that which is prescribed by human law and that which is prescribed by natural or divine law, we should take divine law as the criterion for what is licit and illicit. Furthermore, divine law includes natural law, in the second meaning of the term: a "dictate of right reason."

With Marsilius's definitions of "licit" and "illicit," as we saw, it is unclear whether he regards these notions as depending on human or divine law. In the passage on natural law (II, 12), we can distinguish three possible positions in which, according to Marsilius, something can be judged "licit" or "illicit": a) according to human law (in this case the *licitum* overlaps with the *iustum* of the *lex perfecta*); b) according to divine law; and c) in absolute terms (*simpliciter*). Marsilius identifies b and c. Therefore, for Marsilius, determining that which is "licit" or "illicit" in absolute terms consists in ascertaining whether a judgement, an action, or a thing accords with divine law or goes against it. This reading of Marsilius is confirmed at the beginning of II, 12, 6, where he uses the word "licit" as a synonym for the word *fas*. As Brett confirms in her own translation of the *Defender*,[47] where *fas* is translated as "allowable," it has a heavily sacral and religious connotation. Therefore, in using this word as a synonym of *licitum*, Marsilius is confirming what he says in II, 12, 7, where he implies that "licit" refers indistinctly to human or divine law. However, when the idea of *licitum* is considered as a criterion for estab-

---

will see in the next paragraph, for Aquinas, unlike Marsilius, any law that deviates from natural law is a perversion of law and technically cannot be called law in the first place.

45. *The Defender of Peace*, 254.

46. *The Defender of Peace*, 254.

47. "Hence too we can see what it is that is habitually called 'allowable'. For in one signification, what is allowable is the same thing as what is licit, the two terms being almost convertible." *The Defender of Peace*, 252.

lishing right and wrong in absolute terms, it is identified with divine law.

As Marsilius observes, there is a problem when we compare the second definition of natural law to the first. That is, when defined as a "dictate of right reason," even if natural law seems to be universally valid because of its being based on divine law, as we saw, many human laws clearly do not agree with the commands and prohibitions of that law. This would seem to mean that, for Marsilius, the two meanings of natural law that he provides must be kept separate. This reading of his position finds support in the following sentence, where he says, "in truth, the term "natural" is used equivocally here and above."[48] To clarify the meaning of this sentence, one must interpret the meaning of the word *equivoce* in light of Marsilius's overall reasoning.

Above, we saw that the Paduan appears to follow Aristotle by claiming that the word "natural" cannot be used to describe anything that is not universally valid. In this case, the word natural does not reflect something that is simply accepted by agreement among all people; it refers to convention. Therefore, that which is usually defined as natural law by virtue of being universally accepted among different people is not natural at all but rather conventional or artificial.

At the same time, Marsilius seems to imply that the word "natural" can be applied to "dictates of right reason" that, being truly universally valid, are natural and correspond to divine law. For Marsilius, a law can be defined as "natural" if it corresponds to the "dictate of right reason" under divine law. To interpret his view we have to assume that, in his two definitions of natural law, the word "natural" has two different meanings. According to the first meaning, "natural" refers to human convention or human politics. Therefore, we can take Marsilius's words to imply that the word "natural" is used equivocally in this respect. In the second instance, "natural" refers to the objective validity of the "dictates of right reason" that are included in, and in fact based on, divine law. We could then summarize Marsilius's position by claiming that he provides a correct and a false definition of natural law. We have already explained what motivates his equivocal use of the word "natural" in his first definition. The correct notion of natural law includes divine law and thereby provides an extra-legal standard for establishing right and wrong. Simply

---

48. *The Defender of Peace*, 254. Here is the original Latin: "Verum naturale hic et supra equivoce dicitur."

put, for Marsilius, the correct natural law *is* divine law. This difference between a correct and a false notion of natural law explains the meaning of *equivoce*. For Marsilius, the equivocal aspect of natural law lies in the fact that there is only one meaning of natural law that seems sustainable. The first definition of natural law is false because it includes rules that are not grounded in divine law and are not truly "natural" or universal.

The objective standards of right and wrong established by natural law bear a certain relevance for guiding human acts and define what is necessary for man to obtain salvation. As Marsilius explains in I, 2, 9, the evangelical law cannot regulate "the contentious acts of men" in the present life because these constitute the domain of the human legislator.[49] However, the divine law provides guidelines for the present life in order to establish right and wrong. Marsilius says that "we are adequately directed by evangelical law in what we should do or avoid in this present life, but this is nevertheless the matter of the world to come, or for gaining eternal salvation and avoiding eternal punishment."[50] This means that the evangelical law helps to understand what men ought or ought not to do in the present life if they want to achieve salvation in the next life.

THE RELATIONSHIP BETWEEN NATURAL AND HUMAN LAW IN MARSILIUS

Aquinas very much agrees with Marsilius's idea that we have to define "licit" and "illicit" in absolute terms in order to make a judgement about human conduct. However, he also adds a caveat that makes the precepts of divine law binding for human law. In his view, since natural law absolutely determines that which is "licit" and "illicit," human laws should simply abide by natural law. Aquinas does not thereby limit himself to embracing positions b and c, as Marsilius does, but also position a. This is precisely what Marsilius refuses to do. For this reason, several scholars rightly see his stance on natural law as original. Usually, his espousal of this position is taken to mean that he rejects or does not have a theory of natural law. However, I hope to have shown that this claim should be qualified. He does indeed have a theory of natural law if by having a theory of natural law we mean that one has an objective standard for judg-

---

49. *The Defender of Peace*, 230.
50. *The Defender of Peace*, 230.

ing right and wrong in absolute terms. Even though this standard can only be punished in the heavenly life, this does not diminish the moral value that the precepts of divine law have in the present life. Marsilius's position on natural law is thus original, not because he lacks a theory of natural law, but because of the function he ascribes to natural law within his overall political thought. To see which function he ascribes to it, we must turn to his assessment of the relationship that exists between human and natural law. To this end, I will outline the typical Thomistic position and highlight in what sense Marsilius's position departs from it.

In the *Summa Theologiae,* there is a *quaestio* in which Aquinas deals with the derivation of human law from natural law. It is worth citing this *quaestio* in full:

> Now in human affairs a thing is said to be just, from being right, according to the rule of reason. But the first rule of reason is the law of nature, as is clear from what has been stated above (Q[91], A[2], ad 2). Consequently every human law has just so much of the nature of law, as it is derived from the law of nature. But if in any point it deflects from the law of nature, it is no longer a law but a perversion of law. But it must be noted that something may be derived from the natural law in two ways: first, as a conclusion from premises, secondly, by way of determination of certain generalities. The first way is like to that by which, in sciences, demonstrated conclusions are drawn from the principles: while the second mode is likened to that whereby, in the arts, general forms are particularized as to details: thus the craftsman needs to determine the general form of a house to some particular shape. Some things are therefore derived from the general principles of the natural law, by way of conclusions; e.g. that "one must not kill" may be derived as a conclusion from the principle that "one should do harm to no man": while some are derived therefrom by way of determination; e.g. the law of nature has it that the evil-doer should be punished; but that he be punished in this or that way, is a determination of the law of nature. Accordingly both modes of derivation are found in the human law. But those things which are derived in the first way, are contained in human law not as emanating therefrom exclusively, but have some force from the natural law also. But those things which are derived in the second way, have no other force than that of human law.[51]

In this long quotation, Aquinas makes two main claims. First, he argues that every human law is derived from the law of nature because the

---

51. *ST* I-II, q. 95, a. 2, co.; Benziger Edition, 1:1358.

"just" in human affairs must be established according to the rule of reason, which is the law of nature. Clearly, for Aquinas, we need to resort to natural law to determine the "just" in absolute terms. As we saw, natural law corresponds both to right reason and to participation in the eternal, divine law of God. Second, Aquinas holds that the law *qua* law depends on its being derived from natural law. This means that a proper human law must follow from natural law or it cannot even be considered a law in the first place. This is also why he goes on to state that, when human laws divert from the law of nature, they are no longer laws but "perversions" of it.

The derivation of human law from natural law can proceed in two different ways. On the one hand, human laws can be deduced from natural law by a kind of cause-effect relationship. This is what he calls "conclusion from premises" derivation. On the other hand, human laws can be derived from natural law through a natural process of specifying general rules, a practice common in the arts. Aquinas further clarifies the distinction between these two different possible derivations by explicitly linking them to either the sciences or the arts. He then provides the example of murder and the punishment of murder. There is no doubt that, according to the law of nature, all evildoers should be punished. This rule, which is often contained in human laws, is directly derived from the natural law that "one must not kill." The derivation from the first to the second here is that of the "conclusion from principle" sort. However, other human laws are derived from the natural law by determining some particular application of a general case. In this specific case, the particular determination of the law of nature can be seen in the nature of the punishment that is chosen to sanction the evildoer. This is not established by the law of nature but by human laws. The difference that Aquinas draws between these two ways of deriving human from natural law can be explained through his distinction between primary and secondary precepts of natural law. For Aquinas, secondary precepts are "certain detailed proximate conclusions drawn from the first principle." However, the deontological nature of human laws is entirely determined by their relationship to natural law.

No doubt, Marsilius presents a powerful case against Thomas's position. Chapters 11, 12, and 13 of the first *dictio* of the *Defender* are essential for outlining the Paduan's understanding of the foundation of human law. Previously we saw that actual human law is a *lex perfecta*, which combines a "just" norm and a coercive power through which this norm is enforceable. In I, 12, Marsilius provides his famous definition of the legislator:

> The "legislator", i.e. the primary and proper efficient cause of the law, is the people or the universal body of the citizens or else its prevailing part, when, by means of an election or will expressed in speech in a general assembly of the citizens, it commands or determines, subject to temporal penalty or punishment, that something should be done or omitted in respect of human civil acts.[52]

Marsilius says that the legislator is the *populus seu civium universitas* or its *valentior pars*. The citizens among the people make the laws and, when they elect the *valentior pars*, they remain in charge as the primary legislators.

Apart from I, 12, 3, there are many other passages from *dictio* I in which Marsilius claims that the many make the laws. He explicitly grounds the impartiality of *lex perfecta* in his explanation of the creation of the laws themselves. At the beginning of I, 11, Marsilius explains that the necessary purpose of the law is two-fold: first, the need to keep the common good and civil justice in the *communitas politica* and, second, the goal of guaranteeing the safety of those who are subject to this law.[53] The Paduan argues that the governor must execute the rule according to the law, which itself requires impartial judgment. Such impartiality presupposes that the law must be free of any empirical or contingent influence and thereby provide for a balanced assessment in regulating human acts. To achieve this balance, the Paduan explains that the law needs to clearly specify that which is and is not fair. As he explains in paragraph 3 of chapter 10, the *lex perfecta* contains an almost complete definition of the "just" and "unjust," advantageous or harmful, with respect to any and every human civil act.

To ground his notion of *lex perfecta*, Marsilius draws on a specific concept of knowledge as *prudentia* and not, as we saw in Aquinas, on the definition of natural law as the "dictate of right reason." He says that the

---

52. *The Defender of Peace*, 66.

53. This is a summary of the argument that Marsilius presents in 1, 10, where he talks about the foundations of human law. On this see Alessandro Mulieri, "Marsilius of Padua and Peter of Abano: The Scientific Foundations of Law-making in Defensor Pacis," *British Journal for the History of Philosophy* 26, no. 2 (2018): 281–83.

law is a science or doctrine (*scientia seu doctrina*), or a form of prudence (*prudentia*) that presupposes a certain idea of experience. As I have argued elsewhere, Marsilius's theory of experience is among the most original contributions from the *Defender* as a work of political theory.[54] Indeed, it presupposes a collective notion of experience. In order to formulate good and useful laws, we need *experience*, which Marsilius sees as the collective sum of experience from previous to current generations of men.[55] This particular epistemological theory of the creation of laws fits very well with, and constitutes the theoretical presupposition of, the radical theory of popular sovereignty that Marsilius develops, particularly in chapters 12 and 13 of the first *dictio* of the *Defender*. In I, 13, drawing on Aristotle's *Politics*, he argues that the many are better suited than the individual for realizing the common good. Moreover, in I, 13, 6 he provides a vivid description of citizens' deliberative participation in making and endorsing laws for the political community. His positive attitude toward the role of the people in law-making clearly shows a "democratic" mentality that pervades his description of the legislative procedure.[56]

Based on these chapters of the *Defender*, Marsilius clearly founds human laws in a collective form of knowledge and in a theory of the multitude rather than in any of the two notions of natural law provided above. We saw that, for Marsilius, the *lex perfecta* must reflect ideas of the "just" (*iustum*) and the "unjust" (*iniustum*) and has coercive power over men in the present life. This notion of the "just" identifies that which is *licitum* according to human law. However, it does not overlap at all with the absolute ideas of *licitum* and *illicitum* that are established through natural law as the "dictate of right reason," which is itself placed under divine law. We saw that the latter, the absolute standards of the *licitum* and the

---

54. Mulieri, "Marsilius of Padua and Peter of Abano."

55. On the likely origin of this theory in the Paduan environment where Marsilius lived, see Mulieri, "Marsilius of Padua and Peter of Abano." For an overall reconstruction of the Paduan context of Marsilius's theory, see Paolo Marangon, "Marsilio tra preumanesimo e cultura della arti, ricerca sulle fonti padovane del I discorso del 'Defensor Pacis,'" in *Ad cogitationem scientiae festinare: gli studi delle università e nei conventi di Padova nei secoli XIII e XIV*, ed. Paolo Marangon (Trieste: Lint Editoriale, 1997), 89–119.

56. Marsilius only defines the *civis* as someone who is *secundum graduum*. In I, 12, 4, he defines citizenship as determined according to a person's social and economic ranking in society (*The Defender of Peace*, 67), a claim that makes Marsilius's democratic views closer to the Communal reality of his time. On this, see Jeannine Quillet, *La Philosophie politique de Marsile de Padoue* (Paris: J. Vrin, 1970), 31–48.

illicitum, can provide a moral teaching that can guide human conduct in the present life but can only be punished in the future life. On the contrary, the idea of the "just" to be found in the perfect law is always also legally coercive but, most importantly, is the result of a collective effort to accumulate knowledge and not of natural law as is found in Aquinas. This means that, even if Marsilius's second definition of natural law as a "dictate of right reason" can help identify absolute criteria for determining right and wrong, it does not provide a solid ground for human laws, which very often clash with divine law. As rightly emphasized by Brett, for Marsilius there are two notions of right and wrong, one that is legal/political and another which is moral. Very often, that which is *licitum* only according to human law, the *iustum*, clashes with that which is *licitum* in absolute terms, i.e., according to divine and natural law.

CONCLUSION

In this chapter, we saw that there are two different meanings of natural law to be found in Marsilius of Padua. The first, which Marsilius clearly rejects, identifies the natural with something that should be valid among people from different lands whereas the second considers natural law as a "dictate of right reason" that is placed under divine law. While Marsilius sees the first as natural law in the equivocal sense, i.e., because "natural" here is a synonym of conventional, he considers the second to be the true example of "natural" law since it provides a criterion for establishing the difference between right and wrong: it sets an extra-juridical standard for assessing human conduct via its grounding in divine law. As I have attempted to demonstrate, Marsilius's second definition of natural law elaborates an extrapolitical dimension of right that can be used as a normative standard for determining that which is absolutely right or wrong. This extrapolitical dimension of justice bears some relevance for guiding human conduct in the present life, but transgressions against it can only be punished in the next life.

Marsilius combines his interpretation of this Thomistic position with an original reinstatement of Averroes's position on natural law and confines them to completely different realms. On the one hand, he reaffirms the conventional aspect of natural law by claiming that only the human legislator can be the author of perfect and enforceable human laws. On the other hand, he also isolates a realm of extralegal justice that helps to establish what is right and wrong in absolute terms while emptying this realm of any political relevance. If we compare Marsilius's two definitions of natural law to his account of human law, Marsilius clearly identifies a normative dimension of the autonomous political sphere that, though compatible with Christian ethics, can exist without the latter.

As I have argued elsewhere, Marsilius does not object to the view that, in principle, it is possible to have an idea of either the common good or of right and wrong. Such ideas also contribute to drawing universal normative standards for establishing right and wrong. However, he thinks that those ideas provide no practical guidance in establishing the most appropriate political conduct in specific circumstances. Marsilius claims that natural law can help establish what is right and wrong and draw up an idea of the common good in absolute terms. However, he thinks that such standards have no relevance for the political life of men in the political community. In the political sphere, Marsilius replaces natural law with a theory of the legislator that creates perfect laws based on the *iustum* and that is grounded solely in human experience. Marsilius's refusal to grant natural law the same status as all other classical republicans leads him to find another source of legitimation. He situates it directly in a "secular" form of rationality, one that entails a very high esteem for philosophy and politics as an autonomous branch of thought apart from theology.

Bibliography

Aertsen, Jan A. "Avicenna's Doctrine of the Primary Notions and Its Impact on Medieval Philosophy." In *Islamic Thought in the Middle Ages: Studies in Text, Transmission and Translation, in Honour of Hans Daiber*, edited by Anna Akasoy and Wim Raven, 21–42. Leiden: Brill, 2008.

Ahmed, Rumee. *Narratives of Islamic Legal Theory*. Oxford: Oxford University Press, 2012.

Albert the Great. *Super Ethica: Commentum et Quaestiones*. Edited by Wilhelm Kübel. 2 vols. Münster Westphalia: Aschendorff, 1968–1972.

Alexander of Hales. *Glossa in quattuor libros sententiarum Petri Lombardi*. 4 vols. Quaracchi: Typographia Collegii S. Bonaventurae, 1951–1957.

———. *Summa theologica Halensis: De legibus et praeceptis. Lateinischer Text, deutsche Übersetzung und Kommentar*. Edited by Michael Basse. 3 vols. Berlin: De Gruyter, 2018.

Alexandrov, Victor. *The Syntagma of Matthew Blastares: The Destiny of a Byzantine Legal Code among the Orthodox Slavs and Romanians, 14–17 Centuries*. Frankfurt: Löwenklau-Gesellschaft, 2012.

Anscombe, Gertrude Elizabeth Mary. "Modern Moral Philosophy." *Philosophy* 33, no. 124 (1958): 1–13.

Anthologion (Ἀνθολόγιον τοῦ ὅλου ἐνιαυτοῦ). 3 vols. Rome: Sacra Congregatio Ecclesiarum Orientalium, 1967.

Aristotle. *Analytica posteriora*. In *Analytica priora et posteriora*, edited by William David Ross and Lorenzo Minio-Paluello, 114–83. Oxford: Clarendon, 1964.

———. *Ars rhetorica*. Edited by William David Ross. Oxford: Clarendon Press, 1959.

———. *Ethica Nicomachea*. Edited by Ingram Bywater. Oxford: Clarendon Press, 1963.

———. *Metaphysica*. Edited by Werner Jaeger. Oxford: Clarendon Press, 1957.

———. *Nicomachean Ethics*. Translated by Roger Crisp. Cambridge: Cambridge University Press, 2004.

———. *Aristotelis Opera cum Averrois Commentariis*, 11 vols. Venice: apud Iunctas, 1562–1574.

———. *Politica*. Edited by William David Ross. Oxford: Clarendon Press, 1957.

Arnim, Hans Friedrich von. *Stoicorum veterum fragmenta*. 4 vols. Leipzig: Teubner, 1903.

Athenagoras. *Athenagorae qui fertur De resurrectione mortuorum.* Supplements to Vigiliae Christianae. Vol. 53. Edited by Miroslav Marcovich. Leiden: Brill, 2000.

Aubert, Jean-Marie. *Le droit romain dans l'œuvre de saint Thomas.* Paris: Vrin, 1955.

Auda, Jasser. *Maqasid Al-Shariah as Philosophy of Islamic Law: A Systems Approach.* Herndon, Va.: IIIT, 2008.

Avicenna. *Liber de philosophia prima sive Scientia divina, I-IV.* Edited by Simone van Riet. 3 vols. Louvain: E. Peeters, 1977.

Babie, Paul. "Natural Law in the Orthodox Tradition." In *Christianity and Natural Law: An Introduction*, edited by Norman Doe, 36–57. Cambridge: Cambridge University Press, 2017.

Badr al-Dīn al-ʿAynī. *Al-Bināya Sharḥ Al-Hidāya.* Edited by Ayman Ṣāliḥ Shaʿbān. Beirut: Dār al-Kutub al-ʿIlmiyya, 2000.

Baḥya ben Joseph ibn Paḳuda. *The Book of Direction to the Duties of the Heart.* Translated by Menahem Mansoor. Oxford: The Littman Library of Jewish Civilization, 2004.

Basil of Caesarea. *Homélies sur l'Hexaéméron.* Sources Chrétiennes. Vol. 26. Edited by Stanislas Giet. Paris: Éditions du Cerf, 1949.

———. *Homilia in principium Proverbiorum.* Patrologia Graeca. Vol. 31, 385–424. Paris: Jacques-Paul Migne, 1885.

Bastit, Michel. *Naissance de la loi moderne: la pensée de la loi de saint Thomas à Suarez.* Paris: Presses Universitaires de France, 1990.

Bhuta, Nehal. "Rethinking the Universality of Human Rights: A Comparative Historical Proposal for the Idea of 'Common Ground' with Other Moral Traditions." In *Islamic Law and International Human Rights Law: Searching for Common Ground?*, edited by Anver M. Emon, Mark S. Ellis, and Benjamin Glahn, 123–43. Oxford: Oxford University Press, 2012.

Biblia latina cum glossa ordinaria: Facsimile reprint of the Editio Princeps (Adolph Rusch of Strassburg 1480/81). 4 vols. Turnhout: Brepols, 1992.

Bonaventure. *Collationes in Hexaëmeron et Bonaventuriana quaedam selecta.* Bibliotheca Franciscana scholastica medii aevi. Vol. 8. Edited by Ferdinand M. Delorme. Florence: Ex Typographia Collegii S. Bonaventurae, 1934.

———. *Opera omnia.* 11 vols. Florence: Ex Typographia Collegii S. Bonaventurae, 1882–1902.

———. *Sermones dominicales.* Bibliotheca franciscana scholastica Medii Aevi. Edited by Jacques Guy Bougerol. Grottaferrata: Collegio S. Bonaventura Padri Editori di Quaracchi, 1977.

———. *Sermons "de diversis."* Edited by Jacques-Guy Bougerol. 2 vols. Paris: Éd. franciscaines, 1993.

Bougerol, Jacques Guy. *Introduzione generale.* Opere di san Bonaventura. 9 vols. Vol. 1. Rome: Città Nuova, 1990.

———. "Jean de La Rochelle: les oeuvres et les manuscrits." *Archivum Franciscanum historicum* 87, no. 3–4 (1994): 205–15.

Bouillard, Henri. *Conversion et grâce chez Saint Thomas d'Aquin: étude historique.* Paris: Editions Aubier-Montaigne, 1944.

Brett, Annabel. "Political Right(s) and Human Freedom in Marsilius of Padua." In *Transformations in Medieval and Early-Modern Rights Discourse*, edited by Virpi Mäkinen and Petter Korkman, 95–116. Dordrecht: Springer, 2006.

Brundage, James A. *The Medieval Origins of the Legal Profession: Canonists, Civilians, and Courts.* Chicago: University of Chicago Press, 2008.

Bychkov, Oleg. "'In Harmony with Reason': John Duns Scotus's Theo-aesth/ethics." *Open Theology* 1, no. 1 (2014): 45–55.

Calasso, Francesco. *Medio Evo del diritto.* 2nd ed. Milan: Giuffrè 2005.

Canning, Joseph. "Law, Sovereignty and Corporation Theory, 1300–1450." In *The Cambridge History of Medieval Political Thought c. 350–c. 1450*, edited by J. H. Burns, 454–76. Cambridge: Cambridge University Press, 1988.

Casagrande, Carla, and Vecchio, Silvana. "La classificazione dei peccati tra settenario dei vizi e decalogo." *Documenti e studi sulla tradizione filosofica medievale* 5 (1994): 331–95.

Ceccarelli Morolli, Danilo. *Il diritto dell'Impero Romano d'Oriente. Introduzione alle fonti e ai protagonisti.* Rome: Lilamé, 2016.

Cicero, Marcus Tullius. *De natura deorum.* Loeb Classical Library. Vol. 268. Edited by Harris Rackham. Cambridge, Mass.: Harvard University Press, 1951.

———. *De officiis.* Oxford Classical Texts. Edited by Michael Winterbottom. Oxford: Clarendon Press, 1994.

———. *De re publica.* In *De re publica, De legibus, Cato Maior de senectute, Laelius de amicitia*, edited by Jonathan G. F. Powell, 1–154. Oxford: Clarendon Press, 2006.

———. *Treatises of Marcus Tullius Cicero.* Translated by Charles Duke Yonge. London: H.G. Bohn, 1853.

Clement of Alexandria. *Stromata I-VI.* Edited by Otto Stählin. Leipzig: J.C. Hinrichs'sche Buchhandlung, 1906.

———. *Stromate I.* Sources Chrétiennes. Vol. 30. Introduction and notes by Claude Mondésert. Translated by Marcel Caster. Paris: Éditions du Cerf, 1951.

Constas, Nicholas. *Proclus of Constantinople and the Cult of the Virgin in Late Antiquity: Homilies 1–5, Texts and Translations.* Supplements to Vigiliae Christianae. Vol. 66. Leiden: Brill, 2003.

Copleston, Frederick. *A History of Philosophy.* 11 vols. New York: Image Books, 1993.

Costa, Iacopo. "Reflets théologiques et psychologiques sur l'élaboration du concept de droit (XIIIe-XIVe siècle)." In *Frontières des savoirs en Italie à l'époque des premières universités XIIIe-XVe siècle*, edited by Joël Chandelier and Aurélien Robert. Collection de l'École française de Rome, 177–97. Rome: École française de Rome, 2015.

Crisp, Roger. *The Oxford Handbook of the History of Ethics.* Oxford: Oxford University Press, 2013.

Cross, Richard. "Duns Scotus on Goodness, Justice, and What God Can Do." *The Journal of Theological Studies* 48, no. 1 (1997): 48–76.

———. "Natural Law, Moral Constructivism, and Duns Scotus's Metaethics: The Centrality of Aesthetic Explanation." In *Reason, Religion, and Natural Law: From Plato to Spinoza*, edited by Jonathan A. Jacobs, 175–97. New York: Oxford University Press, 2012.

Crowe, Michael Bertram. *The Changing Profile of the Natural Law.* The Hague: M. Nijhoff, 1977.

Cyril of Alexandria. *Glaphyra in Pentateuchum.* In Patrologia Graeca, vol. 69, edited by Jean Aubert, 9–678. Paris: Jacques-Paul Migne, 1864.

Daiber, Dietrich Lorenz. "Santo Tomás de Aquino y el Islam en la *Suma contra los gentiles.*" *Philosophica* 24–25 (2001–02): 123–37.

Di Maio, Andrea. *Il vocabolario bonaventuriano per la natura.* Rome: Edizioni Miscellanea Francescana, 1988.

———. *La dottrina bonaventuriana sulla natura.* Roma: Miscellanea francescana, 1989.

———. *La concezione Bonaventuriana della natura quale potenziale oggetto di comunicazione.* Roma: Miscellanea francescana, 1990.

———. "'Secundum dictamen legum politicarum..., sicut philosophus loquendo.' Ermeneutica dei testi e del lessico di Bonaventura di Bagnoregio sulla comprensione della dimensione politica fra eredità classica, innovazione cristiana e peculiarità francescana." In *I francescani e la politica atti del convegno di studio, Palermo, 3–7 dicembre 2002*, edited by Alessandro Musco, 307–42. Palermo: Officina di studi medievali, 2007.

Di Salvatore, Antonio. "La legge naturale in S. Bonaventura da Bagnoregio." Doctoral Dissertation, Pontificia Universitas Lateranensis, 2000.

Diodore of Tarsus. *Commentarii in psalmos.* Edited by Jean-Marie Olivier. 2 vols. Corpus Christianorum Series Graeca. Vol. 6. Turnhout: Brepols, 1980.

———. *Commentary on Psalms 1–51.* Translated by Robert C. Hill. Atlanta: Society of Biblical Literature, 2005.

Doucet, Victorin. *Prolegomena in librum III necnon in libros I et II Summae Fratris Alexandri. Summa Theologica seu sic ab origine dicta Summa fratris Alexandris.* 4 vols. Vol. 4/1. Florence: Typographia Collegii S. Bonaventurae, 1948.

Dragas, George. "The Blessed Basil of Seleucia: The Great Antiochian Theologian of the 5th Century A.D. and His Homily 39 on the Annunciation of the Theotokos." *The Patristic and Byzantine Review* 25, no. 1–3 (2007): 172–200.

Dufourcq, Élisabeth. *L'invention de la loi naturelle. Des itinéraires grecs, latins, juifs, chrétiens et musulmans.* Montrouge: Bayard, 2012.

———. *Intuitions et pièges de la loi naturelle.* Paris: Éditions du Cerf, 2019.

Emon, Anver M. "Huqūq Allāh and Huqūq Al-ʿIbād: A Legal Heuristic for a Natural Rights Regime." *Islamic Law and Society* 13, no. 3 (2006): 325–91.

———. *Islamic Natural Law Theories.* New York: Oxford University Press, 2010.

———. "On Islam and Islamic Natural Law: A Response to the International Theological Commission's 'Look at Natural Law.'" In *Searching for a Universal*

Ethic: Multidisciplinary, Ecumenical, and Interfaith Responses to the Catholic Natural Law Tradition, edited by William C. Mattison and John Berkman, 125–35. Grand Rapids, Mich.: William B. Eerdmans, 2014.

Emon, Anver M., Matthew Levering, and David Novak. *Natural Law: A Jewish, Christian, and Islamic Trialogue*. Oxford: Oxford University Press, 2014.

Epictetus. *Epicteti Dissertationes ab Arriano digestae, ad fidem Codicis bodleiani*. Edited by Heinrich Schenkl. Leipzig: B.G. Teubner, 1916.

Ercole, Francesco. *Il pensiero politico di Dante*. Milan: Alpes, 1927–28.

Eustratii et Michaelis et anonyma in ethica Nicomachea commentaria. Edited by Gustav Heylbut. Berlin: Reimer, 1892.

Farrell, Dominic. *The Ends of the Moral Virtues and the First Principles of Practical Reason in Thomas Aquinas*. Analecta Gregoriana 318. Rome: Gregorian and Biblical Press, 2012.

———. "Two Visions of Moral Virtue? Aquinas on Moral Virtue in Revelation and Reason." In *The Virtuous Life. Thomas Aquinas on the Theological Nature of the Moral Virtues*, edited by Harm Goris and Henk Schoot, 221–43. Leuven: Peeters, 2017.

Farrell, Patrick M. "Sources of St. Thomas' Concept of Natural Law." *The Thomist* 20, no. 3 (1957): 237–94.

Finegan, Jack. *The Archeology of the New Testament: The Mediterranean World of the Early Christian Apostles*. Boulder, Colo.: Westview Press, 1981.

Finnis, John. *Natural Law and Natural Rights*. 2nd ed. Oxford: Oxford University Press, 1980, 2011.

Foot, Philippa. *Natural Goodness*. Oxford: Clarendon, 2001.

Gardet, Louis. "La connaissance que Thomas d'Aquin put avoir du monde islamique." In *Aquinas and the Problems of His Time*, edited by Gerard Verbeke and Daniel Verhelst, 139–49. Louvain: Leuven University Press Nijhoff, 1976.

Gewirth, Alan. *Marsilius of Padua: The Defender of Peace*. Vol. 1, *Marsilius of Padua and Medieval Political Philosophy*. New York: Columbia University Press, 1951.

Goodman, Lenn Evan. *Judaism, Human Rights, and Human Values*. New York: Oxford University Press, 1998.

Gregory Nazianzen. *Discours 27–31 (Discours théologiques)*. Sources Chrétiennes. Vol. 250. Edited by Paul Gallay and Maurice Jourjon. Paris: Éditions du Cerf, 1978.

Gregory of Nyssa. *In sextum psalmum*. In *Gregorii Nysseni In inscriptiones psalmorum, In Ecclesiasten homiliae*, edited by James McDonough and Paul Alexander, Gregorii Nysseni opera, vol. 5, 187–93. Leiden: E. J. Brill, 1962.

Gregory Palamas. *Ἀντιρριτικός*. Edited by Panagiótīs K. Chrístou. *Γρηγορίου τοῦ Παλαμᾶ Συγγράμματα*. Vol. 3 (Thessaloniki, 1970).

———. *Λόγος ὑπὲρ τῶν ἱερῶς ἡσυχαζόντων*, Edited by Panagiótīs K. Chrístou. *Γρηγορίου τοῦ Παλαμᾶ Συγγράμματα*. Vol. 1 (Thessaloniki: 2010).

———. *Saint Gregory Palamas: The Homilies*. Edited by Christopher Veniamin. Waverly, PA: Mount Tabor Publishing, 2014.

Halevi, Judah. *The Kuzari (Kitab Al Khazari): An Argument for the Faith of*

Israel. Translated by Hartwig Hirschfield. New York: Schocken Books, 1964.

Hamilton-Bleakley, Holly. "Marsilius of Padua's Conception of Natural Law Revisited." In *The World of Marsilius of Padua*, edited by Gerson Moreno-Riaño, 125–41. Turnhout: Brepols, 2006.

Hankinson, R. J. "Stoic Epistemology." In *The Cambridge Companion to the Stoics*, edited by Brad Inwood, 59–79. New York: Cambridge University Press, 2009.

Harakas, Stanley S. "The Natural Law Teaching in the Ante-Nicene Fathers in Modern Greek Orthodox Theology." PhD Dissertation, Boston University School of Theology, 1965.

———. "Eastern Orthodox Perspectives on Natural Law." *Selected Papers from the Annual Meeting (American Society of Christian Ethics)* 18 (1977): 41–56.

———. "Eastern Orthodox Perspectives on Natural Law." *American Journal of Jurisprudence* 24, no. 1 (1979): 86–113.

Helmholz, Richard H. "Citations and the Construction of Procedural Law in the Ius Commune." In *The Creation of the* Ius Commune: *From* Casus *to* Regula, edited by John W. Cairns and Paul J. du Plessis, 247–75. Edinburgh: Edinburgh University Press, 2010.

———. *Natural Law in Court: A History of Legal Theory in Practice.* Cambridge, Mass.: Harvard University Press, 2015.

Henquinet, François-Maire. "Ist der Traktat De legibus et praeceptis in der Summa Alexander von Hales von Johannes von Rupella?." *Franziskanische Studien* 26, no. 1 (1939): 1–22, 234–58.

Honoré, Tony. *Ulpian: Pioneer of Human Rights.* 2nd ed. Oxford: Oxford University Press, 2002.

Hourani, George F. "Divine Justice and Human Reason in Mu'tazilite Ethical Theology." In *Ethics in Islam*, edited by Richard G. Hovannisian, 73–84. Malibu, Calif.: Undena Publications, 1985.

Hursthouse, Rosalind. *On Virtue Ethics.* Oxford: Oxford University Press, 1999.

Ierodiakonou, Katerina. "Some Observations on Michael of Ephesus' Comments on *Nicomachean Ethics* X." In *Medieval Greek Commentaries on the Nicomachean Ethics*, edited by Charles Barber and David Jenkins, 185–201. Leiden: Brill, 2009.

Ingham, Mary Beth. "Letting Scotus Speak for Himself." *Medieval Philosophy and Theology* 10, no. 2 (2001): 173–216.

International Theological Commission. "In Search of a Universal Ethic: A New Look at the Natural Law." In *Searching for a Universal Ethic: Multidisciplinary, Ecumenical, and Interfaith Responses to the Catholic Natural Law Tradition*, edited by William C. Mattison and John Berkman, 25–92. Grand Rapids, Mich.: William B. Eerdmans Publishing Company, 2014.

Irenaeus of Lyons. *Contre les Hérésies (Adversus Haereses).* Sources Chrétiennes. Vols. 100, 152–53, 210–11, 263–64, 293–94. Paris: Cerf, 1965–82.

Irwin, Terence. *The Development of Ethics: A Historical and Critical Study.* 3 vols. Oxford: Oxford University Press, 2007–09.

Jacobs, Jonathan. "The Epistemology of Moral Tradition: A Defense of a Maimonidean Thesis." *The Review of Metaphysics* 64, no. 1 (2010): 55–74.

———. "The Reasons of the Commandments: Rational Tradition without Natural Law." In *Reason, Religion, and Natural Law: From Plato to Spinoza*, edited by Jonathan A. Jacobs, 106–29. New York: Oxford University Press, 2012.

Jedan, Christoph. *Stoic Virtues: Chrysippus and the Theological Foundations of Stoic Ethics*. New York: Continuum, 2009.

Johansen, Baber. "Apostasy as Objective and Depersonalized Fact: Two Recent Egyptian Court Judgments." *Social Research: An International Quarterly* 70, no. 3 (2003): 687–710.

John Duns Scotus. *Lectura in Librum primum sententiarum Prologus et distinctiones a prima ad septimam*. Opera omnia. Vol. 16. Edited by Karlo Balić. Vatican City: Typis polyglottis Vaticanis, 1960.

———. *Ordinatio: Liber primus, distinctio prima e secunda*. Opera omnia. Vol. 2. Edited by Karlo Balić. Vatican City: Typis polyglottis Vaticanis, 1950.

———. *Ordinatio: Liber primus a distinctione vigesima sexta ad quadragesimam octavam*. Opera omnia. Vol. 6. Edited by Karlo Balić. Vatican City: Typis polyglottis Vaticanis, 1963.

———. *Ordinatio: Liber quartus, a distinctione quadragesima tertia ad quadragesimam nonam*. Opera omnia. Vol. 13. Edited by Barnaba Hechich. Vatican City: Typis Vaticanis, 2011.

———. *Ordinatio: Liber secundus, a distinctione quarta ad quadragesimam quartam*. Opera omnia. Vol. 8. Edited by Barnaba Hechich. Vatican City: Typis Vaticanis, 2001.

———. *Ordinatio: Liber tertius, a distinctione vigesima sexta ad quadragesimam*. Opera omnia. Vol. 10. Edited by Barnaba Hechich. Vatican City: Typis Polyglottis Vaticanis, 2007.

———. *Reportata Parisiensia* III. In *Opera omnia II 2 Opera theologica*, edited by Giovanni Lauriola. Opera omnia: Edito minor. Vol. 14. Alberobello: Editrice AGA, 1999.

———. *Reportatio I-A = The Examined Report of the Paris Lecture: Latin Text and English Translation*. Edited by Allan B. Wolter and Oleg Bychkov. St. Bonaventure, N.Y.: Franciscan Institute, 2004.

———. *Selected Writings on Ethics*. Edited and translated by Thomas Williams. Oxford: Oxford University Press, 2017.

John of Damascus. *An Exact Exposition of the Orthodox Faith (De fide orthodoxa)*. Translated by Frederic Hathaway Chase. In John of Damascus. *Writings*, 165–406. New York: Fathers of the Church, 1958.

———. *Expositio fidei*. Edited by Bonifatius Kotter. Berlin: Walter De Gruyter, 1973.

———. *Philosophical Chapters*. Translated by Frederic Hathaway Chase. In John of Damascus. *Writings*, 3–110. New York: Fathers of the Church, 1958.

Justin the Martyr. *Dialogus Cum Tryphone*. In *Die ältesten Apologeten*, edited by Edgar Johnson Goodspeed, 90–265. Göttingen: Vandenhoeck & Ruprecht, 1914.

Justinian. *Digesta Iustiniani Augusti.* Edited by Theodor Mommsen and Paul Krueger. 2 vols. Berlin: Weidmann, 1870.

———. *Imperatoris Justiniani Institutionum libri quattuor.* Edited by Philipp Eduard Huschke. 4 vols. Leipzig: B.G. Teubner, 1868.

———. *Novellae.* Corpus Iuris Civilis. Edited by Rudolf Schöll and Wilhelm Kroll. Berlin: Weidmann, 1895.

Käppeli, Thomas M. *Scriptores Ordinis Praedicatorum Medii Aevi.* 4 vols. Rome: Typis Polyglottis Vaticanis, 1970–73.

Kellner, Menachem Marc. *Dogma in Medieval Jewish Thought: From Maimonides to Abravanel.* Oxford: Littman Library of Jewish Civilization, 1986.

Kelly, John M. "*Audi alteram partem.*" *Natural Law Forum* 9 (1964): 103–10.

Korsgaard, Christine M. *The Sources of Normativity.* Cambridge: Cambridge University Press, 1996.

Lagarde, Georges de. *La naissance de l'esprit laïque au déclin du Moyen Âge.* 6 vols. Vol. 6. *L'individualisme ockhamiste (3me fascicule): La morale et le droit.* Saint-Paul-Trois-Châteaux: Éditions Béatrice, 1946.

Lambertini, Roberto. "Marsilius and the Poverty Controversy in Dictio II." In *A Companion to Marsilius of Padua*, edited by Gerson Moreno-Riaño and Cary J. Nederman, 229–64. Leiden: Brill, 2012.

Larson, Atria A. *Master of Penance: Gratian and the Development of Penitential Thought and Law in the Twelfth Century.* Studies in Medieval and Early Modern Canon Law 11. Washington, D.C.: The Catholic University of America Press, 2014.

Lee, Alexander. "Roman Law and Human Liberty: Marsilius of Padua on Property Rights." *Journal of the History of Ideas* 70, no. 1 (2009): 23–44.

Levine, Michael P. "The Role of Reason in the Ethics of Maimonides: Or, Why Maimonides Could Have Had a Doctrine of Natural Law Even If He Did Not." *The Journal of Religious Ethics* 14, no. 2 (1986): 279–95.

Lewis, Ewart. "The 'Positivism' of Marsiglio of Padua." *Speculum* 38, no. 4 (1963): 541–82.

Lottin, Odon. *Le droit naturel chez saint Thomas d'Aquin et ses predecesseurs.* 2nd ed. Bruges: Charles Beyaert, 1931.

———. *Psychologie et morale aux XIIe et XIIIe siècles.* 5 vols. Louvain: Abbaye de Mont César, 1942–59.

MacIntyre, Alasdair. *After Virtue: A Study in Moral Theory.* London: Duckworth, 1981.

Maglio, Gianfranco. "Il diritto e la legge naturale in Bonaventura da Bagnoregio." In *L'uomo nel pensiero di Bonaventura da Bagnoregio*, edited by Irene Zavattero, 233–69. Rome: Aracne, 2019.

Maimonides, Moses. *The Book of Judges.* Translated by Abraham M. Hershman. Yale Judaica Series. Vol. 3. The Code of Maimonides 14. New Haven: Yale University Press, 1949.

———. *Eight Chapters.* Translated by Raymond L. Weiss and Charles E. Butterworth. In *Ethical Writings of Maimonides*, 59–104. New York: New York University Press, 1975.

———. *The Guide of the Perplexed.* Translated by Shlomo Pines. 2 vols. Chicago: University of Chicago Press, 1963.

———. *Laws Concerning Character Traits.* Translated by Raymond L. Weiss. In *Ethical Writings of Maimonides,* 27–58. New York: New York University Press, 1975.

———. *Treatise on the Art of Logic.* Translated by Charles E. Butterworth. In *Ethical Writings of Maimonides,* 155–63. New York: New York University Press, 1975.

Makdisi, George. "Ethics in Islamic Traditionalist Doctrine." In *Ethics in Islam,* edited by Richard G. Hovannisian, 47–63. Malibu, Calif.: Undena Publications, 1985.

Mäkinen, Virpi. *Property Rights in the Late Medieval Discussion on Franciscan Poverty.* Louvain: Peeters, 2001.

Mantzaridis, Georgios I. *Grundlinien christlicher Ethik.* St. Ottilien, Ger.: EOS Verlag, 1998.

Marangon, Paolo. "Marsilio tra preumanesimo e cultura della arti, ricerca sulle fonti padovane del I discorso del 'Defensor Pacis.'" In *Ad cogitationem scientiae festinare: gli studi delle università e nei conventi di Padova nei secoli XIII e XIV,* edited by Paolo Marangon, 89–119. Trieste: Lint Editoriale, 1997.

Marcus Aurelius. *The Meditations of the Emperor Marcus Aurelius.* Edited by Arthur Spencer Loat Farquharson. 2 vols. Oxford: Clarendon Press, 1944.

Marsilius of Padua. *The Defender of the Peace.* Translated by Annabel S. Brett. Cambridge: Cambridge University Press, 2005.

———. *Defensor pacis.* Edited by Richard Scholz. Monumenta Germaniae Historica. Fontes iuris germanici antiqui in usum scholarum separatim editi. Hannover: Hahnsche Buchhanldung, 1933.

Martens, John W. "Romans 2.14–16: A Stoic Reading." *New Testament Studies* 40, no. 1 (1994): 55–67.

———. *One God, One Law: Philo of Alexandria on the Mosaic and Greco-Roman Law.* Ancient Mediterranean and Medieval Texts and Contexts. Vol. 2. Boston: Brill Academic Publishers, 2003.

Matteo d'Acquasparta, francescano, filosofo, politico. Atti del XXIX convegno storico internazionale, Todi, 11–14 ottobre 1992. Spoleto: Centro italiano di studi sull'alto Medioevo, 1993.

Matthew of Acquasparta. *Quaestiones disputatae de anima separata, de anima beata, de ieiunio et de Legibus.* Florence: Typographia Collegii S. Bonaventurae, 1959.

Maximus the Confessor. *On Difficulties in Sacred Scripture: The Responses to Thalassios.* Translated by Maximos Constas. The Fathers of the Church: A New Translation 136. Washington, D.C.: The Catholic University of America Press, 2018.

———. *On Difficulties in the Church Fathers: The Ambigua.* Edited by Nicholas Constas. 2 vols. Dumbarton Oaks Medieval Library. Vols. 28–29. Cambridge, Mass.: Harvard University Press, 2014.

Mercken, H. P. F. "The Greek Commentators on Aristotle's *Ethics.*" In *Aristotle*

Transformed: The Ancient Commentators and Their Influence, edited by Richard Sorabji, 407–43. London: Duckworth, 1990.

Michael of Ephesus. *In Ethica Nicomachea IX–X Commentaria.* In *Eustratii et Michaelis et Anonyma in Ethica Nicomachea Commentaria*, edited by Gustav Heylbut, 461–620. Berlin: Reimer, 1892.

Möhle, Hannes. "Scotus's Theory of Natural Law." In *The Cambridge Companion to Duns Scotus*, edited by Thomas Williams, 312–31. New York: Cambridge University Press, 2003.

Mulieri, Alessandro. "Marsilius of Padua and Peter of Abano: The Scientific Foundations of Law-making in Defensor Pacis." *British Journal for the History of Philosophy* 26, no. 2 (2018): 276–96.

———. "Against Classical Republicanism: The Averroist Foundations of Marsilius of Padua's Political Thought." *History of Political Thought* 40, no. 2 (2019): 218–45.

Murphy, Mark C. *Natural Law in Jurisprudence and Politics.* New York: Cambridge University Press, 2006.

Musonius Rufus. *Dissertationum a Lucio digestarum reliquiae.* In *Musonii Rufi Reliquiae*, edited by Otto Friedrich Hense, 1–116. Leipzig: Teubner, 1905.

———. *Lectures and Sayings.* Translated by Cynthia King. Edited by William B. Irvine. Scotts Valley, Calif.: CreateSpace, 2011.

Nassery, Idris, Rumee Ahmed, and Muna Tatari. *The Objectives of Islamic Law: The Promises and Challenges of the MaqāṢId Al-Shariʿa.* Lanham, Md.: Lexington Books, 2018.

Nicholas, Barry. *An Introduction to Roman Law.* Clarendon Law Studies. 3rd ed. Oxford: Clarendon Press, 1987.

Novak, David. *Natural Law in Judaism.* New York: Cambridge University Press, 1998.

———. "Maimonides and Aquinas on Natural Law." In *St. Thomas Aquinas and the Natural Law Tradition: Contemporary Perspectives*, edited by John Goyette, Mark Latkovic, and Richard S. Myers, 43–65. Washington, D.C.: The Catholic University of America Press, 2004.

Origen. *Contre Celse.* Edited by Marcel Borret. Sources Chrétiennes. Vols. 132, 136, 147, 150, 227. Paris: Cerf, 1967.

O'Sullivan, Declan. "Hisba Law and Freedom of Expression in Islam: Two Case Studies of Prosecution in Contemporary Egypt." *Journal of Mediterranean Studies* 14, no. 1 (2004): 213–35.

Papini, Matteo. *Il diritto è estraneo al bene. Lo scandaloso pensiero di Simone Weil.* Assisi: Cittadella, 2009.

Passerin D'Entréves, Alessandro. *Natural Law. An Introduction to Legal Philosophy.* London: Hutchinson's University Library, 1951.

Petrà, Basilio. "La legge naturale nella teologia ortodossa." *Rivista di teologia morale* 40, no. 159 (2008): 325–32.

Philo of Alexandria. *De opificio mundi.* In *Philonis Alexandrini opera quae supersunt*, edited by Leopold Cohn, 1–60. Berlin: Georg Reimer, 1896–1930.

———. *The Works of Philo: Complete and Unabridged (New Updated Edition).*

Translated by Charles Duke Yonge. Peabody, Mass.: Hendrickson Publishers, 1993.

Plato. *Republic*. Translated by Paul Shorey. In *The Collected Dialogues of Plato, Including the Letters*, edited by Edith Hamilton and Huntington Cairns, 575–844. Princeton: Princeton University Press, 1961.

Plested, Marcus. *Orthodox Readings of Aquinas*. Oxford: Oxford University Press, 2012.

Pseudo-Basil of Seleucia. *Oratio XXXIX: In sanctissimae Deiparae assumptionem*. In Patrologia Graeca, vol. 85, 425–52. Paris: Jacques-Paul Migne 1964.

Quillet, Jeannine. *La Philosophie politique de Marsile de Padoue*. Paris: J. Vrin, 1970.

Reck, Erich H. *The Historical Turn in Analytic Philosophy*. Basingstoke, UK: Palgrave Macmillan, 2013.

Rosenfeld, Sophia A. *Common Sense: A Political History*. Cambridge, Mass.: Harvard University Press, 2011.

Rudavsky, Tamar. "Natural Law in Judaism." In *Reason, Religion, and Natural Law: From Plato to Spinoza*, edited by Jonathan A. Jacobs, 83–105. New York: Oxford University Press, 2012.

Runia, David T. *Philo in Early Christian Literature: A Survey*. Assen: Uitgeverij Van Gorcum, 1993.

Saadia Gaon. *The Book of Beliefs and Opinions*. Translated by Samuel Rosenblatt. New Haven: Yale University Press, 1976.

Saccenti, Riccardo. "'Impressio legis aeternae.' La legge naturale nel trattato *De legibus* di Giovanni de La Rochelle." In *Rappresentazioni della natura nel Medioevo*, edited by Giovanni Catapano and Onorato Grassi, 125–38. Florence: SISMEL 2019.

Schumacher, Lydia. *Early Franciscan Theology: Between Authority and Innovation*. Cambridge: Cambridge University Press, 2019.

Seneca, Lucius Annaeus. *Epistles 1–65*. Loeb Classical Library 75. Edited by Richard M. Gummere. Cambridge, Mass.: Harvard University Press, 1917.

———. *L. Annaei Senecae opera quae supersunt*. Edited by Friedrich Haase. 3 vols. Leipzig: B.G. Teubner, 1898.

Shany, Yuval. "Toward a General Margin of Appreciation Doctrine in International Law?." *European Journal of International Law* 16, no. 5 (2005): 907–40.

Sharpe, Matthew. "Stoic Virtue Ethics." In *The Handbook of Virtue Ethics*, edited by Stan Van Hooft, 28–41. Durham, UK: Acumen, 2014.

Solmi, Arrigo. *Il pensiero politico di Dante: studi storici*. Florence: La Voce, 1922.

Sorell, Tom, and G. A. J. Rogers. *Analytic Philosophy and History of Philosophy*. Oxford: Clarendon Press, 2005.

Spielmann, Dean. "Whither the Margin of Appreciation?" *Current Legal Problems* 67, no. 1 (2014): 49–65.

Steele, Jeff. "Duns Scotus, the Natural Law, and the Irrelevance of Aesthetic Explanation." *Oxford Studies in Medieval Philosophy* 4, no. 1 (2016): 78–99.

Steinberg, Justin. *Dante and the Limits of the Law*. Chicago: University of Chicago Press, 2013.

Steineger, Joseph Edward. "The Naturally Implanted Knowledge of God's Existence: Two 13th Century Scholastic Interpretations of John of Damascus and Anselm of Bec." PhD Dissertation, University of Chicago, The Divinity School, 2014.

Strauss, Leo. *Natural Right and History*. Chicago: University of Chicago Press, 1953.

Taylor, Charles. *Sources of the Self: The Making of the Modern Identity*. Cambridge, Mass.: Harvard University Press, 1989.

Tertullian. *Adversus Iudaeos*. In *Opera*, edited by Emil Kroymann, 2 vols., Corpus Christianorum Series Latina, vols. 1–2, 2:1337–96. Turnhout: Brepols, 1954.

———. *De corona*. In *Opera*, edited by Emil Kroymann, 2 vols., Corpus Christianorum Series Latina, vols. 1–2, 2:1037–65. Turnhout: Brepols, 1954.

Theophilus Antecessor. *Institutionum graeca paraphrasis*. Edited by Contardo Ferrini and Karl Eduard Zachariae von Lingenthal. 2 vols. Berlin: S. Calvary, 1884.

———. *Theophili antecessoris paraphrasis institutionum*. Edited by J. H. A. Lokin, R. Meijering, B. H. Stolte and N. van der Wal. Groningen: Chimaira, 2010.

Thomas Aquinas. *Catena aurea in quatuor Evangelia*. Edited by Angelico Guarienti. 2 vols. 2nd ed. Turin: Marietti 1953.

———. *De Regno ad regem Cypri*. Edited by Hyacinthe-François Dondaine. In Editio Leonina, vol. 42, 417–71. Rome: Editori di San Tommaso, 1979.

———. *De unitate intellectus contra Averroistas*. Edited by Hyacinthe-François Dondaine. In Editio Leonina Vol. 43, 243–314. Rome: Editori di San Tommaso, 1976.

———. *Liber de veritate catholicae fidei contra errores infidelium seu Summa contra Gentiles*. Edited by Ceslao Pera, Pierre Marc, and Pietro Caramello. 3 vols. Turin: Marietti, 1961–67.

———. *Quaestio disputata de virtutibus in communi*. In *Quaestiones disputatae*, 2 vols., edited by Egidio Odetto, 10th ed., 2:707–51. Turin: Marietti, 1965.

———. *Quaestiones disputatae de veritate*. Edited by Antoine Dondaine. Editio Leonina. Vol. 22. Rome: Editori di San Tommaso, 1970.

———. *Scriptum super Libros Sententiarum Magistri Petri Lombardi*. Edited by Pierre Mandonnet and Marie-Fabien Moos. 5 vols. Paris: Lethieilleux, 1929–56.

———. *Sententia libri Ethicorum*. Edited by René-Antoine Gauthier. Editio Leonina Vol. 47. Rome: Commissio Leonina, 1969.

———. *Summa Theologiae*. 5 vols. Ottawa: Harpell's Press, 1941–45.

———. *Summa Theologica*. Translated by Fathers of the English Dominican Province. 3 vols. New York: Benziger Brothers, Inc, 1948.

———. *Super Evangelium S. Ioannis Lectura*. Edited by Raffaello Cai. 6th ed. Turin: Marietti, 1972.

Thompson, Michael. *Life and Action: Elementary Structures of Practice and Practical Thought*. Cambridge, Mass.: Harvard University Press, 2008.

Tierney, Brian. "Marsilius on Rights." *Journal of the History of Ideas* 52, no. 1 (1991): 3–17.

———. *The Idea of Natural Rights: Studies on Natural Rights, Natural Law, and Church Law, 1150–1625.* Atlanta: Scholars Press, 1997.

———. "Natural Law and Natural Rights: Old Problems and Recent Approaches." *The Review of Politics* 64, no. 3 (2002): 389–406.

———. *Liberty and Law: The Idea of Permissive Natural Law, 1100–1800.* Studies in Medieval and Early Canon Law. Vol. 12. Washington, D.C.: The Catholic University of America Press, 2014.

Torrell, Jean-Pierre. "Les 'Collationes in decem praeceptis' de saint Thomas d'Aquin. Édition critique avec introduction et notes." *Revue des sciences philosophiques et théologiques* 69, no. 1 and 2 (1985): 5–40, 227–63.

Trizio, Michele. "Byzantine Philosophy as a Contemporary Historiographical Project." *Recherches de théologie et philosophie médiévales* 74, no. 1 (2007): 247–94.

Twersky, Isadore. *Introduction to the Code of Maimonides (Mishneh Torah).* New Haven: Yale University Press, 1980.

van der Ploeg, Johannes Petrus Maria. "Le traité de saint Thomas de la loi ancienne." In *Lex et Libertas: Freedom and Law According to St. Thomas Aquinas,* edited by Leo Elders and Klaus Hedwig, 185–99. Vatican City: Libreria Editrice Vaticana, 1987.

van Riet, Simone. "La *Somme contre les Gentiles* et la polémique islamo-chrétienne." In *Aquinas and the Problems of His Time,* edited by Gerard Verbeke and Daniel Verhelst, 150–60. Louvain: Leuven University Press Nijhoff, 1976.

Veatch, Henry Babcock. *Human Rights: Fact or Fancy?* Baton Rouge: Louisiana State University Press, 1985.

Vecchio, Silvana. "La riflessione sulla legge nella prima teologia francescana." In *Etica e politica: le teorie dei frati mendicanti nel due e trecento,* 119–51. Spoleto: Centro Italiano di Studi sull'Alto Medioevo, 1999.

———. "Precetti e consigli nella teologia del XIII secolo." In *Consilium. teorie e pratiche del consigliare nella cultura medievale,* edited by Carla Casagrande, Chiara Crisciani, and Silvana Vecchio, 33–56. Florence: SISMEL Edizioni del Galluzzo, 2004.

Villey, Michel. *Leçons d'histoire de la philosophie du droit.* Paris: Librairie Dalloz, 1957.

Vos, Antonie. "The Scotian Notion of Natural Law." *Vivarium* 38, no. 2 (2000): 197–221.

———. *The Philosophy of John Duns Scotus.* Edinburgh: Edinburgh University Press, 2006.

Waltz, James. "Muāmmad and the Muslims in St. Thomas Aquinas." *The Muslim World* 66, no. 2 (1976): 81–95.

Wei, John C. *Gratian the Theologian.* Studies in Medieval and Early Modern Canon Law. Vol. 13. Washington, D.C.: The Catholic University of America Press, 2016.

Weigand, Rudolf. *Die Naturrechtslehre der Legisten und Dekretisten von Irnerius bis Accursius und von Gratian bis Johannes Teutonicus.* Munich: Max Hueber, 1967.

Williams, Bernard. *Ethics and the Limits of Philosophy.* London: Fontana, 1985.

Williams, Thomas. "Reason, Morality, and Voluntarism in Duns Scotus: A Pseudo-Problem Dissolved." *The Modern Schoolman* 74, no. 2 (1997): 73–94.

Wolter, Allan B. *Duns Scotus on the Will and Morality.* Washington, D.C.: The Catholic University of America Press, 1997.

Contributors

ANDREA DI MAIO is an associate professor of the Faculty of Philosophy of the Pontifical Gregorian University, Rome. His research focuses on Christian philosophy and the philosophical and theological hermeneutics and lexicography of Augustine, Bonaventure, and Thomas Aquinas. He has published numerous articles and various books in Italian, including volumes on the concept of communication in Aquinas and an introduction to the thought and lexicography of Bonaventure.

ANVER M. EMON is Professor of Law and Canada Research Chair in Religion, Pluralism and the Rule of Law at the University of Toronto Faculty of Law. His research focuses on pre-modern and modern Islamic legal history and theory, pre-modern modes of governance and adjudication, and the role of Shari'a both inside and outside the Muslim world. In addition to numerous articles, he is the author of *Islamic Natural Law Theories* (2010), *Religious Pluralism and Islamic Law: Dhimmis and Others in the Empire of Law* (2012). As coeditor, he has published *Islamic Law and International Human Rights Law: Searching for Common Ground* (2012), and *the Oxford Handbook on Islamic Law* (2018). He is the founding editor of *Middle East Law and Governance: An Interdisciplinary Journal* and *General Editor of Oxford Islamic Legal Studies Series*.

DOMINIC FARRELL, LC, is a Professor of Philosophy at the Pontifical Athenaeum *Regina Apostolorum*, Rome. His research focusses on ethics, political philosophy, and Aquinas. He has published several articles and book chapters on the virtues and natural law in Aquinas, and the book *The Ends of the Moral Virtues and the First Principles of Practical Reason in Thomas Aquinas* (2012)

JONATHAN JACOBS is Presidential Scholar, Director of the Institute for Criminal Justice Ethics, Chair of the Department of Philosophy at John College of Criminal Justice and a member of the Doctoral Faculty of Philosophy at the CUNY Graduate Center. Author of nine books and editor of two, he works primarily in moral philosophy, moral psychology, and philosophy of law and punishment. Among his books are *Law, Reason, and Morality in Medieval Jewish Philosophy* (2010), *Dimensions of Moral Theory: An Introduction to Metaethics and Moral Psychology* (2002), and *Aristotle's Virtues: Nature, Knowledge, and Human Good* (2004). He is editor of *The Routledge Handbook of Criminal Justice Ethics* (2016) and editor of *Reason, Religion, and Natural Law: From Plato to Spinoza* (2012).

CHRISTIAAN KAPPES is the Academic Dean of Saints Cyril and Methodius Byzantine Catholic Seminary in Pittsburgh, USA, where he teaches patristics and dogmatics. His research and publications are centre on Greco-Latin intellectual interaction in the Roman East and West and on the reception of Latin texts in the Palaiologian period. He is a researcher for the *Thomas de Aquino Byzantinus* project, which produces critical editions of fourteenth and fifteenth century Greek translations of Thomistic texts. He has published on the Greco-Latin interaction in the fields of biblical studies, philosophy, canon law, and liturgy.

MARTYNA KOSZKAŁO is an Associate Professor at the Department of History of Ancient, Medieval and Modern Philosophy, Institute of Philosophy, Sociology and Journalism at the University of Gdańsk, Poland. Her research focusses on ancient and medieval philosophy, modern scholasticism, and philosophy of religion. She has published articles and book chapters on Augustine, Aquinas, John Duns Scotus, Francis Suarez, Leibniz, and the books *Individual and Individuation. The Analysis of John Duns Scotus' Works* (2003, in Polish), and *The Nature of Will. Freedom and Necessity. The Analysis of John Duns Scotus' Theory in Comparison to St. Augustine, St. Anselm of Canterbury, and St. Thomas Aquinas* (2019, University of Gdańsk Press, in Polish).

ALESSANDRO MULIERI is a post-doctoral research fellow at the Research Foundation – Flanders of the Institute of Philosophy at Katholieke

Universiteit Leuven. His research focuses on political philosophy and late medieval and early modern political thought. He has published in journals such as *Philosophy and Social Criticism* and *British Journal for the History of Philosophy.*

RICCARDO SACCENTI teaches History of Medieval Philosophy at the University of Bergamo and is member of the team of the ERC research project *Authority and Innovation in Early Franciscan Thought* based at King's College London. He is the author of *Debating Medieval Natural Law: A Survey* (2016), *La ragione e la norma: Dibattiti attorno alla legge naturale fra XII e XIII secolo* (2019), and the coeditor of *In the Image of God: Foundations and Objections within the Discourse on Human Dignity* (2009).

Recent titles in Studies in Philosophy and the
History of Philosophy

General Editor, John C. McCarthy